INSIDE GREEK U.

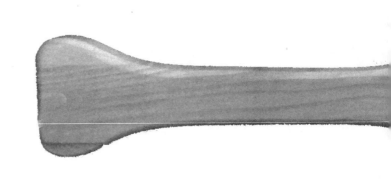

INSIDE GREEK U.

Fraternities, Sororities, and the Pursuit of Pleasure, Power, and Prestige

ALAN D. DESANTIS

THE UNIVERSITY PRESS OF KENTUCKY

Publication of this volume was made possible in part by a grant
from the National Endowment for the Humanities.

Editorial and Sales Offices: The University Press of Kentucky
663 South Limestone Street, Lexington, Kentucky 40508-4008
www.kentuckypress.com

13 12 11 10 09   6 5 4 3 2

Library of Congress Cataloging-in-Publication Data

DeSantis, Alan D.
  Inside Greek U. : fraternities, sororities, and the pursuit of pleasure,
power, and prestige / Alan D. DeSantis.
    p. cm.
  Includes bibliographical references and index.
  ISBN 978-0-8131-2468-1 (hardcover : alk. paper)
  1. Greek letter societies—United States. 2. College students—United
States—Conduct of life. I. Title.
  LJ51.D47 2007
  371.8'50973—dc22   2007019779

This book is printed on acid-free recycled paper meeting
the requirements of the American National Standard
for Permanence in Paper for Printed Library Materials.

Manufactured in the United States of America.

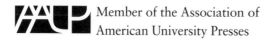 Member of the Association of
American University Presses

To my brothers

Contents

Introduction

Life at Greek University

In *Reviving Ophelia: Saving the Selves of Adolescent Girls* (1994), Mary Pipher detailed the struggles of America's adolescent girls with depression, eating disorders, self-esteem, suicide, sexuality, and a culture that narrowly defines womanhood. In *Raising Cain: Protecting the Emotional Life of Boys* (2000), Dan Kindlon and Michael Thompson similarly discussed the struggles of America's boys with anger, violence, the inability to express themselves emotionally, drinking and drugs, and a culture that narrowly defines manhood.

But what happens when Ophelia and Cain grow up, go away to college, and pledge a fraternity or a sorority, that is, "go Greek"? Do they become better adjusted, happier, and healthier? Are their levels of self-esteem higher and their rates of eating disorders lower? Does college free them from the narrowly defined ideas of femininity and masculinity that caused them so much dissonance in their childhood? Or does this elite learning experience simply reinforce all the previous cultural messages that they have received about sexuality, independence, conflict, violence, aggression, passivity, and their freedom (or lack thereof) to deviate from these ideals?

At its most essential, this book explores the role played by fraternities and sororities at what I refer to as Greek University (GU) in shaping the gender identities of its members. As a college professor who is also a faculty and alumni adviser in the Greek system, I have witnessed thousands of Ophelias and Cains entering college, pledging organizations, falling in (and out of) love, drinking to excess, and, eventually, growing up and starting their postcollege lives. But what kind of college graduates are we producing? Do we have

1

reason to celebrate or cause to worry? The answer is a resounding both!

Working toward this general conclusion, *Inside Greek U* examines the ways fraternities and sororities both challenge and reinforce traditional conceptions of gender in their everyday practices. Given the disturbing trends on college campuses toward increased aggression and violence among men and eating disorders and victimization (e.g., date rape) among women, understanding how these students conceive of gender, sex, relationships, and power is of significant social importance.

My ultimate goal, however, is to do more than just report on the sensational exploits of decadent Greeks. I want to critically and sympathetically examine the way these students are having their potential limited by a rigid gender classification system that insists that "real men" must be tough, unemotional, promiscuous, and violent and "nice girls" nurturing, passive, nonconfrontational, and domestic.

My hope is that the next generation of Ophelias and Cains will be freer to deviate from the narrow and confining conceptions of masculinity and femininity and to explore the new potential that becomes possible only through increased choices and expanded identities.

Understanding the Greek System?

Because of the highly secretive and protective nature of fraternities and sororities, most Americans, even those non-Greeks who have attended American colleges with Greek systems, know little about the inner workings of these groups—except perhaps for what has been portrayed in movies such as *Animal House, Old School, Revenge of the Nerds, Legally Blonde,* and *Sorority Strip Party.* Consequently, before an investigation of gender in the context of America's Greek system can be undertaken, it is necessary to give an overview of that system, including its history and definitions of key practices, rituals, and terms.

To begin with, "being Greek" has nothing to do with Hellenic culture, Plato, or "big fat weddings." In fact, the only Greek aspect of the Greek system is the letters—Sigma Pi, Alpha Delta Pi, Alpha Delta Pi, Delta Delta Delta, etc.—arbitrarily used to differentiate organizations. Why, then, are Greek letters used? In the eighteenth and nineteenth centuries, when fraternities first appeared on American college campuses, ancient Greek studies were academically in vogue.[1]

However, not all Greek-letter organizations are the same. The institution writ large is actually divided into three categories. There are *professional* fraternities and sororities that bring students together on the basis of their professional or vocational field (e.g., Phi Delta Phi, founded in 1869, is a coeducational fraternity for students interested in the study of law). There are *honor* societies that are composed mainly of students who have achieved distinction in scholarship (e.g., Tau Beta Phi, founded in 1885, is a coeducational fraternity for students who have excelled in the study of engineering).[2] And, finally, there are *social* fraternities and sororities, the organizations that are commonly associated with big parties, pledging and hazing, and communal housing. These are the groups on which my investigation focuses.[3]

The first of these *social* organizations appeared on the campus of the College of William and Mary in Williamsburg, Virginia, in 1776. The five white male students who formed Phi Beta Kappa wanted to create a men's club that offered camaraderie, secrecy, and intellectual discussion to its members.[4] Needless to say, beer kegs, toga parties, and goldfish eating were not yet part of the Greek curriculum (Winston, Nettles & Opper, 1987).

In the century that followed, modest numbers of new fraternities, inspired by the high ideas of the Phi Beta Kappas, began springing up throughout the nation. On campuses as varied as Yale, Jefferson College, Dartmouth, Union College, Miami (of Ohio), Virginia Military Institute, Harvard, and the University of Alabama, today's largest and wealthiest white male social fraternities took root. By

1900, such groups as Kappa Alpha (1825), Phi Gamma Delta (1848), Sigma Chi (1852), Sigma Alpha Epsilon (1856), Alpha Tau Omega (1865), and Sigma Nu (1869), were all firmly established and preparing for their subsequent expansion throughout the United States.[5]

As hard as it may be for some to believe, given the contemporary reputation of fraternities, these early Greek-letter societies were considered "valuable adjuncts of student life and, instead of opposing them, most institutions decided that they might be put to work helping run the school, keeping recalcitrant students in line, acting as convenient units of discipline in college life" (Ferguson, 1937, p. 40). As high-minded as they inspired to be, these groups were also segregated institutions, reserved only for wealthy, white, Christian men. Women, blacks, non-Christians, and the poor need not apply.

Consequently, disenfranchised segments of the student body—beginning with a handful of industrious college women in the Midwest—began their own elite and segregated social clubs. By the late nineteenth century, Pi Beta Phi (1867), Kappa Alpha Theta (1870), Kappa Kappa Gamma (1870), Delta Gamma (1872), Alpha Delta Pi (1904), and Phi Mu (1904) sororities were established to give educated white women a forum in which to discuss literature, poetry, and morality.[6]

By the turn of the twentieth century, African Americans also began forming their own Greek organizations. Alpha Phi Alpha Fraternity (1906), Alpha Kappa Alpha Sorority (1908), Kappa Alpha Psi Fraternity (1911), Omega Psi Phi Fraternity (1911), and Delta Sigma Theta Sorority (1913) were the first to take advantage of the financial, intellectual, social, and networking benefits of elite Greek institutions (Ross, 2000).[7]

Regardless of race or gender distinctions, however, *all* of America's social Greek organizations experienced a period of dramatic transformation in the second half of the twentieth century. With the ending of World War II in 1945—and the subsequent economic/ baby boom that followed—men and women began attending college in record numbers. And, as David Halberstam (1994) has argued, higher education quickly became democratized. Working-class men and women, minorities, and newly arrived immigrants, people who in years past would never have contemplated attending college, were now matriculating—and pledging social Greek organizations.

As a result, new Greek organizations were materializing at an unprecedented rate, old Greek organizations were expanding onto new campuses, membership for both was steadily climbing, and, partially because of the increasing need for university housing, fraternities and sororities began building their own domiciles—complete with bedrooms, kitchens, dining rooms, and "social" rooms. These developments played no small part in precipitating one of the most significant (and troubling) changes to the institution of the social Greek organization: The older organizations, which brought members together for conversation and camaraderie, were transformed into social clubs dedicated primarily to amusement. Poetry readings, literary circles, and dining were replaced with beer, sex, and rock and roll.

In 1957, the University of Chicago administrator and Phi Delta Theta alumni Ray Blackwell politely summarized this new Greek situation: "Perhaps most students would agree that the ever widening expanse of fraternity activities in the past few decades has caused some lessening of the emphasis of earlier days. In some chapters it may be the modern emphasis [i.e., partying] has relegated those ideals of the founders to secondary importance. . . . [Many have been] exceedingly critical . . . of fraternity membership for its failures to live up to the high ideals for which the fraternity has stood since the very beginning of the American nation" (p. vii).

However, not everything from the earlier years was discarded. Many of the older practices and rituals remained steadfast—albeit many ignobly augmented for a *different* generation of students. Fraternities and sororities, for instance, still "rush"—the process of membership recruitment where organizations evaluate potential new members (and vice versa). Those students deemed worthy are still "bid" or invited to "pledge"—pledging usually being a semester-long activity where new members learn about their organization, its members, activities, and responsibilities. At times, especially for fraternities, pledging involves the secret and now illegal act of "hazing"—behavior that often endangers, abuses, degrades, humiliates, and/or intimidates pledges.[8] Finally, for those who make it through the sometimes arduous and trying pledging process, there is still "initiation"—the secret induction ritual where new "brothers" and "sisters" learn the confidences, codes, passwords, and handshakes of their forefathers and foremothers.

These practices, rites, and rituals have remained relatively consistent over the years, as have two other aspects of Greek life. First, the social Greek system remains almost as segregated today as it was in 1776. No real interest in or commitment to the idea of integration, whether gender or racial, has been demonstrated. It can be argued, in fact, that the social fraternity/sorority remains the most segregated institution in America. Second, while a few Canadian universities have been colonized, fraternities and sororities both black and white have remained a uniquely American phenomenon.

Why Study the Greek System?

Given this contemporary, and often unflattering, description of social Greek organizations, some may wonder why I investigate Greeks—and not, for example, the basketball team, the cheerleaders, or the math club. After all, Greeks constitute a minority of students on most college campuses and are a relatively homogeneous group—namely, white, middle- to upper-class students. The answer to this question is threefold.

First, because of the secretive nature of the Greek system, most studies of it consist of reports from outside observers or quantitative survey research counting number of drinks consumed or parties attended. What has not been undertaken is research conducted from an insider's perspective, research that not only observes the way these students live their lives but also ascertains their perspectives, beliefs, hopes, and fears about being young in America in the twenty-first century.

Second, while Greeks constitute an average of only 8.5 percent of American college students,[9] they produce from among their ranks a staggering number of American leaders (NIC, n.d.). According to the Center for the Study of the College Fraternity (n.d.), Greeks, especially white fraternity members, dominate the elite realms of politics, law, and business, constituting, for example:

- 76 percent of U.S. senators;
- 71 percent of the men listed in *Who's Who in America*;
- 85 percent of the Fortune 500 executives;
- 120 of the *Forbes'* 500 CEOs, 10 in the top 30 alone (see table 1);
- 63 percent of U.S. presidents' cabinet members since 1900;
- 85 percent of the U.S. Supreme Court justices since 1910;
- 18 U.S. presidents since 1877 (see table 2).

This is to say nothing of the prominent positions held on most campuses by Greeks. As one of my students recently comment

Table 1. The Top 10 Greek CEOs on the *Forbes'* 500 List for 2003

Forbes Rank	Company	CEO	Fraternity
1	Citigroup	Sanford Weill	Alpha Epsilon Pi
4	American International Group	Maurice Greenberg	Sigma Alpha Mu
12	J.P. Morgan Chase	William B. Harrison Jr.	Zeta Psi
19	Goldman Sachs	Jenry Paulson	Sigma Alpha Epsilon
21	Procter & Gamble	Alan Lafley	Psi Upsilon
24	Wachovia	G. Kennedy Thompson	Beta Theta Pi
25	Berkshire Hathaway	Warren Buffett	Alpha Sigma Phi
27	Home Depot	Robert Nardelli	Tau Kappa Epsilon
28	BellSouth	F. Duane Ackerman	Lambda Chi Alpha
29	General Motors	G. Richard Wagoner	Delta Tau Delta

Note: These facts and figures are taken from http://www.forbes.com/2003/cx_dd_0131frat.html.

Table 2. Greek U.S. Presidents since 1877 and Their Fraternity Affiliations

President	Years in Office	Fraternity
Rutherford B. Hayes	1877–81	Delta Kappa Epsilon
James Garfield	1881	Delta Epsilon
Chester Arthur	1881–85	Psi Upsilon
Benjamin Harrison	1889–93	Phi Delta Theta
William McKinley	1897–1901	Sigma Alpha Epsilon
Theodore Roosevelt	1901-09	Delta Kappa Epsilon/ Alpha Delta Phi
William Howard Taft	1909–13	Psi Upsilon
Woodrow Wilson	1913–21	Phi Kappa Psi
Calvin Coolidge	1923–29	Phi Gamma Delta
Franklin D. Roosevelt	1933–45	Alpha Delta Phi
Harry S. Truman	1945–53	Lambda Chi Alpha
Dwight D. Eisenhower	1953–61	Tau Epsilon Phi
John F. Kennedy	1961–63	Phi Kappa Theta
Gerald R. Ford	1974–77	Delta Kappa Epsilon
Ronald Reagan	1981–89	Tau Kappa Epsilon
George H. W. Bush	1989–93	Delta Kappa Epsilon
George W. Bush	2001–	Delta Kappa Epsilon

ed: "Those damn Greeks run everything." It is not uncommon to find sorority and fraternity members who are student government presidents, homecoming kings and queens, student activity chairs, and department and college ambassadors. On all the five campuses on which I have spent significant amounts of time, it is virtually impossible to be elected to a prominent position without either being a Greek or having the support of the Greek voting bloc. At the University of Alabama, this voting bloc has even been given the ominous moniker "The Machine."

Third, the members of America's Greek system do not remain isolated on college campuses forever. They eventually grow older, leave their Greek houses, and enter the general population. Given the fact that there are already millions of Greek alumni in America today and that their ranks are augmented by 200,000 graduating seniors every spring, they are necessarily and inevitably to be found among our neighbors, our teachers, our police officers, our child-care professionals, our doctors, our school board representatives, our sons and daughters. Far from being an academic exercise, understanding the Greek system is a part of understanding America.

Methodology

The data that inform *Inside Greek U* were obtained through three separate but interdependent methods.[10] First, statistical data from institutional, academic, and government research supplied demographic figures on membership, pledging, GPAs, alcohol consumption, hazing fatalities, and postgraduate occupations and salaries nationwide. These numbers helped establish the scope and influence of America's Greek system.

The book also draws on my extensive involvement with fraternity and sorority life. I have been a part of the Greek experience for over twenty-five years. For the first four of those years, I was an undergraduate student and an active fraternity brother at Brandywine College, Wilmington, Delaware (A.A. 1982–84), and James Madison University, Harrisonburg, Virginia (B.A. 1984–86). I spent the next seven years in graduate school at the University of Alabama, Tuscaloosa (M.A. 1986–88), and Indiana University, Bloomington (Ph.D. 1988–1993), working toward advanced degrees in rhetoric and communication and, when time and opportunity permitted, remaining active as a Greek alumnus on two very pro-Greek campuses. By the end of those eleven years, I had experienced Greek life from a student's perspective on campuses that ranged from a private college in the Northeast with seven hundred students to public Research I institutions in the Deep South and Midwest with more than twenty and thirty thousand students, respectively.[11]

By 1993, it was time, to quote my mother, "to finally begin my life as a full-fledged working adult." I accepted a professorship in the Department of Communications at GU, an average-size (twenty-five to thirty thousand students) public Research I university currently hosting forty-one Greek organizations (thirty-four white and seven black) with approximately thirty-one hundred active members (around 13 percent of the full-time undergraduate population). The majority of undergraduate students on campus range in age from eighteen to twenty-five and come from white, middle-class families; freshman have an average incoming high school GPA of 3.1 and an average ACT score of 25 or an average SAT score of 1,100. GU is located in the middle of the eastern half of the United States and is a member of a major NCAA sports conference. Consequently, it attracts students from all fifty states searching for a typical college experience, complete with Saturday afternoon football games, great teachers, diverse courses, and, of course, fraternity and sorority life.

Given the nature of this dynamic university and its energetic students, it was only two semesters before I found myself drawn back to the Greek system—albeit this time as an alumni adviser with twenty-twenty hindsight. Fourteen years later, along with being a tenured professor, I am also the chapter director for the GU branch of my own fraternity and the faculty adviser for twelve different white social Greek organizations, one black social Greek organization, and two white social Greek governing organizations.[12]

While the amount of time I spend with each of these organizations as a director or an adviser varies greatly in any given year, depending as it does on the needs and personalities of each chapter, I have generally invested an average of two to three hours per week interacting with, mentoring, eating with, listening to, emceeing for, moderating among, socializing with, and, at times, reprimanding these groups. While university administrators have expressed their appreciation for my participation in student life (an activity that most professors avoid), the real benefit for me has been getting to know the university's thousands of brothers and sisters, both in the formal setting of *my* classroom and, more important, in the informal settings of *their* tailgates, Monday night dinners, chapter meetings, rush functions, fund-raisers, and graduation parties.

The nature of my participation in GU's Greek life was transformed, however, in September 2001, when I began gathering data for this book. Not only did I begin to increase the amount of time I spent with GU's Greeks (from two to three hours per week to four to five), but I also began keeping systematic field notes of my observations of and thoughts about how fraternity and sorority members negotiate their gender roles and identities through their daily performances.

Specifically, I entered salient conversations verbatim and detailed interactions (activities, practices, rituals) that took place at formal and informal Greek events. I also recorded my responses, both intellectual and emotional, to those conversations and interactions. On those occasions where doing so was neither conspicuous nor disruptive (e.g., chapter meetings, campus debates), I took notes on the spot. Most often, however, I recorded my thoughts immediately after an encounter, using a Sony portable digital recorder that, because of its small size (1½ × 2 inches), I was able to carry with me almost everywhere and, thus, capture spontaneous conversations as well.

Finally, this book is informed by focus group and individual interviews with 217 fraternity and sorority members conducted on the GU campus. Since I had worked so closely with the Greek system and was perceived as a pro-Greek faculty member, recruiting students for my videotaped focus group interviews was relatively easy. The real problem that I encountered was managing the logistics of getting large numbers of Greeks from different organizations to the right place at the right time. With the help of two graduate students—Erin (a Pi Beta Phi Sorority alumna from GU) and Amy (a Tri Delta Sorority alumna from GU)—I devised a plan using undergraduate *point people.*

Point people were GU Greek students whom I had previously, and successfully, worked with and trusted (most were either former students or members of a Greek organization that I had helped or advised), who were willing to serve as representatives and liaisons for their fraternity or sorority, and who were active members of one of the nineteen Greek organizations I wanted to study. The primary responsibilities of these students were to recruit eight to twelve interviewees who represented what *they* thought was an accurate and balanced cross section of their chapter and arrange a time that they could all meet for a two-hour focus group interview.[13] With the support and organizational skills of my nineteen enthusiastic point people, I conducted nineteen different focus-group interviews with five elite and four aspirer fraternities and six elite and four aspirer sororities.[14]

The elite organizations were GU's first-tier Greek organizations. They were well established, influential, wealthy, popular, and large, and their members lived in a fraternity or sorority house. They wielded a disproportionate influence on campus, were unanimously recognized by the Greek community and university officials as GU's top Greek organizations, and had produced the wealthiest, most influential alumni. They were also the most homogeneous groups, composed of attractive, middle- to upper-class, popular, white, Christian, heterosexual men and women who behaved in traditionally masculine and feminine ways.

The aspirer organizations were GU's second-tier Greek organizations. They were not as wealthy, selective, or influential as the elites, and membership in them was not as coveted. Their ranks were often filled with students who *just* missed the elite cut but still wanted to experience Greek life. Consequently, their membership was slightly more diverse: a little less attractive, popular, and wealthy, a little more ethnic,[15] and a little more likely to think and behave androgynously. It is important to remember, however, that they accepted these "differences," not because they were more self-actualized and enlightened (they did, ultimately, aspire to elite status), but because they were forced, by university-imposed quotas and their own financial exigencies, to be less selective when recruiting pledge classes.

Together the elites and the aspirers accounted for nineteen of GU's thirty-four fraternities and sororities. The remaining fifteen can be classified as the struggler organizations. These Greek pariahs were significantly smaller (many had fewer than twenty or thirty members), did not participate in collective Greek activities (fund-raisers, mixers/parties, talent shows, intramural sports), did not own/lease/rent a communal living space, were much newer (many were less than a decade old), were far less influential and visible on campus, and had virtually no alumni support. Their members were too ethnic, too heavy, too unattractive, too unpopular, too uninvolved, too unmasculine/unfeminine, too uncool, to receive bids from the aspirers or the elites. To highlight how invisible these groups were, most aspirers and elites were unaware of their existence.[16] Since the strugglers were so peripheral to campus life, I decided not to interview their members in focus groups but, instead, to select a representative sample of their membership for dyadic interviews.

Along with choosing which organizations to interview, I also had to decide on the composition of the focus groups. After much thought, I opted *not* to mix and match members from different organizations. I knew from experience that many of these groups had long-standing rivalries and, as a result, would have been far less forthcoming in mixed company. Instead, I interviewed each fraternity and sorority separately, keeping brothers and sisters together. Knowing how intimate and familiar they would be with each other, I was hoping for a more honest and open exchange. The quality of the interviews far exceeded my expectations.

To begin with, there were no periods of awkward silence, trepidation, or mistrust during the early stages of the interviews—a problem that arises when interviewing groups whose members have no shared history. These students, having already established intimacy, jumped into conversation almost immediately once the video recorder was turned on. Next, I discovered that, because of these students' shared history, memories and thoughts expressed by one often triggered memories and thoughts in the others. It was not uncommon for an innocuous topic, such as a party, to snowball into an intensely meaningful group conversation about the excessive drinking, the interpersonal conflict, and the sex that took place there. Finally, these brothers and sisters served as a great source of collective and corrective memory. Sometimes someone would forget key elements of a story; within seconds, the others would join the conversation and share in the story's expansion and development. Other times multiple interpretations of the same event would arise; in these cases, fun but passionate debate would take place over the contradictory perceptions. The important thing for me as a researcher was, not necessarily to work toward a unanimous resolution, but to record the multiple perspectives on a shared event.

Focus groups constituted only part of the interviewing process. In order to check the reliability of the focus groups, reach members of struggler organizations, obtain information about points that had not yet been covered, and seek clarification as new questions arose, I also conducted twenty-seven audiotaped individual interviews with students from twenty different white social Greek organizations. These interviews ranged in length from fifteen minutes to two hours, forty-five minutes. The students who participated in them were selected on the basis of personal insight, organizational affiliation, communication skill, leadership role, and/or diversity (what little there is in the white Greek system).

During both the focus group and the individual interviews, the questions that I asked and the discussions that were thereby generated addressed issues germane to gender. Specifically, the interviews were designed to cover six general, but interrelated, areas: how participants conceived of their own gender, how they conceived of the opposite gender, how their particular Greek organization defined appropriate gender behavior, how they supported and/or challenged their organization's conception of gender, what role they thought the Greek system played in their own conception of gender and in their development as men and women, and what they thought needed to be done to improve the Greek system in terms of gender relations.

Besides the questions of whom and how to interview, there were other significant issues that I wrestled with as a researcher. The most important of these was how my sex, age, Greek affiliations, and professional position would influence the content and nature of the interviews. Would the men react to me by being competitive and aggressive, the women by being secretive and circumspect? Would both perceive my project as exploitative (as most similar projects have been)? Or would they perceive it as legitimate and worthwhile and, thus, choose to trust me?

With the final interviews transcribed, coded, and analyzed, I feel confident in claiming that both the men and the women who participated in my study were extremely honest and forthright with me. This assertion—which speaks to the reliability and validity of my project—is supported by at least four verifying techniques. First, a cross-referencing of the facts, figures, and narrative accounts supplied by the interviewees uncovered no instances of concealment, deception, or lying. While there were clearly multiple *evaluative* perspectives on issues—for example, whose organization was best—no two interviewees ever supplied contradictory or incongruent *factual* accounts. Second, in the almost eighty hours of taped interviews, I captured no statements significantly contradicting what I had observed in my thirteen years at GU as a professor, chapter director, or faculty adviser. Third, as I began finishing drafts of chapters, I asked interested sorority and fraternity members to read and respond to my interpretations and assertions. In all cases, I was told that both my descriptions and my discussions were accurate and informed, albeit sometimes painful and embarrassing to read. Finally, all my point people claimed—in exit interviews conducted with them—that their groups were "surprisingly honest," "really truthful," and "pulled no punches." They also reported that their members thought that, given my history with the Greeks, I could be "definitely trusted" and that they believed that I would use this research "to help the Greek system get stronger."

This is not to claim, however, that my results are absolute or that my sex, race, age, and professional position did not influence—positively or negatively—what was said (or what was asked) in the interviews. It is inevitable, as Gadamer's (1975) idea of philosophical hermeneutics reminds us, that, regardless of how neutral, objective, and unbiased I strive to be, who I am affects not only how I interact with others and how others interact with me but also how I perceive the problem I am investigating, what questions I ask, what questions I don't ask, and how I interpret the answers I receive. Consequently, the best I can do as a researcher is to be academically responsible and ethical, acknowledge that I can tell only *my* story, not *the* story, and reflect constantly on how my position in this project might affect the story I tell.

Finally, this work is a case study of one public university in America. The goal of this project is not to draw absolute conclusions about America or American college life in general. I do believe, however, that my results are reliable enough to allow readers to draw their own cautious inferences about other white fraternity and sorority systems in America, especially those at large, public universities.

General Overview

I have chosen to allow the organization of this book to be guided by the students who shared their stories and lives with me. Consequently, after a brief discussion of gender identity and theory, I move on to discussions of the five aspects of gender identified by them as most important: sexuality, aggression and competition, body image, relationships, and postcollege careers. More specifically, the book unfolds as follows.

In chapter 1, "Understanding Gender," I discuss the ways in which identity formation, gender construction, and performativity theory function as a critical lens for this study. I also preview the seven most significant conclusions to be drawn from it, conclusions that will serve to unify subsequent chapters and underscore overarching themes.

In chapter 2, "Studs and Virgins," I consider the ways in which men and women conceive of sexuality and relationships. Men, for example, are encouraged to sleep with as many women as possible, objectify women through both dehumanizing actions and misogynistic discourse, view acceptable relationships within the confines of a fraternity house, and are driven by homophobic fears to eliminate any effeminate or sensitive personality from their organization. Women, by contrast, search for "virtuous" sisters through the rush and pledge process, eliminate any woman with a questionable sexual reputation, redefine oral and anal intercourse as nonsexual activities in order to maintain their vestal identities, prevent pregnancies, and appease their dates, and perform for men (through suggestive dance, provocative dress, and bisexual flirting) to obtain both power and attention. When all is said and done, however, a brother who gets laid is still a stud and the sister who gets laid still a whore.

In chapter 3, "The Tough Guy and His Date (Rape)," I explore how Greek men and women manage their emotions and actions in same-sex and opposite-sex relationships. For example, GU's fraternity men practice a hyperaggressive and competitive masculinity with each other. The most coveted man in any house is the brother who is successful both in the bedroom and on the battlefield. Fighting, however, is not only a way to climb the fraternal caste system; it is also a means of male bonding. As these men testify, there is nothing that brings brothers together like "going to war" with another fraternity. Tragically, aggression also often figures prominently in these men's relationships with women.

In chapter 4, "Her Laxatives, His Steroids," I explore how Greeks today think about body shape and size. I discovered, not surprisingly, that the overwhelming majority of sorority women suffer from what can best be described as an unhealthy relationship with food. They perpetually diet, suffer from eating disorders, obsessively count calories, carbs, and fat, view food as an enemy, exercise compulsively, and no longer enjoy eating. Ironically, fraternity men are becoming just as obsessive about body image as sorority women have traditionally been. More and more are lifting weights, taking supplements, using steroids, shaving, waxing, and tanning their bodies, and primping, preening, and grooming themselves to death. In the end, the men are never big enough, the women never small enough.

In chapter 5, "Bros before Hos," I examine how Greeks are taught to think about the platonic and romantic relationships in their lives. Interestingly, there is not in this case a split along gender lines. Both fraternity men and sorority women are encouraged to be interdependent, not individualistic. In fact, as most sorority women admit, fraternity brothers are bonded emotionally in ways that non-Greek men, women, and even sorority sisters are not. Unfortunately, this may be the only time in their lives that such a bond exists for them. Masculine individuality and isolation become the norms after men graduate and exit the fraternity house.

In chapter 6, "Soccer Moms and Corporate Dads," I address my subjects' postcollege hopes and dreams. Not surprisingly, fraternity men do not make academics a priority but still dream of high-paying, socially prestigious jobs. They also take for granted that there will be women in their lives who will assume complete responsibility for the domestic sphere. Interestingly, most sorority women envision a postcollege life that privileges the domestic over the professional even though they work harder and earn better grades than most other students on campus.

In the final chapter, "Cleaning Up after the Party," I summarize my major findings and evaluate the Greek system's strengths and weaknesses. Most important, however, I offer concerned faculty, alumni, students, parents, and administrators practical suggestions for moving fraternities and sororities closer to the idealized goals of higher education.

1. Understanding Gender

It is no exaggeration to say that this book has taken me over two decades to conceptualize. From the first day that I began pledging my fraternity in 1982, I remember being both intrigued by the Greek system's secrecy, friendships, and social life and disturbed by its elitism, sexism, and hazing. My ambivalence, however, did not prevent me from becoming—and remaining—an ardent, but critical, supporter of Greek life.

In the years that followed my graduation and subsequent departure from my fraternity house, I conceived of at least a dozen ill-fated research projects, all attempting to address the nature of the Greek system's strengths and weaknesses. None was quite right. Then, in the summer of 2000, after returning from a four-day fraternity conference where I spoke—or, more accurately, hung out—with hundreds of undergraduate brothers from around the nation, I had a breakthrough, an epiphany of sorts. Fraternities and sororities can be best understood as *gendered clubs* where traditional ideas of masculinity and femininity are reaffirmed—and, in some cases, even reformed or replaced.

This book, therefore, is about the symbiotic relation that the Greek system has with its members. It influences their gender conceptions; they influence its gender practices. And, when they leave college, they disproportionately influence America. It is crucial, then, that we understand fraternities and sororities not only as institutions but also as they affect and are affected by their members.

The following discussion details the theoretical lens used to investigate that intersection between the individual and the institution. Specifically, I discuss why I chose to privilege gender over other aspects of identity, elaborate on the ideas of gender construction and performativity theory, and preview the nine most significant conclusions to be drawn from my work.

Aspects of Identity

While this book focuses on *gender*, masculinity and femininity are only part of the factors that inform the complex web of human identities. Other frequently discussed aspects of identity, as Gauntlett (2002) summarized, "include class, age, disability and sexuality" (p. 13). In addition, geographic origins (I'm from New Jersey), education, ethnicity (I'm an Italian American), and occupation (I'm a percussionist and a professor) can also shape an individual's sense of self.

Which variables come to the forefront in the process of self-definition, however, are often determined by contextual and relational factors. For example, I think of myself as an Italian American only when I am around other Italian Americans or when the topic of Italian culture is broached. Similarly, I never thought of myself as a Yankee until I attended the University of Alabama. Before then, being from New Jersey was inconsequential to how I defined myself. After all, everyone I ever knew was from New Jersey—*what was the big deal?* In Tuscaloosa, however, my birthplace *was* a big deal; it was the major factor by which my Alabama peers (endearingly) defined me and, thus, became a major factor in my self-definition (see Hewitt, 1991, pp. 124–129).

Such redefinitions affect not only the way we think about ourselves but also the way we act toward others. For example, when individuals or situations bring my Italian American identity to the forefront, my communication style changes noticeably. I become more ethnic in the way I talk, act, and walk. This transformation is made even more complex by the fact that my conception of what it means to be/act Italian is informed by my ideas of traditional, tough-guy masculinity and an aggressive Northeastern attitude, à la Marlon Brando's Vito Corleone or James Gandolfini's Tony Soprano.

Because identity is so fluid and layered, multiple self-definitions are commonplace. Depending on the contextual factors at play at any given time, ethnicity, class, race, or gender will be thrust to the forefront of consciousness or relegated to its deepest recesses (Hewitt, 1991, pp. 121–123). What distinguishes people, therefore, is not necessarily their identities themselves but how often they are forced to think about and even redefine their identities. Generally speaking, those with power and in the majority (two factors that often accompany one another) are far less likely to have to think about or redefine their identities (Flagg, 1997; McIntosh, 1997; Morrison, 1993; Ross, 1997).

Nowhere is this privilege illustrated better than in America's white social Greek system. Once young students pledge an organization and move into the Greek community, they are, for all intents and purposes, surrounded by a stable, homogeneous group of brothers and sisters for the next four to five years of their lives. And, since the overwhelming majority of their brothers and sisters are white, middle- to upper-class,[1] Christian, and heterosexual, *gender* and Greek affiliation become the sole factors informing their self-identities. We should not be surprised, therefore, that, almost without exception, the men and women who participated in this study thought of themselves as *just* Greek men and women.

But there is a price to pay for such comfortable conformity. When individuals are placed in such protective communities, other aspects of their identity become invisible to them. Those who never encounter African Americans never have to think about *their* own whiteness. Those who never encounter poverty never have to think about *their* own economic privilege. Those who never encounter homosexuals never have to confront the meaning of *their* own heterosexuality. Their own race, class, ethnicity, and sexual orientation, therefore, are free to masquerade as natural and universal.

The segregation in the lives of these men and women, however, is no accident or coincidence. Maintaining sameness is built into the very nature of these selective and secretive organizations. Nowhere is this more in evidence than during the all-important rush process, where the worth and fit of potential new members is deliberated. For over two decades, I have witnessed sameness methodically reproduced at rush not just by the favoritism shown to those rushees most similar to the older brothers and sisters but by the absolute exclusion of those who are significantly different—a practice that Cornell West (1994) has called *racial nepotism.*

This selective exclusion is so well known on most campuses, in fact, that the large majority of black, Hispanic, Asian, homosexual, non-Christian, and disabled students do not even bother attending rush functions. For those brave, uninformed, and/or optimistic students who do, however, almost certain rejection—and, in many cases, humiliation—awaits them.

Last semester, for example, I witnessed three international students from Saudi Arabia walk into one of GU's top fraternity houses looking for the all-American college experience. Unfortunately, but unsurprisingly, they were treated as trespassers. Not only did every active fraternity brother avoid conversation with them; none greeted, smiled, or even made eye contact with them. Within minutes of their entrance, they unceremoniously left. While I later apologized to them for their treatment and assured them that not all student organizations on campus were so unfriendly, I could not in good conscience encourage them to visit other fraternity houses, knowing that the same reception awaited them there too.[2]

This type of treatment of nonwhite students is not uncommon on GU's campus, or, for that matter, on most campuses that I have experienced. African American men and women (GU's largest minority group) who walk through white rush, for instance, often receive a similar collective cold shoulder. I have been in deliberative meetings, in fact, where blocs of members have convinced their chapters to exclude blacks because of the "dangerous" precedent it would set. At one such rush meeting, Mark, a senior Kappa, asserted that, if the chapter extended a bid to Jason, a young black man from Chicago, the floodgates would soon open, and the chapter would become "one big ghetto," inundated with "niggers." "Is that what you guys want?" The chapter answered with a resounding no. Jason never received a bid.

While the fear of being ghettoized may motivate some organizations to remain segregated, other fraternities claim to have retained their all-white status out of fear of sorority rejection and isolation. At a 2004 international fraternity conference in Chicago, I asked a group of delegates representing four large Southeastern universities to explain this particular concern:

AD: Tell me why extending a bid to a black member would be bad for your organization?

Michael: The sororities won't socialize with you. No date parties. And, hell, no overnight formals.

Sean: Exactly, especially like old row houses.

AD: What are old row houses?

Sean: The oldest sororities. . . . They are the richest and best. The really good ones.

Spencer: They are just as bad as we are. Mommy and daddy would not like it if little Susie was fraternizing with black men. [*Collective agreement.*]

Michael: Now, the bad sororities will still party with you.

Spencer: Yeah, but they're desperate. Those cows will party with anybody. [*Group laughter.*]

Some elite houses will, however, make the rare exception for certain African American rushees. At one of the best and richest fraternities on GU's campus, for instance, two black members, Kevin and Carl, have pledged and been initiated in the last four years. For this to have happened, the older brothers had to be convinced that Kevin and Carl were not "niggers." As Smitty explained: "We don't hate black people; it's only the niggers that we don't want. . . . But if you are *cool,* you know, *normal,* then I don't think many of us would—well some would—really have a problem pledging a *cool* black guy."

But to be classified as *cool* and *normal* by Smitty, his brothers, and the white Greek system in general, African American students must be black in skin color only. That is, to have any chance of acceptance, they must talk white, dress white, act white, have no black friends, reject black culture and tradition, and be light skinned. And, even then, the possibility of rejection remains disturbingly high, especially at universities in the Deep South.

Some exclusionary practices that keep fraternities and sororities dangerously homogeneous, however, are not as consciously blatant or malicious. Sometimes, brothers and sisters naively vote for or against rush candidates solely on the basis of whether they like and feel comfortable with them. "I don't care whether you are black, white, pink, green, who cares," explains John, Omega's vice president. "When I cast my vote, I only think about whether I like you as a human or not. Period." What John and many of his fellow Greeks don't acknowledge, however, is that, as over fifty years' worth of social-psychological research has demonstrated, liking and comfort levels are highly correlated with perceived commonalities (Byrne, 1971; Cialdini, 2001). Thus, the more you think you have in common with people—for example, race, nationality, religion, and sexual preference—the more likely you are to enjoy their company and conversation and, by extension, rush, bid, pledge, and befriend them (Brewer, 1979; Tajfel, 1981).

This link between similarity and liking, therefore, explains the absence of malice in the many good-hearted, moral students who, in choosing new brothers and sisters, favor similarity and exclude difference. The absence of malice, however, does not mitigate the effect. Sameness is perpetuated, the status quo is reinforced, and the organization is deprived of diverse perspectives and talents.

As a researcher, I have found that this troubling absence of difference informing and complicating my subjects' identities has allowed me to isolate gender as key to understanding how fraternity brothers and sorority sisters define themselves, their compatriots, and their organizations. They see themselves, living in their homogeneous community where only gender and Greek affiliation separate one from another, as *just* Greek men and women talking, studying, playing, and partying with other Greek men and women just like them.

The Theoretical Foundation of This Book

This book adopts the general perspective that our ideas of gender (i.e., masculine and feminine) are shaped and constructed by social forces and discourse—such as media, family, societal traditions, and peer groups—not innate to the human biological form. That is to say, while after birth we have little say regarding our gender designation (male or female), how we come to understand our specific gender *role* is an ongoing cultural process. Parents and teachers, cartoons and toys, religion and MTV, all influence the way we come to understand what it means to be a "man's man" or a "good girl."

This is not to imply, however, that gender is fixed or something that one *is*. Rather, as Judith Butler (1990) has argued, gender is something that one *does*. It is, as Salih notes, "an act, or more precisely, a sequence of acts, a verb rather than a noun, a doing rather than a being" (2002, p. 62). Butler expands on the idea of performativity: "Gender is always a doing, though not a doing by a subject who might be said to preexist the deed. . . . There is no gender identity behind the expressions of gender; that identity is *performatively* constituted by the very 'expressions' that are said to be its results" (1990, p. 25). Thus, gender should be seen, not as a fixed attribute or idea, but as a "fluid variable which can shift and change in different contexts and at different times" (Gauntlett, 2002, p. 139). On my college campus, for instance, I find men and women adopting myriad different gender performances, some, admittedly, more encouraged and rewarded than others. Lisa, a Kappa sister, for example, told me how she "kicked ass and took no prisoners" in her finance report on Wednesday, dressed provocatively and "danced dirty" at the clubs on Saturday, and presided over a meeting of her 160-member chapter on Monday. Similarly, Mark, a Chi brother, proudly told me how he spent his Saturday afternoon encouraging and hugging Special Olympic athletes and his Saturday night drinking, fighting, and aggressively pursuing women.

Lisa and Mark's activities, as different as they may seem on the surface, highlight the fluid and mercurial nature of gender in practice. With each new performance, their gendered identities changed, illustrating that no single performance is more essential or authentic to their core. Or, to put it another way, there is no "core gender identity that produces one's gendered activities." "Rather," as Eckert and McConnell-Ginet have argued, "it is those very activities that create the illusion of a core. And it is the predominance of certain kinds of performances that support the illusion that one's core is either 'male' or 'female'" (2003, p. 316).

Conceiving of gender as performance, however, is not to imply that men and women are *free* to perform where, when, and how they wish. Our choices of gender scripts are set within a "highly rigid regulatory frame that congeals over time to produce the appearance of substance, of a natural sort of being" (Butler, 1990, p. 33). To pick the wrong performance within the wrong context can, as many gay men and lesbian women can testify, result in ridicule, ostracism, violence, and even death.

For most of the fraternity brothers and sorority sisters who participated in this study, however, the process of selecting the most culturally appropriate gender script has been largely unconscious and effortless. Because traditional masculine and feminine behaviors repeat themselves over time, most subjects viewed their performances as following natural, ahistoric, and God-given paths. It is this masquerade of neutrality that prevents them from both seriously contemplating the logic or saneness of their gendered actions and conceiving, much less adopting, new and unconventional scripts. Indeed, for many of these students, only the insane (including queers, fags, dykes, queens, etc.) and the misanthropic (including hippies, punk rockers, druggies, etc.) disobey the natural dictates of appropriate gender behavior.

However, this resistance to nontraditional gender roles and the durability of the status quo does not eliminate the possibility of change and subversion: "If gender is a performance, then it can be turned on its head—or turned into anything" (Gauntlett, 2002, p. 139). We need not wait for an uprising demanding, or a constitutional amendment dictating, tolerance. Gender can be reinvented by anyone who breaks expectations, challenges taken-for-granted ideas, or parodies stereotypical routine in his or her gender performances (Butler, 1990, pp. 30–34). David Bowie's gender-bending Ziggy Stardust in the 1970s, Dustin Hoffman's Tootsie in the 1980s, and Madonna's dominatrix stage and screen persona in the 1990s come to mind as popular subversive examples. The public performances of all three figures challenged traditional ideas of gender, thus expanding the possibilities for future gender performances by others.

But engendering change is not reserved only for the famous. As Butler reminds us, we are all either part of the problem or part of the solution—whether we want that responsibility or not. The question becomes, therefore, not *whether* to perform—for all identity is already performance—but *what* to perform. If we simply follow convention, the path that most of us blindly and unquestionably take, then not only do we perpetuate the illusion that gender is permanent and neutral, but we also limit the possibilities open to others who wish to operate outside traditional gender categories.

In many ways then, the American Greek system is Butler's worst theoretical nightmare. As will be argued throughout this book, fraternities and sororities proudly and fiercely reproduce *many* of the most traditional and harmful ideas about gender through their scripted performances. These are places where men are expected to act like "real" men, not sissies, women are coerced into acting like "real" women, not sluts, and those who are too androgynous or ambivalent in their gendered performances are denied entrance. In the end, the rigidity of the Greek institution produces a subculture where deviant performances—performances that are potentially liberating because of their ability to expand brothers' and sisters' gendered repertoire—are prohibited.

Learning the Right Performance

For most of the men and women in my study, blending in, being popular, and fulfilling social expectations on GU's campus have come easily. By the time students enter Greek row, they have already undergone eighteen years of intensive gender lessons—from their mothers and fathers, their coaches and teachers, Disney films and MTV videos—impressing on them the proper performances to enact in order to be welcomed into traditional elite white society.

When asked to discuss these lessons, most of these students had indelible, and, at times, painful, memories of being shaped and molded. Grace, an eighteen-year-old Alpha sister, remembers the toys she and her brother would receive at Christmas. She recalls always getting "Barbies, Easy-Bake Ovens, and pretty dresses." Her brother, however, always got the "cool stuff." He would have "the living room filled with guns, balls, erector sets." The message, she remembers, was clear: "Girls cook and take care of baby dolls, and boys build and shoot things."

Sally, a twenty-year-old Epsilon sister, remembers being shunned by the girls and not asked out by the boys because she "loved sports and getting dirty." "I knew what was expected of me," she remembered. "You know, sit on the sidelines and cheer while the boys play, . . . wear uncomfortable dresses, . . . just look pretty." "You pay the price," she told her focus group. "Act unfeminine, and you are just not popular."

Many of the males I interviewed also had memories of gender lessons. Interestingly, many entailed hypermasculine coaches and homophobic fathers. Bill, a senior from Michigan, remembers his Pop Warner football coach who "would actually rub dirt in your cuts, it would make you a man or something, and smack you in your helmet if you cried." Josh remembers gaining increased popularity after getting into his first playground fight in the fifth grade. "It was funny," he said, "but no one really saw me as a tough guy. Then I hit this kid in the face, his nose bled, and all of a sudden I'm cool.

Even my dad was psyched. You know, he was like, 'Yeah! My son's not gay.'"

Others recall the gender lessons derived from books, magazines, videos, music, and television. A very enlightened Nancy remembers never seeing any women represented in school textbooks. "They were all white men . . . presidents, generals, politicians, scientists, . . . women were nowhere. No wonder so many of us [referring to her sisters] go into elementary education and not into medicine or engineering. Those jobs just seem like male things to do." Robert remembers playing with his sisters, who always wanted to watch Snow White and the Little Mermaid on video. "They wanted to play 'save the princess' and shit." "For me," he remembered, "I loved the Ninja Turtles and the Batman cartoons. I wanted to chop things and run around the house and punch bad guys." Finally, Alice, a twenty-year-old Beta sister from Louisiana, like many of her contemporaries, recalls the impact that MTV had on her understanding of femininity. "My girlfriends and I used to love Madonna," she recalled. "We thought she was so sexy and nasty. We would dress up and grab ourselves [meaning their crotches]." One evening, however, her father caught them "acting out." He was "so angry. He and my mom gave us this big talk about being inappropriate and how nice girls were supposed to act. It was such drama in our house, but we never did it again."

But just because gender is a controlling force in our lives does not mean that masculinity and femininity are stable and static. Like everything else in our linguistically constructed world, they too will inevitably change with time and vary from culture to culture. Prior to the Industrial Revolution, for example, very few gender distinctions were made in America between the domestic and the professional spheres of labor. Both men and women participated in farming, raising the children, running the business, and homemaking (Ryan, 1979). And, while it may seem difficult to believe given contemporary standards, industry and strength were prized attributes in women as well as men (Cancian, 1989).

An investigation of world cultures further illustrates just how arbitrary many Western gender ideas are. On the island of New Guinea, for example, Margaret Mead found at least three different gender patterns. Wood (2005, p. 24) summarizes Mead's findings:

Among *Arapesh* people, both women and men conform closely to what we consider feminine behavior. Both are passive, peaceful, and deferential, and both nurture others, especially young children. The *Mundugumor* tribe socializes both women and men to be aggressive, independent, and competitive. Mothers are not nurturant and spend very little time with newborn babies, but instead wean them early. Within the *Tchambuli* society, genders are the converse of current ones in America. Women are domineering and sexually aggressive, while men are considered delicate and are taught to wear decorative clothes and curl their hair so they will be attractive to women.

In Tahiti, David Gilmore (1990) found a "bizarre lack of sexual differentiation." Wives can dominate and "even beat their husbands." Tahitian women also participate in all sporting events, even wrestling, equally with men (p. 202). One also finds village transsexuals, called *mahu,* "who elect to be honorary women. More than simply tolerated, they are . . . often highly respected." As anomalous as Tahitian *mahu* may seem, similar gender benders can be found in the *berdache* of the North American Plains Indians, the *xanith* of the Omani Muslims, and the *eunichs* of India (p. 207).

As these examples illustrate, gender is not a fixed, absolute standard, but a fluid, ever-shifting idea, influenced by customs, epochs, economics, media, religion, politics, and, of course, individual performances. On American college campuses at the turn of a new century, a unique ideal of femininity and masculinity has developed. In my attempt to understand its meaning and its influence on the lives of sorority sisters and fraternity brothers, a number of salient theoretical findings emerged, findings that undergird the rest of this project.

The Theoretical Findings Informing This Book

Seven significant conclusions drawn from this research serve as the theoretical foundation for this book. Some of these conclusions build on previous findings, others cut against the prevailing theoretical grain, and still others discuss new areas not previously addressed by gender researchers. All these conclusions, however, highlight the social and performative nature of gender and the interconnection between masculinity and femininity and between the individual and the institution.

The Masculine/Feminine Dichotomy

Most gender researchers agree that the categories *masculine* and *feminine* are socially constructed and that there is nothing natural about this binary division according to which all individuals born with penises are expected to be masculine (e.g., assertive, promiscuous, independent, and successful) and all those born with vaginas are expected to be feminine (e.g., nurturing, monogamous, interdependent, and domestic). Given the complexity of human personality, this dualistic, oppositional view is not only ridiculously simplistic; it is also oppressively limiting. Consequently, many scholars advocate the proliferation of new gender categories based, not on sex organs, but on personality traits and free choice (Bem, 1993), and some even champion the complete abolishment of all categories. For, as Foucault has asserted, all categorization, regardless of its intention, is oppressive (Foucault, 1994).

The fraternity brothers and sorority sisters whom I interviewed and observed for this project, however, did not view gender so poststructurally. In their eyes, there are only the two God-given gender roles—masculinity and femininity—each composed of five innate characteristics.[3] This binary worldview was so ingrained in their thinking that they could conceive of themselves and others in no other terms. Not even the performance of nontraditional gender roles could break its hold. Consequently, I have organized this book around the notions of masculinity and femininity. For, if we are to understand what gender means to my subjects, we must view the world through their cognitive and linguistic divisions.

The first half of the students' binary worldview highlighted their conception of masculinity and the five performances and/or attributes that they believe constitute it. But this conception is by no means uniformly held in America. Trujillo (1991), for example, argues that masculinity is made up of "physical force," "occupational achievement," "familial patriarchy," "frontiersmanship," and "heterosexuality." To this list, House, Dallinger, and Kilgallen (1998) and Wood (2005) add "rational thinking" and "emotional control," and Connell (1990) highlights the importance of "toughness/power," "competitiveness," the "subordination of women," and the "marginalization of gay men."

Analyzing masculinity from a more multilayered perspective, Connell (1995) has argued that there is no one monolithic idea of the ideal man but, instead, multiple conceptions influenced by myriad social and personal factors, for example, blue-collar (physical) versus white-collar (technical) American workers. Following a similarly more complex path, Brod's (1994) study of Jewish men, Mac an Ghaill's (1994) analysis of African Americans, and Hondagneu-Sotelo and Messner's (1994) work on Mexican immigrants have all highlighted cultural influences that affect the way different ethnicities conceptualize the ideal American man. Other noteworthy attempts to understand this illusive and ever-changing conception include Bordo (1999), Brod and Kaufman (1994), Connell (1987, 2002), Gilmore (1990), Kiesling (2001), Kimmel (2003), Miedzian (1991), and Whitehead and Barrett (2001).

For the white men and women in this study, however, prototypical masculinity is composed of five interrelated themes.

Heterosexual Promiscuity. This is the idea (discussed in chapter 2) that having as much sex and with as many women as possible increases a man's rank and prestige. The objects of the male sexual conquest, however, must be female, for homosexual activity is *the* great taboo in the world of fraternities. Consider the response of Mike, a twenty-one-year-old Omega brother who threatened to "throw any fag living in [his] house out the fucking window."[4]

Toughness and Assertiveness. This is the idea (discussed in chapter 3) that no real man takes shit from anyone and that fighting to establish one's reputation as a tough guy is not just tolerated but encouraged. As John, a twenty-year-old Alpha brother, put it, nothing makes a man quite like "beating the crap out of someone while your buddies watch."

Imposing Physical Type. This is the idea (discussed in chapter 4) that, the more muscular and imposing one is, the more one meets ideal standards of masculinity. Consequently, according to John, at least 60 percent of his Delta chapter "goes to Gold's Gym five times a week to get cut, you know, defined." As one of John's brothers remarked: "When you have the cannons [i.e., muscular arms], the guys fear you, and the chicks dig you."

Relational Independence. This is the idea (discussed in chapter 5) that real men are self-reliant, needing no other male, and, of course, no other female, to accomplish tasks, manage their emotions, or be complete. While the Marlboro Man may be ancient history to this generation, the prototypical masculine concept that he stood for is alive and well.

Professional Orientation. This is the idea (discussed in chapter 6) that men should be, first and foremost, successful in the public or business realm. This drive toward professional achievement in the public sphere stands in contrast to notions of appropriate behavior in the private sphere, where, as Ron, a twenty-year-old Beta put it, "the wife takes care of the kids and keeps the house nice."

FEMININITY AND ITS FIVE GENDER THEMES

The second, but equally necessary, half of the student's binary conception of gender highlighted their conception of femininity and the five performances and/or attributes that they believe constitute it.

In attempts to understand the notion of femininity, scholars such as Cancian (1989), Riessman (1990), and Wood (1993) have asserted that to be feminine in America is to be "attractive" (preferably thin and white), "deferential," "unaggressive," "sensitive," and "emotional." A "good woman" should also be "nurturing," "concerned with people and relationships," "an adoring mother," and a "meticulous housekeeper." For all the developments in women's rights, asserts Wood, "the basic blueprint remains relatively constant" (1999, p. 23).

Others, such as Gauntlett (2002), however, have argued that notions of femininity *have* been significantly transformed in the last thirty years. Today's women, he argues, "are not generally bothered about fitting their identity within the ideal of [traditional] femininity" (p. 10). Instead, femininity is just one of many performances that modern women employ. Similarly complicating the idea of *the* American woman, hooks's (2000) and Joseph and Lewis's (1981) research on African American women, Beemyn and Eliason's (1996) work on lesbians, Anzuldúa's (1999) ideas on Latino femininity, and Espiritu's (1997) analysis of Asian Americans have all argued for a more complex and multicultural understanding of femininity.

The white middle-class men and women in this study, however, conceived of femininity as the sum of five traditional, interrelated categories that antithetically mirrored their traditional ideas of masculinity.

Monogamy and Virginity. This is the idea (discussed in chapter 2) that nice girls don't—or, if they do, it is with only one man to whom they are deeply, emotionally connected. The worst infraction, in fact, that any sorority sister can commit is to be "trashy, easy, or slutty." For such transgressions, offenders will be reprimanded by the organization's judicial board, ostracized by their own sisters, or even blackballed.

Nurturing and Caring. This is the idea (discussed in chapter 3) that good women are caregivers and nurturers, whether they are tending to children, boyfriends, or sorority sisters. As Alice, a nursing major, asserted: "This thing [caregiving] is what makes women women. We naturally care and worry about others. Men just don't think about that stuff."

Petite Physical Type. This is the idea (discussed in chapter 4) that women should be petite and thin. Any variation, for example, being overly muscular, large, or overweight, is seen as a serious flaw in the female form. This motif was so punctuated by the women that I interviewed that most openly admitted to having a very unhealthy relationship with food. "I can't remember the last time I really enjoyed pizza or ice cream because you know you always feel so guilty, bad, like you did something wrong like getting fat," Deborah, an Alpha, remarked.

Relational Interdependence. This is the idea (discussed in chapter 5) that, to be fulfilled and happy, a woman needs others in her life to complete her. She is a daughter to her father, a wife to her husband, a mother to her children, and a friend to her friends. Across college campuses, for instance, while fraternity men are ridiculed for having a girlfriend, sorority sisters are celebrated for falling in love, thus fulfilling their relational destiny.

Domestic Orientation. This is the idea (discussed in chapter 6) that, whether she chooses to work outside the home or not, a good woman always prioritizes the domestic sphere. For many of the women I interviewed, a college degree is more a safety net in case of divorce or a way to supplement her husband's salary (the family's primary income) than a means to a fulfilling professional career. As Nancy, a senior education major in the Gamma house, told me: "I will teach first or second grade after my kids start school so that I will have a schedule that will allow me to be at home with my kids and husband."

Symmetrical Gender Pairings

In the coding and analysis of my interviews and interactions with students, the ten themes listed above formed a *gendered pairing sys-*

tem in which each concept was aligned with its binary opposite. As Wood (2005) has argued, the two genders as our society conceives them are always defined "relationally" and, as such, make sense only "in relation to each other." Our society, she continues, "defines femininity in contrast to masculinity, and masculinity as a counterpoint to femininity" (p. 27). Or, in Doyle's (1995) conception, each gender serves as a "negative touchstone" for the other. To be a real man means not to be feminine or risk being ridiculed as a sissy, fag, or mama's boy. Conversely, to be a good woman means not to act masculine or risk being disparaged as a bitch, butch, or dyke.

Gender Themes of Masculinity		Gender Themes of Femininity
Heterosexual Promiscuity	↔	Monogamy and Virginity
Toughness and Assertiveness	↔	Nurturing and Caring
Imposing Physical Type	↔	Petite Physical Type
Relational Independence	↔	Relational Interdependence
Professional Orientation	↔	Domestic Orientation

Figure 1. Symmetrical pairing.

As is outlined in figure 1, the men in this study could not explain what it means to be tough and assertive without referring to the antithetical feminine theme of being nurturing and caring. Conversely, the women could not articulate their understanding of what it means to be interdependent without referring to the masculine theme of being independent. Consequently, the only way to understand the complexity of any of the ten gender themes is to view it as it relates to its antithesis.

The Blurring of These Gender Categories

Positioned on a graph, or discussed in isolation, these ten gender themes can give the false impression that they exist in strict isolation, to the exclusion of cross-gendered performances. In practice, however, the boundaries between them often overlap, students' gendered performances regularly crossing the borders between masculinity and femininity.

In chapter 2, for example, we hear both women and men discussing sexual experimentation (masculine theme) and their search for soul mates (feminine theme). The lines are similarly blurred in chapter 6 when both men and women discuss the anxiety they feel when thinking about how they might balance their private (feminine theme) and public (masculine theme) lives after graduation. Finally, in chapter 5, both the fraternity brothers and the sorority sisters, using almost identical language, verbalize the intensely competitive relationship (masculine theme) they have with rival organizations and the unconditional support (feminine theme) they give to their own Greek families.

These ten gender categories are, thus, best conceptualized as, not fixed, but fluid, continually shaped by social discourse and performance, as templates that arrange the world into simplistic and comprehensible segments for the men and women who use them. Thus, while this gender matrix may appear to be orderly and clearly defined, it is, in fact, messy and blurred.

Cohesive Fabric of Gender

Messy as they might be, these ten gender themes also provide a cohesive and comprehensive basis for gender identity. Each theme influences, and is influenced by, its cohorts. For example, if we know that men are taught the importance of relational independence, then it makes sense that they would also be promiscuous (avoiding connection with others), competitive (viewing others as adversaries, not partners), and tough, assertive, and physically imposing (struggling to attain sole control of their surroundings). Similarly, if we know that women are taught the importance of relational interdependence, then it makes sense that they are also monogamous (maintaining connection with others), cooperative (playing nicely with others), and nurturing and caring (supporting others).

The interconnected nature of the gender themes has an interesting consequence for gender development. Namely, if any one theme is to change, all the others must change as well. For, in symbiotic relationships, what affects one part also affects all the other parts. For example, if women shift their emphasis from a domestic orientation to a professional one, their ideas about interdependence, monogamy, and cooperativeness will almost certainly shift as well. Likewise, if men change their focus from the professional sphere to the domestic, then their conceptions of individuality, promiscuity, and competitiveness will almost certainly change as well.

The Relation between Popularity and Traditional Gender Conceptions

One aspect of gender that has shown no sign of change, however, is the timeless practice of men and women categorizing and ranking each other. On the GU campus, as on every other campus I have been on, Greek organizations are, as discussed previously, divided into three castes: the elites, the aspirers, and the strugglers. The elites are the organizations that dominate every aspect of Greek life, including popularity. The aspirers are the second-tier organizations that both strive for acceptance from the elites and hope to ascend to their rank. The strugglers are the newer, smaller, less attractive organizations.

Not only was this tripartite division apparent to me; it was also a recurring topic addressed by all the groups under investigation. Furthermore, there was very little debate about which groups fell into which categories. Of the hundreds of people that I interviewed, including members of groups seen as the pariahs of the Greek system, only a very few disagreed about which organizations were hot and which were not. Not only were the former perceived as the best by other Greeks, non-Greeks, and university professors and administrators alike; they also, not surprisingly, had the most members, the most money, and the most social prestige, and they produced the most campus leaders and influential alumni.

While ranking is not unusual among groups, or, for that matter, among individuals, what sets the Greek-system ranking apart is the price a group pays for its popularity. Specifically, the elite groups have far less freedom to deviate from assigned gender roles and embrace a more traditional conception of masculinity and femininity. The elite sororities, for example, were far more concerned about body shape, appearance, and the maintenance of a reputation for sexual virtue than were their lesser-ranked compatriots. Similarly, the elite fraternities were far more violent, promiscuous, misogynistic, and body conscious than were the struggler and, to a lesser extent, the aspirer fraternities.

Ironically, therefore, the less popular strugglers and aspirers were better adjusted, more tolerant, and healthier. The women had a healthier relationship with food, expressed greater acceptance of deviation from gender norms, and adopted a more forceful and assertive interpersonal communication style. Similarly, the men were less concerned with weight lifting and self-image, were less misogynistic, and maintained more significant interpersonal relationships (both platonic and romantic) with the opposite sex.

The Interplay between Groups, Recruits, and Culture

Why are these elite organizations more traditional and dogmatic? The answer is found in the complex interplay between the group, the recruit, and the organizational culture. To begin with, elite groups are far more likely to rush, bid, and pledge physically attractive and wealthy students with traditional personality types. Young men who are athletic, aggressive, fun loving, and promiscuous have a much better chance of being welcomed into the elite fraternity fold than those who are not. Elite sororities, on the other hand, are ideally searching for young women who are cute, nonaggressive, sexually conservative, studious, and nurturing.

Elite recruits/rushees, however, are just as discerning as elite organizations. Recruits who are physically attractive, wealthy, and traditionally masculine or feminine gravitate toward elite organizations searching for like-minded/bodied peers. Cool kids, after all, want to hang out with other cool kids. This symbiotic law of attraction is so predictable that I (and most others involved with campus life) can forecast with surprising accuracy which organizations a young rushee will be attracted to, and vice versa:

- The smart and cute women who want to be active participants on campus also want to be Alphas (and vice versa).
- The rich men who are not exceptionally athletic or attractive like the Betas (and vice versa).
- The not so smart but hot women gravitate toward the Gammas (and vice versa).
- The male jocks often find a home with the Omegas (and vice versa).
- The women partiers love the Phis and the male partiers the Pis (and vice versa).
- The privately schooled men with influential family members target the older and more established Chis (and vice versa).
- The wealthy cute women who dream of a comfortable domestic life after college feel comfortable with the Deltas (and vice versa).

This is not to say that I am never wrong. On occasion, I find myself pleasantly surprised when a coveted cool kid pledges an aspiring or struggling organization or when an elite organization bids outside its type. But such cases remain true anomalies on GU's campus, where, as a rule of thumb, elite students join elite organizations, aspiring students pledge aspiring organizations, and struggling students, many times by default, find a home with a struggling organization.

Finally, the organizational culture of the elite groups is far more traditional and dogmatic. Through generations of fine-tuning, these fraternities and sororities have developed a conservative ideology that dictates, encourages, and rewards the performance of traditional gender scripts. These codes of gendered conduct—transmitted through pledging, rituals, contact with alumni, formal meetings, and informal parties—let new and old members alike know what is expected of them. Thus, while elite organizations may search for and attract more traditionally gendered recruits (and vice versa), once these recruits pledge, activate, and become full-fledged members, they will be taught—for four undisturbed years—a far more rigid set of traditional rules and codes.

As we will see in the following chapters, the elite sisters and brothers in this study often confess to (and brag about) being shaped and influenced by their organization's strict and unforgiving edicts regarding behavior. For example, many men have claimed that they became more violent, promiscuous, and body conscious after joining their fraternity. Similarly, many women, especially those in elite organizations, believe they became more prudent sexually and self-conscious about their appearances after they moved in with their sorority sisters.

Contesting Gender Conceptions

Regardless of which of the three organizational castes these young men and women found themselves in, I was always pleasantly surprised to find pockets of critically thinking individuals willing to challenge the rules and roles of gender appropriateness. For example, some of the women I interviewed knew that idealized femininity stresses the importance of the domestic sphere, that is, of staying home to raise children, but openly questioned its place in their internalized conception of womanhood. Similarly, some of the men I interviewed questioned the traditional role of the father. Robert, a freshman from Indiana, told me that he did not want to be like his father: "I want to be with my kids. I want to see them grow up. My dad was always at work or sleeping. I mean, I know you have to make a living, but enough is enough." This is not to say, however, that these students were completely liberated from their society's ideological shackles, but some were at least testing boundaries.

In the chapters that follow, each of these seven undergirding findings will surface at predictable and, at times, unpredictable moments. While they are not intended to drive the content of this book—for it is the students' lives and stories that will take that primary responsibility—they will, I hope, supply interesting lenses through which to view the complex nature of gender at GU.

2. Studs and Virgins

At the Monday-night Alpha meeting, brothers engage in the old fraternal tradition of "kissing and telling," or more aptly put, "fucking
and bragging." Robert, a twenty-year-old accounting major, begins
the always-raucous session by narking on his roommate, Matthew.
Matthew, I came to find out, "picked up a pig" and "snuck her
home" after a party to avoid ridicule. As the yarn evolves, some sixty brothers and twenty new pledges erupt in uncontrollable laughter and high fives. Trying both to defend his actions and to bolster
his reputation, Matthew shouts above the crowd that he was "too
drunk" to know better—and that at least he "didn't kiss her."

Next up is the chapter's president, Nathan, who calls out one
of the new pledges, James. "This dirty dick," he says, pointing
to the neophyte, "nailed the drunkest girl at Saturday's tailgate."
Everyone in the room is already well aware of James's conquest,
but such events always warrant public recapitulation. The chapter
hears how the new stud of the pledge class "got a blow job" in
the girl's dormitory weight room as pedestrians passed by in horror
and amusement. James, following the ironclad script of masculinity,
laughs with pride and assures his brothers that he feels absolutely
no emotional connection to the girl in question. In fact, following
in the footsteps of all his brothers who have gone before him, James
demonstrates contempt for the "trashy whore."

This gossiping ritual continues for another ten minutes until everyone's dirty laundry has been aired. As the meeting adjourns, there
are backslaps for Matthew, James, and the other newly anointed
chapter studs. The sense of brotherhood and camaraderie is palpa-
ble. Perhaps, like storytelling around a community fire in an earlier,
oral age, such collective narrative sessions solidify the bond that
exists between members of any tribe. Whatever the explanation,
however, one can sense that these brothers would go to war for each
other.

Sex, love, and relationships are the most popular topics of conversation at most fraternity houses on GU's campus. They permeate talk at breakfast, lunch, and dinner, while sober or drunk, from freshman-year rush through senior-year graduation. If we move past our initial shock at the discussion's misogynistic tone, we can learn a great deal about the gendered minds of these young men from this "man talk."

Specifically, we learn that, as far as these fraternity brothers are concerned, the ideal masculinity is hypersexual, promiscuous, and heterosexual. This conception mirrors that of the larger society, which, via homophobic peer groups, concerned fathers, and sexist music videos, has taught them that men are "interested in sex—all the time, anytime" (Wood, 2005, p. 161); have multiple sex partners, the more the better (Gaylin, 1992); and do not have "relationships with men that are sexual" (Herek, 1987, pp. 72–73). The young man who acts any differently risks, at best, suspicion and invective and, at worst, alienation and physical violence. The staggering number of sexually ambivalent teenage boys who commit suicide and the increasing number of hate crimes committed against homosexual men speak dramatically to the strength of this social imperative.

In the first half of this chapter, I synthesize my analysis of hundreds of conversations and observations in order to determine GU brothers' views on sex, women, relationships, and homosexuality and what institutional factors reinforce and/or challenge these views. I then move to a similar synthesis of GU sisters' views and the factors reinforcing and/or challenging them.

Men

View of Women and Sex

There is a dualism in the way these college men view women. On the one hand, they have close female friends, sisters, girlfriends, and mothers. They protect, support, and respect these privileged few.

On the other hand, there are the masses of young college women with whom they have no emotional connection. It is this lot that is, if physically attractive, the object of their sexual interest or, if unattractive, the target of their ridicule and contempt.

Michael, a nineteen-year-old Gamma brother, admits that the only reason he has "anything to do with any sorority or group of girls is the sex." Guys, he freely admits, "are cooler—we have more in common with each other, we like the same things." "Women are a lot of work" for what you get out of them. "You gotta wonder why any guy in his right mind would hang with women if he wasn't getting any." Take the sex out of the equation, and women are "just ballbusters."

For some, however, women play a different role. For James and Robert, two brothers at the Beta house, they also serve as the raw material for good healthy masculine competition:

AD: Are you guys competitive with each other?
James: We got a competition of who's fucked the most girls this
    year. We're tied nine to nine right now.
Robert: You got to win by two.
James: It kills me, we'll be out and I see him leave with a girl
    or if I go into his room the next morning and he's not in
    there, I'm worried to death [that he is earning more points
    than I am]. But if I see him later and he gives me the big
    zero [demonstrates a nonverbal zero sign], I'm on cloud nine
    'cause I'm safe.
AD: How do you know that you're not lying to each other
    about your numbers?
James: Trust.
Robert: It's that brotherhood thing.

While indiscriminate sex may be fine for James and Robert's fun-loving competition, to be considered a serious player you must be guided by the *quality* maxim. Jeff, like most of his Sigma brothers, believes that "the ideal guy is one who only gets fucked by the hottest girls." This imperative is demonstrated by Adam, the Sigmas' prototypical chapter stud, who, according to his brothers, "only nails the finest women." According to Jason, it's not just that he has a "lot of numbers chalked up"; it's also "the incredible babes that he picks up." "We wish we could dog him," admits Douglas, "but he never slips us. I admit, he's the man." This last remark elicits group laughter.

Brian, the social chair of the Nus, also believes in the quality maxim and, consequently, will allow his hundred-man chapter to party with only the best sororities on campus. "If we are going to have a date party," he informs me, "it is going to be with the top five." He is referring here to the five top sororities in terms of reputation and attractiveness, attributes that, for all intents and purposes, are identical. "You look better in everybody else's eyes. If you have a date party with the Gamma girls, then people see the shirts later [i.e., the T-shirts commemorating the party], and they're like, 'Oh, these guys hang out with the top sororities.'" When asked why the Gammas were the best, I was told, without hesitation, that "they *look* a lot better," "they're hot," and "they're smokin'." In judging the worth of sororities, therefore, the standard is clear and prioritized. Attractiveness matters above all else.

But only the fortunate few, the Adams and the Brians, can be so selective—and so open about their conquests. For the others, discretion is crucial. When you "nail an ugly one," Jeff tells me, "you cannot let anyone else know. If they find out, you are going to get hazed [i.e., made fun of] in the morning." The degree of hazing, however, depends on the type of physical contact that takes place. James told me that, if you "only get your dick sucked by a skank," the next morning is a little easier. The worst-case scenario, however, is if your brothers "find out you went down [i.e., performed oral sex] on a pig. . . . If that gets out, you are dead!"

After consistently hearing this anticunnilingus maxim, I began wondering when and how such a rule developed. While no one knew its origins—which means it is at least four years old—most admitted that it was a rule that they became aware of only after arriving on campus. I asked Jonathan, a junior from the Beta house, for example, whether performing oral sex on females was taboo in high school. "No, not really," he recalls. "I mean, some guys didn't like it, but I think more girls had more problems with it." "They were uptight," he says, laughing nervously, "afraid they smelled or something." David similarly remembers that "giving a girl head was fine as long as she was clean [and] . . . not slutty." After arriving at the Gamma house, however, he discovered that the rules had changed: "It's just one of those things you don't admit to. . . . A lot of the guys in the house think it's nasty." James, who is still a confessed "carpet muncher," has not given up the habit, although he admits to receiving his fair share of ribbing. "I don't know what the big deal is. They [his brothers] think I'm sick, but fuck 'em. I love it!" At this point the focus group room explodes with laughter.

With the professed sex drive of these young men, it is no wonder that so many break the quality maxim. Indeed, it is amazing that these guys accomplish anything during the day. Michael, a twenty-one-year-old Delta brother majoring in political science, tells me about a man's daily thought process: "Ask the average guy how many times they think of sex. He will tell you hundreds. Just walking though campus. Every bitch we see we think about nailing her. Other guys may not admit it. But even the OK looking ones we still think about hittin' that. We may not want to take her in public, but, you know, getting a blow job. We are pigs, but that is just the way we think. It's biological, evolution baby."

This essentialist view of the male sex drive was not only surprisingly common but also utilitarian. Along with supplying these men with an explanation for their promiscuity, the theory helped many justify their infidelity. Drawing on lessons he claimed to have learned in his psychology class, Sam argued that man is driven to "pregnate [sic] as many women as he can for the survival of the species." It is why "men cheat." It's "just the way we were made." Similarly, Jason "learned" that the seven-year itch is "the way our brains tell us to go out and spread more of your seed." "In earlier times," he elaborated, "death was so high that humans had to keep having children, . . . reproducing again and again."

On other occasions, this belief in the inherent nature of man was used to explain the incompatibility of the sexes. Summarizing this common take on relationships, Sam elaborated on the brains of men and women: "We are just different. . . . We are hardwired to kill things . . . to have a lot more sex. Women are born mothers. They want to make love, not fuck. . . . They want one man, only, to take care of them. . . . We want as many as we can get." This is why, he concluded, "men think about sex all the time."

Such a belief about the male sex drive is not anomalistic; it is the norm. Brian, a prelaw major, supported Michael's and Sam's claims. "When I walk to class and I see a nice ass, all I can think about is nailing that." Brian admits that he may not "even know what her face looks like." But that seems to be unimportant—for it is the "ass and tits" that are important. In the spring it gets so bad, I was informed, that many brothers can barely make it back to the house before they "have to rub one out," that is, masturbate.

Interestingly, and surprisingly, masturbation is not a taboo topic. In fact, it is often referred to and joked about in most houses. Since such conversations were extremely rare when I was an undergraduate (1982–86), I asked some of the brothers to elaborate on the topic's frequency and governing rules. Shane, a junior Rho brother, informed me: "Come on, we all know we're all doing it; you have to mention it, it's like you can't avoid it." For Kevin, it is the ease and access to pornography that spur such discussions: "We all have Internet connections in our rooms now," Kevin explains. "What do you think we spend most of our time looking at? . . . We'll give each other new sites to check out, . . . e-mail each other great pictures. Of course people whack off to them."

There are rules, however, governing both the discussion and the act of masturbation. To begin with, you cannot get caught masturbating. "Talking about it is one thing. If you get caught doing it, it's over," explained Henry, meaning that the culprit would be publicly ridiculed. Also, the discussions must remain lighthearted and humorous. "It's funny shit." No one, according to Shane, wants to hear a serious discussion of a brother's technique or a cataloging of his activities. "That's just creepy."

It appears, however, that this type of open discussion is not a national trend. While a few brothers claimed to have joked about masturbation in high school, most of the men that I interviewed said that it "really is a fraternity thing." Danny expands: "I guess it is because we live so close to each other, you just can't avoid the topic here. In high school at least, you had some privacy from your buds." For Justin, the Rho president, it is the close fraternal bonds that make lighthearted conversations about masturbation acceptable. "You don't talk that way with everybody, like in front of strangers, no, but, you know, brothers are different. There's no secrets here—even if you wanted to keep some." Finally, some brothers, like the Gammas' Justin, think it is the increased visual stimuli at college that engender such conversations. "There's just so much ass on campus," he explains, "how can you not talk about it?" As Alex and his Delta brothers similarly put it, GU "has the hottest girls. Of course pussy is on your mind, 24/7. . . . You have to relieve yourself or explode." Collective laughter and group affirmation follow this remark.

One of the disastrous outcomes of this form of hypersexuality is the reduction of women to soulless body parts, for example, "ass," "pussy," "tits," etc. Time and time again, I was told that no attractive woman escapes the dehumanizing gaze of men. "It is very difficult for any woman who is hot," confessed Douglas, a twenty-one-year-old Mu, "to ever be seen by any man without them thinking about what she looks like naked." A woman's status, education level, or involvement in a personal relationship is no protection from a man's sexual desire. James told me: "She could be your boss, your professor, your friend's mom, it does not matter. If they are hot, every guy, and I mean every guy, thinks of having sex with them."

Mark, another Mu brother, fears that, if "women only knew how much we are *not* listening to what they say but are thinking about them on their hands and knees, they would never talk to any man again." "No wonder," he comments, laughing, "there aren't more women in power in the world." As Brad, a twenty-two-year-old Chi brother, puts it, all men hear is "blah, blah, blah."

View of Relationships and Monogamy

While it may be difficult to believe—given the time and thought that these young men devote to promiscuous sex—some brothers actually maintain steady relationships with women. There is Zack, for example, an eighteen-year-old pledge who has been dating the same girl since he was a freshman in high school. He is a loyal, loving boyfriend who sticks out like the proverbial sore thumb at his house. Most significant relationships of this sort, however, do not develop until the brothers reach their early twenties. Around their junior year, some begin to outgrow the one-night stands that marked so much of their freshmen and sophomore years. Aaron, for example, a twenty-one-year-old junior majoring in engineering, was a typical frat playboy. Late in his junior year, however, he met his girlfriend, Alice, and things changed dramatically. He spent less time partying with his brothers and more time in meaningful interpersonal interactions with Alice. He was, in short, becoming a man in the best sense of the word. Zack and Aaron are not alone. Roughly 10 percent of all fraternity members find themselves committed to a woman before they graduate. These relationships, of course, vary in their duration and intensity, but they nonetheless illustrate the capacity for emotional growth and sensitivity.

Such attached brothers, however, quickly become the bane of their houses. Interestingly, this is *not* solely because they have lost their masculine individuality and independence. Instead, their steady relationships threaten to undermine brotherhood and fraternal values. Or, to put it another way, intimate relationships with women challenge intimate relationships with men.

"This house gets intense," claims Robert, a Chi brother who has had a steady girlfriend for two years. "At home, you know, it was cool, I mean, your friends were happy if you were happy. Not in this fuckin' house. These guys do not want any competition." Paul, a Psi brother, tells an almost identical then-and-now story. "My brothers hate me having a girlfriend. I just don't get it. In high school we all had steady girls. Here [the Psi house], it's like you can't see anyone for more than a week, or they start in on you."

"Girlfriends change guys," Mark angrily proclaims. This twenty-year-old Kappa brother gets pissed because "you never see them [attached brothers] around." They "stop hanging at the house; they don't party anymore with you." And, when you can sneak them out "with the boys, you are looking to hook up, and they can't." They just hang out at the bar like a "wet rag." Similarly, Jason, an Omega brother, claims that "girlfriends take over your life" and "turn you into a pussy." To illustrate his point, Jason singles out one of his brothers, Jamie, who is sitting to his left during the interview. "This guy here," he says caustically, pointing at Jamie, "he's with his girlfriend more than he's over at the house, and that kind of pisses me off more than anything." Dave, another brother at the focus group table, concurs with Jason's sentiments: "Yeah, he doesn't ever want to do anything. And, when he does hang out, he is always on the phone with her." "If guys are cool its one thing," Andy joins in, "but, if they don't talk or hang out, then it's different. You always have to remember: 'It's bros before hos.'"

This platonic jealously does not go unnoticed by the girlfriends. Many of the women I interviewed told me that a relationship's worst enemy is the man's friends. Lisa, a twenty-two-year-old senior, relates the ridicule she and her boyfriend go through just to maintain their relationship. "I go over to the house," she says, "and they give him crap whenever he goes out with me." It is not that they don't like her personally, she informs me; it is that she "take[s] him away from them." Lisa is not alone. Many of the women I talked to told similar stories of the ribbing and teasing that their boyfriends put up with just to go on a date. One Chi brother even admitted that he actively tries to break up his brothers' relationships if they do not spend enough time at the house.

Not every committed brother, however, receives the same scornful treatment. John, a twenty-year-old marketing major, tells us that he has a steady girlfriend but doesn't get "much shit for it." When I inquire about the secret of his success, he informs me that she "lives in Orlando, Florida," roughly fifteen hours away by car, and he "only sees her a few times a semester." Consequently, he boasts: "I'm pretty much like a guy now. . . . They're not like: 'Dude, you always hang out with your girl.'"

If one is not lucky enough to have a girlfriend who lives a time zone away, there are other strategies that can make the committed life easier. First: "You can't stop hanging with your buds." Al tells me how he "dated a girl for a year and a half but still came out and drank." The secret, he continues, is that "you have to divide your time" between your brothers and your girlfriend. Similarly, Robert warns: "You can't fall into that trap that all the time, twenty-four hours a day, you're with your girlfriend—you gotta stay cool."

The committed woman can also attenuate the severity of the relational ridicule. The brothers are far more tolerant, for instance, if girlfriends "hang at the frat house." Life is a lot easier if, as Seth puts it, "she is willing to become friends with your friends." In some rare cases, girlfriends can even become beloved. The brothers at the Sigma house, for example, talk protectively about Mary Katherine, Brian's girlfriend, who "loves the guys as much as she loves Brian." They tell me how she "stops by the house to visit his brothers, even if Brian is nowhere around," "makes cookies for the chapter before meetings," and even serves as the fraternity psychologist for the brokenhearted. In the eyes of the Sigmas, Mary Katherine is not a meddling bitch set on wrecking Brian's social life; she is their little sister.

A girlfriend's stock can also rise, I am told, if "she is hot" and if she "brings her hot sisters around the house" so that the "brothers can get some ass off." Derek, for example, started dating Missy, a member of the coveted Omega sorority. As the story goes, the Omegas had traditionally nothing to do with Derek's Chi brothers. Since the pairing, however, more and more sisters have found their way to the Chi house for parties. Far from being a hindrance to brotherhood, Derek's relationship was the proverbial foot in the door the Chis had been waiting for.

Regardless of attempts to appease the brothers, the concept of monogamy within a committed relationship leaves a lot more wiggle room for the man than it does for the woman. Straying, or getting some on the side, is not just tolerated; it is encouraged by the other men. Of the hundreds of brothers I surveyed, more than three-quarters admitted to straying while in relationships. Mark, however, is far less optimistic: "Maybe one out of every hundred or thousand won't cheat." John thinks that "any guy will cheat if given the right setup, you know, the right girl and no chance of being caught." According to him, anyone who thinks otherwise is "all full of shit" and anyone who tells you different "is a fucking liar," pronouncements greeted with laughter and applause. A man's monogamy, therefore, is seen not as a sacrifice for love but only as a lack of opportunity.

Consequently, most men admitted that they see no inconsistency in loving a girl and, as Dave, a Sigma brother, puts it, "getting blown by some whore." John, a senior business major in the Psi house, elaborated: "A guy can love his girl but still want a little stray ass. It has nothing to do with the girlfriend. There is something really strong about picking up a total stranger, one with no ties or commitment, getting her naked, and fucking her. I mean, you look down at her face when you are on top of her, and you are like: Who is this person? It is hot. 'Cause you got her naked and there she is under you. Crazy. Just don't get caught."

A brother can rest assured knowing that the only person he needs to hide his indiscretions from is his girlfriend—and, of course, all his girlfriend's friends. His brothers are, to borrow a term from modern-day psychology, enablers. They encourage, reward, support, arrange, and even cover up a brother's duplicity. "It's a brotherhood thing," explained Phil. Not only is the committed brother protected from his girlfriend's indictment; he also remains an active participant in the fraternity's social rituals, hanging out at the house, drinking, and picking up women. Infidelity allows him to straddle the divide between being a boyfriend and being a brother. He maintains his relationship with his girlfriend, who is appeased by the illusion that she is in a monogamous relationship, and he maintains his relationship with his brothers, who are reassured that they have not been forgotten or replaced.

View of Homosexuality

While infidelity is both common and encouraged, homosexuality is neither. It is the one unforgivable sin in any fraternity house. Mike, the twenty-one-year-old Omega president, highlighted its severity when he threatened to "throw any fag living in [his] house out the fucking window." John, one of Mike's nineteen-year-old brothers, even offered to help by "running [the fag] over with my truck after he hits the ground."

While homophobia permeates American notions of masculinity, it is especially acute in fraternity houses, where young men, many still struggling with their sexuality, share a confined living space. Brothers typically sleep two to four per bedroom, share a common bathroom unlikely to have toilet-stall doors or shower curtains, and seldom knock before invading a brother's privacy.

Brothers also share emotional space. For the first, and, perhaps, the last, time in their lives, these men communicate their most intimate secrets and their most private hopes and dreams with other men. More than any other topic, however, they talk to each other about love, sex, relationships, and heartbreak. Consequently, to discover that there is a homosexual in their midst means, not only that a fag has been watching them shower, but also that they have been deceived during their most vulnerable moments of self-disclosure.

Because the fear of being so deceived is so great, considerable effort is expended during rush and pledging on weeding out sexually ambivalent personalities. It is not uncommon, for example, to hear heated debates during the rush process over a visitor's supposedly effeminate qualities. Applications have been rejected, for example, because a rushee talked like a girl, dressed like a fag, associated with feminine men, walked like a queer, avoided fights or conflicts, or was unathletic. These so-called indisputable early warning signs of homosexuality are taken as serious harbingers.

On rare occasions, however, the weeding-out process fails. Even the president of the most prestigious fraternity on GU's campus admitted, "Sometimes *they* slip through the cracks." Charlie, being less optimistic about the system's firewall, realizes that "if the statistics are right . . . every fraternity on campus has gays." He just does not want them in *his* fraternity.

Charlie was, indeed, right. Every fraternity has gay brothers. In most cases, however, they do not come out until they graduate, leave school, and start their new lives independent of the chapter. On very rare occasions, however, some brothers disclose their homosexuality during their undergraduate years.

Patrick

Patrick, now a twenty-four-year-old advertising executive, came out to his Delta brothers during his junior year. Far from being thrown out a window and run over by a truck, Patrick maintained most of his friendships and continued his leadership role with the chapter. This is not to say that his disclosure was unconditionally welcomed by all his brothers. Some feared that, if "word got out that we had a fag in the house, no one would want to pledge us." Others simply "did not want a homo around [them]." Most of the brothers, however, generally accepted Patrick as part of the family—albeit the black sheep.

When I inquired as to why the Delta brothers were so atypically understanding, especially given the hostile responses that homosexuals invoked from every other fraternity I studied, one brother told me: "[Patrick] was our friend first before we knew he was gay." As

Jason humorously remarked, by the time Patrick came out, "it was a little late to decide we didn't like him." It was quite clear, however, that the love felt for Patrick is an exception. What would happen if some gay rushee no one knew wanted to become a member? "He would never make it through our front doors." The brothers told stories of how effeminate boys were laughed out of their rush parties for such unforgivable transgressions as "wearing a cheerleading shirt," "playing volleyball like a girl," or just being "horribly unmasculine."

Patrick's ability to maintain his sense of humor (and his thick skin) also made the brothers more comfortable around him and his sexuality. Mark told me that "he was the coolest guy ever about his homosexuality." He remembered Patrick coming in the bathroom when he was showering: "I was like: 'Don't you come sneaking up on me.' . . . He knew I was joking, and he was like: 'You're not my type.'" The brothers would "joke with him," but "he knew it was out of love." Sometimes, however, the humor was not so funny. Sean, a twenty-year-old accounting major, admits that guys would slip and make gay jokes or absentmindedly call each other fags when Patrick was around. "Patrick never got pissed, though. He always laughed that stuff off."

Finally, Patrick avoided certain taboo behaviors that would have turned the house against him. First, he did not publicize his homosexuality—he told only his brothers and a few close friends. As a result, neither his sexuality nor his fraternity became the fodder for universitywide gossip. Second, he was not, as one brother put it, "a flamer." Mark assured me that I "could not tell he was gay just by looking at him." Patrick's ability to pass helped the Deltas keep their dirty little secret in the closet. Finally, he did not flaunt his sexuality by "bringing guys back to the house" or discussing his sexual preferences with the brothers. Mark recalls: "[Once] he told us that he was messing around with a Sigma and a Chi brother, and we were like, 'Don't even fuckin' tell us about that.'" He never talked to his brothers about that aspect of his life again.

Patrick remains an active alumnus, returning to the house on homecoming weekends and holiday breaks. Even given the occasional humiliation that he has had to endure, his fraternity continues to be a source of brotherhood for him. Not every gay brother, however, enjoys such tolerance or understanding.

ALLEN

When I first met Allen, he was a handsome eighteen-year-old freshman from Ohio looking for friendship and camaraderie. He was drawn to the Pi fraternity because of the "cool brothers, good intramural sports, and big parties." On the surface, it appeared that he found the perfect home. He was popular, respected, and even elected to the executive council as a sophomore.

Then, at the end of his second year, Allen left the fraternity. Tired of living a lie about his sexuality, he moved out of the house, resigned his leadership role, and found a new group of friends who were, as he put it, "more tolerant and accepting people." It did not take long before his old chapter heard the news: *Allen was a fag!* Over the next few months, speculation, rumormongering, innuendo, and homophobic humor dominated fraternity gossip. Even today, Allen remains the dirty little secret that most of the brothers try to bury under the floorboards.

During my last interview with Allen, I asked him why, unlike Patrick, he never again visited to the fraternity after leaving. Solemnly, he responded that he "would not have been welcomed back." When asked why he thought that, he told me that, as a gay man, you remember certain poignant moments that let you know whether a situation is safe. He recalls, for instance, how "vicious the discussions were during rush" over any young man who was the "least bit feminine." "We once kicked a kid out just because he talked with a lisp and the brothers thought that meant he was gay." He remembers the day that an older effeminate alumni came back for a visit and the brothers "freaked out." They were laughing and joking, "purposely making him feel uncomfortable until he left." Then there was Mike, a sweet-hearted pledge and close friend of Allen's, who exhibited too many sissy qualities for the older brothers. After a few weeks of merciless hazing, Allen told me, "Mike had enough and quit." And, of course, there was the antihomosexual rhetoric that was a staple at every social gathering. "Somebody was always saying something about fags or homos." One night during dinner, Allen recalls, "a few brothers were even laughing at a story on the news about hate crimes against gays." They were saying that "those fags had it coming to them" and that "that's what they get." A gay man does not forget moments like those.

Remarkably, Allen does not regret his decision to pledge Pi. When I asked him what was the most important thing he took away from the fraternity experience, he laughed and said: "Robert." Robert was his partner; at that point they had been together for five years. As the story goes, Allen met Robert during his freshman year while waiting in line for beer at the Pi house. "Just think about it," Allen said. "It's great irony. I met my lover at my fraternity house." Allen also discovered that his closest brothers did not abandon him. He has remained friends with almost a quarter of his pledge class. While, after graduation, he did not see them as often as he would have liked, he still enjoyed drinking a beer and talking about old times with them. He hoped, in fact, to see some of them at his and Robert's upcoming wedding/commitment ceremony.

Women

Since gender is structured in terms of oppositional pairs by the men and women at GU, it was no surprise to discover that the sexual freedom enjoyed by men in fraternities was not afforded to women in sororities. For, if ideal masculinity is characterized by promiscuity, ideal femininity is characterized by prudence. As a result, sorority sisters spend a great deal of time determining which behaviors are appropriate and which are trashy.

Defining Appropriate Sexuality

June, a Chi sister, Kristi, a Beta sister, Teresa, a Pi sister, and just about every other woman I interviewed told me that trashy is the worst thing you can be. "Girls that are trash," Teresa tells me, "have no respect for themselves." Trashy girls, June claims, "give the whole sorority a bad name on campus." But what constitutes trashy, or slutty, behavior? According to Alice, a trashy girl is one "who goes out on Thursday night and sleeps with a guy, then Friday sleeps with somebody else." Her sister Nancy said it was slutty for a girl to "go through a fraternity, like go down the hall and have a different brother every night." Judy, the president of the Alpha sorority, said that it was in really bad taste to "have sex with random acquaintances . . . night after night." Finally, Erin thought that "sluts are girls that sleep with a different guy every night and don't care about their reputations." When asked whether any sister ever behaved like that, they all cringed in horror: "Of course not." Only *other* girls are like that.

What then, one may wonder, is *appropriate* behavior? I was told that, while "hooking up" or "shacking" (neither term necessarily means having sex) may be generally tolerated, it is not the best way for a woman to manage her reputation. Ideally, Mary, a twenty-year-old Gamma sister, told me, "girls should care about the people they are with." Jessica, an eighteen-year-old Delta sister, thinks that making out is fine but that "anything else [i.e., sex] without love is cheap." Similarly, Jenny does not think that a girl has to wait until marriage, but, ideally, "she should care a lot for the boy before having sex."

I was left wondering whether this way of thinking was representative? Do all GU's Greek women view love and sex similarly? According to the sorority sisters in this study, it depends. The elite houses, I was told, seem to be more prudent, adhering to stricter codes of behavior. Janis, an elite Omega, thinks that her sorority is "more serious about what you can do. . . . In high school, it really was never like that, you know, that old-fashioned."

The aspirers and the strugglers, on the other hand, seem, as one sister reported, to give their girls "more breathing room to have fun." Becky, a sister at the Psi house (an aspirer sorority), thinks that her "sorority gives girls more room to be themselves." "The Chis and the Thetas [two elite sororities]," she observed, "are just so tight about all that." This does not mean, however, that Becky and her fellow aspirers and strugglers are free from societal constraints. The best friends Lisa, an Epsilon aspirer, and Brooke, an Iota struggler, explained it this way:

AD: OK, I'm confused. Help me on this one. Are you saying that your sororities don't care what you do on dates.

Lisa: No no.

Brooke: God no. It's like they care. Sororities, all of them, I think are more conscious of that kind of stuff. I mean we care about our reputations.

Lisa: Yeah, no one wants to be a slut. And I think sororities are really, a lot more, careful about what they let their girls do. But I think that some sororities take it too far. I was going to pledge Kappa [an elite sorority], but I just felt like they were way too uptight about everything. The way you look, who you date, what you do on dates—everything.

Brooke: Me too. I just felt way too nervous at Kappa . . . and the Gamma house [another elite house]. I think Epsilons and the Iotas are a lot alike like that. It's like they give you more freedom to be yourself.

Lisa: All those skinny bitches need to loosen up. [*Both women laugh in agreement.*]

In coming to understand sexual propriety for women, I was also struck by how *trashy* and *appropriate* were defined, especially by the elites, in terms that were both polarized and exaggerated. *Trashy* refers to behavior so outrageous that the sisters were hard-pressed to find any real-life examples in their organization. Antithetically, *appropriate* refers to behavior so puritanical that only a very few sisters in even the most proper chapters could merit being so described. Indeed, most of the women I talked to readily admitted that they "hook up," "make out," or "shack" with the occasional "stray" or "random" guy. While such behavior may not be habitual, it is certainly not uncommon.

I am left to wonder, therefore, what would prompt these women to construct a notion of appropriate behavior that excludes most of them. While the advantages of such an extreme definition of *trashy* are obvious—the term can be applied to none of them—so are the disadvantages of such an extreme definition of *appropriate*. These women have left themselves no room in which to experiment with or explore their sexuality and still stay within the bounds of the appropriate.

Maintaining Appropriate Sexuality

Such a restrictive and ambiguous code of sexual morality would, one would think, be difficult both to communicate and to enforce. Sororities are surprisingly astute, however, at reproducing its traditional ideas. Every chapter I studied, regardless of its composition, size, or location, relied on the same three hegemonic practices to ensure uniformity in the ranks: the rush process, the judicial-board (j-board) review, and personal intervention.

The most important of the three is sorority rush. It is here that sisters can, and do, weed out rushees with questionable morals. The week-long process begins when first-year students visit the sorority houses they are most interested in joining. After a few visits, where introductions are made and personalities evaluated, the active sisters secretly meet to debate the merits of each applicant. While physical attractiveness is the greatest predictor of acceptance, a promiscuous reputation is the greatest forecaster of rejection. All in attendance at Kappa rush meetings, for example, know that, if a candidate is said to have "questionable morals," it means she should be blackballed. More precisely, it means that one or more of the older sisters *heard* that, as it is variously put, she "screws around a lot," "is a slut," "had a disease," "was trashy in high school," or "screwed somebody's boyfriend." Lisa, the rush chair at the Alpha house, unapologetically defended such ruthless weeding out: "We don't want somebody who is like that. We don't want someone who gets that kind of reputation." Elizabeth, the rush chair at the Theta house, even cut a girl from her hometown because it was rumored that "she had multiple partners." For the sororities I studied, therefore, the first, and best, line of defense in protecting their reputation is eliminating the trashy girls before they get in the house.

Like fags in fraternities, sluts in sororities also sometimes slip under the organizational radar. Unlike fraternities, however, sororities have a means of handling such outlaws. Every sorority recognized by the National Panhellenic Conference[1] must have a judicial board (sometimes known as a standards board or a developmental board) to handle sisters who step out of line. While it is possible to be subpoenaed by the board for such benign infractions as overdrinking, underage drinking, or excessive drinking at a date party, sexual impropriety is the only serious issue that it handles.

Erin, a three-year member of the Phi's j-board, told me that, when a girl acts too slutty in public, she will likely be called before the board. She remembered a case of a younger sister who "got drunk at a frat party and was dirty dancing and grinding on about a dozen guys throughout the night. They were grabbing her and rubbing her all over." Needless to say, the next day the sister was reprimanded by the board for "reflecting negatively on her sorority." Sisters can even be called before the board for acting too slutty in private. Elizabeth, a member of the Omegas, retold the story of the now-infamous Chi sister who "gave a strip show to ten or fifteen guys in the living room of the Sigma fraternity. She got on three or four of them—they took her upstairs, and she just didn't care." While no other sorority women actually witnessed these goings-on, the rumor was enough to warrant a j-board investigation. While most houses have a three-strike rule governing expulsion from the organization, the first admonishment is often all that is needed. Erin reported that, most of the time, "the girl is so embarrassed and humiliated she either drops out or becomes one of those born-again virgins."

The final means of controlling the sexual behavior of members is through personal intervention. Sisters reprimand, chastise, and discipline each other for actions unbecoming a Greek. There are times, for example, like the one described by Becky, an Omega sister, when a sister gets a bit too demonstrative in public: "You have to grab her and tell her to put her shoes on and get off the freakin' table." There are other times when sisters collectively intervene, pull a sister aside, and give her a good talking-to. The Alphas, for example, tell how they had to "sit down" with a sister to inform her that "the Beta brothers have been talking shit about her." They told her, "as nicely as possible," to "straighten up" and stop giving the Alphas a bad name. Similarly, Sally, a fourth-year accounting major, remembers one uncomfortable Sunday morning when she and her roommate "sat down" with a younger sister about her inappropriate behavior at a tailgate party. She was "drinking way too much and hanging all over one of the sister's boyfriends." "After that," Sally claims, "Suzie became the model sister and even became rush chair." "I think we have all had to play mom," Jessie says, "at least a couple of times [before graduation]."

This is not to say that there is absolute agreement or compliance with sorority standards. I found a few strong, intelligent voices of dissent emanating from sisters who felt unfairly constrained by the laws of appropriate behavior for women. Alice, a third-year Gamma, expressed frustration over the "sexual double standard": "Our age, our generation is really starting to struggle with dating and sex. We are starting to say that it is OK to date different guys. But, for us to do so, we are called promiscuous. When in fact we are just trying to find out what it is we're looking for in a partner. But yet we're portrayed as being promiscuous."

Katherine, a sophomore from the Rho house, similarly expressed discontent with the limitations placed on women's sexuality. Not all girls, she says, are looking for that "emotional thing" that all girls are suppose to want. "Some girls don't want a relationship with a guy." They just want to have a good time and maybe have sex. But if you do, she warns, "you have to apologize" or lie: "You have to tell people that 'I really liked him' or 'I thought he was really nice and hoped for more' so they don't think you are a slut. We try to make it OK because society tells us that we shouldn't be sleeping around."

The men in this study also told stories of women clandestinely breaking out of the sexual constraints of sorority life. The Delta brothers, for example, explained how sorority women evade their sisters' watchful eyes:

> Brian: I think with sororities, if they are around their sisters, they won't do anything bad. But, by the end of the night, they have moved away 'cause they don't want to be brought in front of their standards [i.e., the j-board].
>
> Mike: So they move away from their sisters so, when they leave with you, no one sees it.
>
> Lenny: Yeah, and the later it gets, the shadier the girls get, especially when there is no one there to see.
>
> Brian: You can tell too. The sister that hangs around long after the rest have left the bar. It's obvious.
>
> Mike: Her sisters will be watching her too. They'll tell her, "Now you come home soon," or, "Don't do anything stupid that you will regret."

What constitutes *stupid* or defines acts that one "will regret," however, is not fixed or stable over time. Within the last ten years, for instance, notions of *virginity, sex,* and *trashy* have all been redefined on college campuses.

Redefining Sex

Twenty-five years ago when I was in college, sex was considered penetration of any kind—oral, anal, or vaginal. Different levels of intimacy, however, were attached to different sex acts. Throughout the 1970s, 1980s, and early 1990s, anal sex was taboo. Oral sex was reserved for intimate partners, given the mouth's association with communication, eating, tasting, and kissing.[2] Vaginal sex was the most common of all sex acts, conceived of by both men and women as more pleasurable, less painful, and more psychologically and emotionally removed (Gates & Sonenstein, 2000; Horan, Phillips & Hagan, 1998).

In the last ten years, however, this prioritization has been turned on its head. The *New York Times,* the *Washington Post,* the *American Journal of Public Health,* and even *Seventeen* and *Twist* magazines have all reported a dramatic redefinition by American adolescents of what constitutes an intimate sex act.[3] Oral sex, according to Jarrell (2000), is something today's girls do with their boyfriends before they are ready to have sex. It is, in the eyes of a growing number of adolescents, an act no longer associated with intense intimacy or commitment—"like a good-night kiss to [middle school students]" (p. 2).

Today's Greeks have not been untouched by this national trend. They too have redefined what constitutes sex and the level of intimacy associated with each act: *Only* vaginal penetration is considered to be sex. Oral sex is something far more casual.[4] The sisters of Omega explained the differences:

Ellie: I've never considered in my life oral sex to be like sex. When I first had oral sex I never thought: "I just lost my virginity." That was always a line to draw. You have oral sex, if you go beyond that, if you do it [vaginal sex], you're not a virgin.
Nancy: Everything but.
Susie: Everything but.
Ellie: Everything but.
Lisa: Everything but. That's the universal slogan. Use that in your book: "Everything but."

Nancy: Everything but. Yeah, we can do everything but.

Susie: Everything but.

In interview after interview, I heard similar delineations. Lori, a second-year Chi sister, told me that no one "would ever convince [her] that oral sex is real sex." Similarly, Julie believed "that sex is sex and that oral sex is like nothing." Consequently, many women, like Stacy of the Theta house, are still considered virgins even though they have had sex with their boyfriends. "I mean," Stacy claimed, "it has never been an issue about how far I had or had not gone with John. The sisters knew that I hadn't had [vaginal] sex. It didn't matter if I did every other kind [i.e., oral or anal]." As the sociologist Debbie Then has pointed out, for today's American girls oral sex has become "a kind of moral freebie" (Bordo, 1999, p. 295).

This redefinition of sex has also become the touchstone for the organizations. When I asked which sex acts were acceptable, everyone, regardless of house, responded that oral sex, in moderation, was fine. The vice president of the Mus, for example, told me, "If you shack with a boy and give him a blow job, you are not considered a slut." If, however, "you sleep [i.e., have vaginal sex] with him, people will think you're a slut." Candice, an elementary education major, claimed that, in her sorority, "a girl would never get called in front of standards for only having oral sex." As long as she did not "overdo it," it was really no big deal.

The men in the study, not surprisingly, are also well aware of this rhetorically constructed loophole in the rules. Michael, for example, tells me, "Blow jobs are no big deal now." Many times, he says, "girls will give a guy head just to get them to stop nagging them about getting laid." When I asked the Beta brothers about "fooling around," they told me that "you will get your dick sucked long before a girl will ever let you fuck her." "Oral is not seen as that big of a deal," Mark concluded. The women "don't feel like sluts or whores afterwards, and they don't get a bad time from their sisters."

The women and men I interviewed did not agree on all points, however. Listening only to the men's bravado, one would conclude that oral sex was performed only by women, that the favor was never reciprocated. In most fraternity houses, in fact, performing cunnilingus is perceived as a sign of weakness. At the Sigma house, there is even a year-end award that pejoratively recognizes the brother who "munches carpet." As Kevin explained it, "Eating pussy is giving up too much power—you are serving her—it is just not right." Derek thinks that "it is just too dirty and smelly." For Jacob, "there is something gay about it. If she fucked a guy, you are now all in his stuff."

When I asked the sorority members about this unequal relationship, they claimed that "those guys are full of shit." Beth, a fifth-year communication major, laughs at the assertion and asks, "Do you really think that we would not expect the favor returned? . . . It may happen like that on a one-night stand, but, after the first one, he better pay back."

Kimi, a Gamma sister, says, "I don't know any guy who doesn't. They may not tell each other, but they all do it." "Return the favor. That's my deal," Andrea claims. Usually, in fact, "he goes first." "You see," she explains, "guys when they are finished don't have anything left for you. They can't move. So most girls get theirs first."

So who is telling the truth? According to national statistics on college sexuality, the women are. When self-defined virgins were surveyed, 37 percent admitted to performing fellatio, while slightly over 48 percent confessed to experiencing cunnilingus (Davidson & Moore, 1994). According to Elliott and Brantley (1997), "a slightly higher percentage of college women—85 percent—have received oral sex than have performed it" (p. 114). When college men were surveyed, the conclusions were not shockingly different: 82 percent of college men claimed to have performed oral sex, 83 percent to have received oral sex. And the percentage increases with years in college, 76 percent of freshman, 83.5 percent of sophomores, 85 percent of juniors, and 88.5 percent of seniors performing cunnilingus (p. 115).

I was also told that "a lot of people are having anal sex." The sisters at the Nu house estimated that "a ton"—"70–80 percent"—of the girls are doing it. The women may not enjoy it, they said, but they do it because "they can't get pregnant" and because "it is not technically sex," thus allowing them to remain reputably chaste.[5] While no one in the room admitted to trying it, I was informed that "it's just been like a recent thing that happened" and "you'd be shocked to know the real numbers." Interestingly, the men in the study rarely mentioned this new trend. One would think that it would be ideal fodder for barroom gossip. Indeed, "nailing a bitch in the ass," as John, an Omega brother, put it, is the subject of many misogynistic jokes and much masculine braggadocio.

One explanation for this omission was supplied by John, Chris, and Jack in a follow-up interview exploring the question. When I asked the three about this void in the male interviews, I was told that "anal sex is never one of those things that you have instead of fucking." Most of the guys they know who have anal are in steady relationships: "Guys will do it with their girlfriends, . . . but a one-night stand would never do it." And, as Jack put it, "A guy is not likely to openly tell everyone that he is doing anal on his girlfriend."

The multifaceted redefinition of sex may not simply be the deterioration of morality, as claimed by some during the Clinton sex scandal. After spending considerable time with these women, I am led to believe that it may be a strategy developed by women that enables them to be more sexually active in a society that demands sexual prudence. Since the cultural mores demand that good girls do not have sex absent a deep, emotional commitment, these women have redefined what acts constitute sex. Thanks to a rhetorically constructed loophole, they are able to explore their sexuality without being trashy or feeling guilty.

Not surprisingly, this redefinition of sex also benefits the Greek system's men. While it appears that the women are demanding more reciprocation, there is clearly still not equality in the bedroom. Most men still expect women to service them, not vice versa. This is especially true in the case of one-night-stand oral sex and, to a lesser extent, anal sex.

Performing for the Boys

That women are expected to service men is also reflected in many Greek rituals. At virtually every institution of higher education in the United States, fraternities sponsor activities, usually under the guise of a fund-raiser, aimed at getting women to perform for them. Be they beauty pageants, talent shows, cheerleading competitions, or dance contests, and regardless of how much money they raise, these "fund-raisers" are at heart exhibitions of women's sexuality.

Far from being outraged by the invitation to be objectified by the male gaze, sorority sisters welcome the opportunity to strut their stuff, especially if the fraternity sponsor is venerated. At such events, according to Emma, the women dress in "outfits that are skintight." "Their shirts are cropped to here," she says, pointing to a spot just below the breast line. "Sometimes they even come off," she continues, to group laughter.

At a recent Halloween fund-raiser, the sisters of the Chi house told of their strategically enticing outfits. "I was a girly devil," Erin confesses. "I wore a short red dress, fishnets with big black boots on. It was really sassy." Jessica went as a Hawaiian: "I had a sarong. It was short, and I had a white halter top." Beth went as a construction worker with "tight jeans and a tied up shirt." Even Alicia, the supposedly shy one of the bunch, went as Jane, without a Tarzan. "I wore a bathing suit with leaves. I was almost naked." Far from being anomalies, these Chi sisters were the norm. Over 90 percent of the women in attendance "sexed it up" for the guys, they said. "It makes you feel sexy, and you get a lot of attention from cute boys."

Their performances at such events are as provocative as their dress. At last year's annual dance fund-raiser sponsored by the Delta brothers, Nancy described how "one sorority piled on top of each other": "They were like licking suckers and throwing them around the guys who were judging." At other times, sisters model their dance performances after strippers and exotic dancers. They will spank each other's asses, push out their breasts, lick their fingers, gyrate their butts, all while maintaining the ever-present invitational stare. As the Delta sisters told me, their goal is to "put the guys in hysteria."

When there is not a competition/fund-raiser to perform at, sisters will find other outlets for their exhibitionism. Around America, bar-top dancing is becoming an increasingly popular trend. For example, at a nationally franchised nightclub targeting college towns, guys can watch the nightly ritual of women patrons dancing on the bar top while the bartenders serve drinks between their legs. As the men begin to cram closer to the bar/stage, the women start to move suggestively to the club's hip-hop grooves. The women's dance is a performance for the men. They invite the voyeurs to sneak intimate glances by lifting their skirts, shimmying their breasts, and provocatively bending over. As this ritual continues, the men in the audience are worked up into a sexual frenzy, shouting encouragement, and glaring hungrily. Even at more traditional nightclubs where bar-top dancing is banned, this choreography is repeated on the dance floor. Walk into any bar or fraternity house in America, and you will see similar behavior. The women are not expressing their passion for music through dance. They are performing for the men.

I remember a night I witnessed over a dozen of my best and brightest women students, all with GPAs of 3.3 or higher, willingly objectify themselves for the validation of a drunk, loud, and rude male audience. The scene was simultaneously shocking and saddening. Why were these wonderful women degrading themselves for cheap applause? Were they that desperate for men's attention and acceptance? The next day I asked a few of these students about the prior night's performance. They told me that "it was fun to get so much attention," "to goof off," "to get drunk and dance," and to have "the boys in the bar in the palm of their hands."

Another increasingly popular exhibitionistic trend that has

emerged during the last few years is the female bisexual kiss. Like the performances discussed above, this one too has as its objective attracting the male gaze:

AD: I have seen more and more pictures from your parties of girls kissing each other. Tell me about that.

Nancy: Yeah, girls kiss each other for the camera all the time. It's no big deal.

Susan: If we are drunk enough. [*Collective laughter.*]

Lisa: It's not as if we are lesbians or anything; it is just a goof thing. I don't think they enjoy it. Certain women may enjoy it, but most are just curious and try it. I think it is curiosity.

AD: Is it an enjoyable experience?

Susan: I mean it's nice, but we don't like get off on it.

Nancy: It drives the guys crazy is why we do it.

Brenda: Yeah, they start yelling and asking us to do it. It is kind of funny. They freak out. One guy actually fell over on his back.

Nancy: At spring break this year, I saw a lot more than kissing. [*Collective laughter.*]

AD: Are there always guys around to watch?

Susan: Of course. It's not as if we are making out in private. It's just funny to see the guys' reactions and everything.

Lisa: Alcohol will make you do the craziest things.

Nancy: Yeah. They [women] just want attention 'cause they'll get it. They'll get it.

And they do get it. These smart, humorous, and thoughtful women end up playing the age-old flirtation game to receive the positive attention from men that they so covet. Sadly, these women have learned that there is no substitute for inviting sexuality. Today, as in generations past, most men are more attracted by the sexual availability of a woman than by her intelligence, spirituality, wit, or strength. But women are not the only losers in this human exchange. Men are also interpersonally cheated by using such narrow and superficial criteria to determine who gets their attention. In the end, these choreographed histrionics reward men's shallowness at the expense of women's multidimensionality while leaving both less vibrant and with less potential.

But this is not the only way in which such performances by women can be interpreted. Some gender theorists (e.g., Paglia, 1992, 1994; Roiphe, 1993; Wolfe, 1993) have argued that women are far more active and conscious in their gendered lives than many have given them credit for. Could it be, therefore, that, instead of being passive agents of the omnipotent patriarchy, many of these women are consciously performing traditional femininity as a means of usurping male power? Are they dirty dancing to take and maintain center stage in social gatherings? Do they find these highly sexual acts erotically stimulating? Or are they simply "having fun," "goofing on" and "making fun of" the hyperactive libidos of drunken fraternity men?

If we listen to what the women in this study say about these sexualized performances, the answer to all these questions is yes. Far from acknowledging their exploitation, these women claim to be having fun, enjoying the attention, and teasing men on their nights out on the town. Lisa, for example, thinks that "the guys are such idiots. It's like they have never seen girls before. So we [her sisters] just like messing with them." Similarly, Deb, a self-professed "big flirt," "love[s] to dance and tease. . . . You can get them to do anything for you if you're good." For Alisa, sexualized performances are also about good, old-fashioned fun and self-confirmation: "Once you get up and start dancing and you're looking good and feeling good, the night is a blast." "All that attention is good for the ego," she continues, eliciting laughter. Lisa, Deb, and Alisa are performing for themselves, not for the men. It is their way of having fun, exerting power, and validating their attractiveness and sexuality.

But, even if we grant legitimacy to this perspective, we still must question a college culture that does not provide women equally stimulating opportunities to exert power or to achieve validation. I would like to think that, if American universities did a better job of stimulating critical thought, affirming personal worth, and empowering female students, female students would be less likely to rely on sexual performances.

Conclusion

While the men and women in this study may use a neat and orderly binary framework to make sense of their world theoretically, in practice they are anything but neat and orderly. We have seen women performing masculinity (being sexual and assertive), men performing femininity (searching for long-term relationships), and both critiquing traditional gender roles. This is not to say, however, that GU's fraternity brothers and sorority sisters are free to bend gender at will. Like most other institutions in America, GU's Greek system primarily rewards men and women for enacting traditional gender scripts. It is also not to imply that there are no significant differences or common denominators in the way these men and women generally act and think. There are. When it comes to dating and sexual activity, fraternity brothers are granted more freedom, sorority sisters less.

This inequality, however, was not of significant concern to these women. Rather, they consistently highlighted the frustration and confusion of maintaining a paradoxical sexual identity. On the one hand, they are expected to be virginal, monogamous, chaste, and virtuous, and, on the other, they are encouraged to be sexual, inviting, provocative, and available. This double bind forces them to walk a thin line between acceptable and unacceptable behavior. To complicate things even more, the line between the trashy and the appropriate is constantly, and capriciously, shifting. Oral sex is acceptable, but vaginal sex is not. Kissing your sorority sister is acceptable, but being trashy is not. No wonder so many of the men I interviewed spoke of receiving "mixed messages." As one Lamda brother confessed: "I am never really sure what *no* means. She hangs all over you and grabs your ass at the bar, but, when you get back to your room, she cools off and leaves. I don't think *they* know what they want."

After listening to hundreds of hours of men's conversations about sexuality, I am not surprised by this ambivalence on the part of women. The fraternity brothers' language, subsequently appropriated by sororities, casts deviant women as sluts and whores. As Lees (1986) notes, there is more at work here than just name-calling, for language limits human possibilities and actions. Such terms, Eder (2001) writes, instill a "double standard of morality directly into our language and thus in our consciousness" (p. 133). Consequently, these labels have a "powerful way of controlling" women's "sexual assertiveness as well as their general life force" (p. 147). And, as Lorde (1984) has argued: "By controlling the life force of erotic energy you can control people" (p. 76). Equally troubling, however, is that restricting women's sexuality also "promotes an image of women as being passive sexually and dependent on men to initiate sexual activity. This image then becomes a societal justification for male sexual domination" (Eder, 2001, p. 147).

Ironically, the men in this study were equally schizophrenic about their sexual identity. The dialectical tension with which they wrestle, however, is between the emotionally removed playboy and the intimate boyfriend. While most of them enjoyed the idea of the promiscuous lifestyle, few lived it. After all, it is hard, expensive, and lonely work picking up a new woman every night. In more private moments away from their brothers, many confessed their desire for a steady girlfriend to "hang out with." These conflicting urges explain why so many brothers engage in so many short-term relationships. The pattern is as follows: pick up, date for a week or two, break up, and repeat. This strategy effectively balances the pull of being single and the push of being committed.

While some brothers may claim that they want the companionship and friendship of women, the organizations they belong to cultivate a climate of malicious misogyny. In fact, of the hundreds of fraternities around the nation with which I have had the opportunity to interact, most reinforce the same four notions: a woman's worth (as well as her sorority's) is based on her physical attractiveness; a woman becomes the object of scorn once she has sexual intercourse (oral, anal, or vaginal) with any man to whom she is not emotionally attached; a promiscuous woman should be used only for discreet one-night stands; and the companionship of women is an unacceptable substitute for that of men. These notions are perpetuated at weekly meetings and Wednesday-night dinners. They are passed on to members through off-color jokes and bad-conduct awards. They are manifested on the backs of T-shirts and in ritualized drinking songs. They are, in short, part of the constant reinforcing of the patriarchy that is the order of the day at most fraternity houses.

3. The Tough Guy and His Date (Rape)

At 3:00 A.M., Scott awoke to the sound of frantic pounding on his door. Without waiting for a response, his big brother, Bruce, stormed into the room. "It's going down, now! Get your shit on! Let's go!" Scott, only half conscious, and still drunk from last night's party, immediately knew the meaning of this encrypted call to arms: the rumble between the Alphas and the Deltas was starting. What began last semester as an isolated exchange of insults between two drunken students from rival fraternities quickly escalated into a full-fledged interhouse brawl. It was inevitable, Scott recalled. "Everybody just knew that all this shit was going to end in one big mass clusterfuck."

Scott was right. Everybody knew that the late-night bang on the door was coming. Even I held out little hope of a peaceful resolution to this conflict after the previous week's five (Alphas) on seven (Deltas) throwdown outside a popular local bar. As I was told the next morning: "Jack [a senior Delta] and six of his faggot-ass brothers were talking shit." Once the two groups got outside, "it just exploded." While the fight was broken up before the cops came or anyone was seriously hurt, the die was cast. Only the where and the when were unknown to the two hundred waiting brothers.

As Scott and the rest of his brothers gathered downstairs in the house's vestibule and shook off their inebriated sleep, Bruce filled everyone in on the events that had transpired over the last hour. After the Alpha party had broken up, a few of the brothers went to the bars for some postparty socializing. To their surprise, they ran into a pack of drunk and angry Delta brothers who were "talking shit 'cause they had the numbers [i.e., they outnumbered the Alphas]." Bruce and the Alphas left promising to return with backup.

"It seemed like there must have been sixty of us walking to the Delta house," recalled Brian. The numbers, needless to say, now favored the Alphas. As the brothers broke through the front doors of the enemy's house, hollering about "respect" and "loudmouth pussies," their alarmed rivals, still half asleep and disoriented, streamed out of their rooms to meet the invading force. With fists flying, the two foes fought to a draw. While the "great rumble of 2003" lasted no more than two minutes, produced no serious injuries, and spawned no definitive winners or losers, the bonding and memories that it engendered for both sides was, as Scott, an Alpha brother, put it, "fucking memorable, fucking great." Mark, a Delta brother, reported: "It really was something cool. I would have been so pissed if I missed it."

The Alphas and Deltas are not alone in the experience of violence. Just about every fraternity that I have spoken with throughout the years has a similar story of warfare and heroics that is retold with pride and hyperbole. In 1982, as a college sophomore, I even found myself in the throes of my fraternity's great rumble. If truth be told, there were only two brothers who actually participated in hand-to-hand combat—and both were unceremoniously expelled from campus the next morning. Nonetheless, all observers in attendance, including myself, took pride and credit for being real men who went to battle when they were called. Not to have answered the door when the knock came, or to have expressed trepidation over the logic or ethics of the rumble, would surely have resulted in a lifetime (or at least a school year) of emasculating ridicule and scorn. Thank goodness I showed up. Thank goodness I didn't have to fight.

This chapter deals with the way in which fraternity men conceive of violence, competition, and aggression. As my informants assert, in no uncertain terms, no man can be truly masculine unless he is ready to go to battle—regardless of whether the fight is verbal, physical, athletic, or sexual.

Men

Whether among the men or the women in this study, discussion of masculinity necessarily involved discussions of aggression, competition, and violence. Along with sexual promiscuity (see chapter 2), these were the ideas that most punctuated their perceptions of manhood. Academics who have studied contemporary American masculinity concur. Connell (1983), Komisar (1980), Messner (1988), Nelson (1994), and Trujillo (1991) all agree that *the* dominant feature of our culture's conception of true manhood is the attainment of status and respect through aggression.

That the successful man is the aggressive man is a lesson that is learned early (Miedzian, 1991; Nelson, 1994). By the time my son was four, for example, he had been so thoroughly inculcated in the world of the Ninja Turtles, the Power Rangers, football action heroes, pirates, and cowboys and Indians that he was chopping, kicking, punching, stabbing, and shooting virtually every nonhuman object he ran across. Much to my dismay—and despite my best efforts to protect him from the worst manifestations of masculinity—he had already learned how to "play man" before his fifth birthday.

Most of the men in this study remember similar childhood experiences that imprinted on them the lessons of aggression and violence. They learned that life is an ongoing battle against other men for women, prestige, popularity, attention, respect, and rank. Fathers, gym teachers, coaches, girlfriends, MTV, and ESPN have all shown/ told them that they are at their most attractive and desirable after having fought their bloody way to the top.

Brian remembers the day, for instance, that he got into his first fight and was subsequently hailed as a hero by his friends. Although he felt bad about beating up a classmate, the positive response he received made it well worth it. "I knew from then on," he said, "that fighting in situations like that was always the right thing to do. . . . After my second or third fight in eighth grade, everyone was like, 'You are a bad ass.' . . . Girls loved it too."

For Jonathan, a young boy being raised by a single mother, it was his football coach that most profoundly affected his ideas of masculinity. "I loved Coach Lewis. I mean he was a real old-school guy.

But I mean he taught me about life. . . . 'Life is football,' he would say. He's right, you know?" To this day, long after his football-playing days in high school ended, he still remembers the lessons of "doing everything hard," "never letting up," and "pushing through the pain." Thanks to Coach Lewis and his wisdom, Jonathan believes that he will be successful in anything he does in life.

Finally, Mark will never forget the masculinity scripts that he learned from his father and grandfather. Mark told me that he comes from a long line of Michigan sportsmen. "Hunting, shooting, fishing, I was raised doing it all. . . . Every winter we go hunting in Canada. . . . Summers we like to fish the lakes." These experiences, he explained, taught him how to be successful. "It is about setting out to accomplish something. It is a challenge, you know? . . . It is you against the animal, or whatever. If you are better, smarter than it, you kill it. You win. That's life."

When Brian's, Jonathan's, and Mark's stories are unpacked and considered alongside the others that have been recorded for this project, a uniquely American narrative about competition, aggression, and violence is told.

Interfraternity Competition and Aggression

Everything in the lives of these men is competitive, and that is the way they profess to like it. From playing basketball and video games to drinking beer and having sex, it is all one great big contest to see who is the Alpha male (no pun intended). Within the Greek system, however, there is no fiercer competition than that between rival fraternities. And every fraternity—from the 150-year-old elite group to the struggling, newly colonized one—has its archnemesis. It is this dynamic that gives definition and direction to the daily practices at each house.

The most obvious form of competition comes every fall during rush, when each house bids for a disproportionate share of the cool kids.[1] "Man, rush is war, really," Jason, a Nu brother, said. "I mean each year you have to re-prove yourself as the best. . . . You can't let off. . . . Everybody wants to take your spot." For Derek and his Psi brothers, rush is their annual opportunity to move up in the pack. "We are new, or newer. We don't have the house or money of some of the others. You know, though, it only takes a couple really great [pledge] classes to change [i.e., move up in the rankings]."

Regardless of where it is in the pecking order, however, each organization has its work cut out for it. The elites want to stay elite, and the aspirers want to move up, not down, and the strugglers don't want to be humiliated. A great pledge class can elevate a group in the eyes of its peers and, of course, intrigue the women on campus; a poor pledge class can engender gossip about an organization's demise and its members' lack of aggression and virility.

Consequently, every chapter dedicates a great deal of time, money, and energy to this competitive male courting ritual. In recent years, for example, fraternities at GU have sponsored female Jell-O and mud wrestling, strippers, wet T-shirt contests, the university dance team, and the Hooters Girls; served all-you-can-eat barbecue ribs, pizza, wings, hoagies/subs, rib-eye steak, and seafood jambalaya; rented stretch limousines (and filled them with attractive women) to lure back lost freshman; hired acoustic guitar players, country bands, hip-hop DJs, and heavy-metal rock groups; handed out cigars, T-shirts, drinking cups, minibasketballs, pens, and gift certificates; taken coveted candidates to restaurants, strip clubs, and bars; bribed sorority women to flirt with prospective pledges; spread rumors about a rival's dangerous hazing practices, lame social events, and sexual orientation; and, of course, maintained a never-ending series of clandestine, after-hour keg parties to lubricate freshman decisionmaking.[2] But, as Derek sees it: "It is all worth it. The money, the time, all the other stuff. You gotta nut-up for rush. You gotta fight for every good guy. That's how you become the best."

While rush may be the single most intense competition between fraternities, it is not the most mean-spirited. That honor goes to interfraternity sports. With the best of intentions, American universities established these programs to encourage exercise, camaraderie, and sportsmanship. The reality at GU, however, is that the Inter-fraternity Council (IFC) sports program has become an officially sanctioned outlet for aggressive, athletic fraternities to publicly humiliate less aggressive, less athletic fraternities. Of course, the larger elite organizations come away with the lion's share of the championships.

In cases when two elite organizations go to war, the match is framed rhetorically as more than just a game; it is transformed into an event where the most hypermasculine attributes of the Greek community are displayed in full force. It indicates to observers which of the two groups is the toughest, the strongest, the most aggressive, the most popular, even the most heterosexual. An e-mail message that I received from the Deltas in the spring of 2005 was typical. In it, I was encouraged to "come out and support the team": "We play tonight at 10:30 at the [university sports center] against [the Alphas]. Those fucking fags are going to have a ton of guys there so we need to have everyone come out and watch us kick the shit out of those pussies. The more people that are there, the easier it will be for those fudge-packers to understand their role on this campus. Let's have a good turnout tonight." Clearly, the game was about more than just football; it was about the masculine drive for supremacy in one of its most dangerous forms.

But not all championships are equal in the eyes of GU's fraternity men. While the yearlong IFC sports season includes such diverse activities as ping-pong, swimming, volleyball, and golf, only the truly masculine sports matter to these men. Only the men who excel at football, basketball, and, to a lesser extent, soccer are perceived as real athletes, masculine and aggressive. The men of Omega elaborate:

AD: Are the Omegas competitive?
Jason: Shit yeah, especially against other fraternities. You know, not so much between ourselves. But, shit, when it comes to sports, it's serious.

Patrick: Oh yeah! [*Group laughter fills the room.*]

Chris: We don't really care about the stupid sports. Ping-pong and swimming, you know, track. That stuff doesn't really mean anything.

Jason: Only to the loser fraternities. [*Group laughter.*]

Shorty: They think they're big shit when they win. Hell, we don't even send guys to those events. . . . They're chick sports. [*More group laughter.*]

AD: What do you mean, *chick sports?*

Chris: Oh [*thoughtful pause*], sports that don't take athleticism. No, I mean sports that don't take strength or speed. Like that.

Shorty: Sports that girls can do as well as guys. Ping-pong, who cares?

AD: So what matters?

Jason: Football!

Patrick: Yeah, football. [*Group consensus.*]

Shorty: Basketball is really important. Soccer too. [*More group consensus.*]

Patrick: These are the guy sports that matter. Stud sports. [*Group laughter.*]

Chris: OK, here it is. I guess the cool sports are sports that you can get hurt doing. Is there blood? Stuff that you need to be in shape to do. If a fat kid can win, or a girl, then, it's not a sport. [*Group laughter.*]

Masculine sports that matter, therefore, should be played by aggressive, strong men not afraid to bleed. In the world of fraternities, the organization with the most aggressive, most fearless men wins more often than not. And winners, regardless of how cocky or disliked they may be, are still respected by other men. A man's character and his achievements are two separate things. The former does not diminish the latter. "I fucking hate the Omegas," confesses Alpha's Nathanial. "They are just dick heads. But they're good. I guess until we can beat them, they can talk all the trash they want." "It's true," agrees Nick. "You know, if you can walk the walk, then talk, man. They're fast. They just outran us [referring to last year's championship football game]. You got to give them their props." Interestingly, the Omegas' IFC championship T-shirts proclaimed a similar sentiment: "YOU DON'T HAVE TO LIKE US, BUT YOU WILL RESPECT US!"

Rush and IFC sports are only the two most obvious aspects of fraternity competition. Less obvious, but equally fierce, is the competition between chapters over such matters as who gets the most attention from the elite sororities, who has the biggest parties, who has the most attractive members, who has the most prestigious campus leaders, who receives the most sorority prizes and awards (Mr. GU, homecoming king, Greek man of the year), who has the most (and the biggest) weight lifters, who has the wealthiest alumni, who holds the most popular tailgates, who has the most high-profile varsity athletes, who has the biggest house in the best location, who has the largest pledge class, and who has been on campus the longest. Sadly, a fraternity's GPA is rarely a point of contention. These men would much rather win the IFC football championship than its Excellence in Academics award. In fact, such a dubious honor can actually work against a fraternity's masculine status—and the not so subtle undercurrent of anti-intellectualism—if not tempered or masked with a healthy dose of public womanizing, fighting, and drinking.

Given the organizational culture that permeates most elite houses, this ubiquitous competition in the lives of these young men is not surprising. From the first day of pledging to graduation day, these brothers are taught to dislike, if not hate, all other fraternities. This us-versus-them mentality doesn't just sanction the expression of meanness, aggression, and violence toward those not in the clan; it encourages it. The inflammatory and threatening customized T-shirts that chapters parade around campus in illustrate this culture of animosity:

"WE DON'T REBUILD, WE RELOAD" (with a picture of a tank
   blowing up fraternity row).

"WE'RE KICKIN' ASS AND TAKING NAMES" (with a cartoon of the muscular Alphas beating up a nerdy Greek).

"WALK IN OUR SHOES OR STAND IN OUR SHADOWS" (with a picture of a big foot stepping on the Sigmas' new house).

"YOU'RE EITHER WITH US, OR YOU'RE AGAINST US" (with a machine-gun-toting Nu shooting his letters into the side of a rival's house).

"YOU MAY NOT LIKE US, BUT YOUR GIRLFRIEND DOES" (with a cartoon of a muscular Chi brother making out with a big-chested cheerleader as her wimpy and emasculated Greek boyfriend watches).

Such isolation and distrust tends not to be found, and is, in fact, discouraged, among sororities. It is common at GU to find older sisters from different sororities living together in off-campus housing. Gammas, Alphas, and Deltas often share living space with their Beta, Pi, and Mu friends. For many of these women, similarities in personality and interests play a much more significant role in determining friendships than does simple Greek affiliation.

Among the men in this study, this type of fraternal mixing and matching is virtually unheard of. In the few cases where it has occurred, the brothers living together have had their loyalty to their respective houses questioned. Benjamin, a Gamma brother, thinks that it is "fucked up" when a brother chooses to move away from his fraternity. "I don't get it, I really don't get it. Why would a guy choose to be best friends with guys from somewhere else? Why doesn't he just pledge them?" In the case of Robert, an Iota brother who lives with three Nu brothers in an off-campus apartment, things have actually, as he said, "gotten ugly." "I get shit all the time. They're like little jealous girls. . . . I get shit said to me all the time about living with those guys. It's like, 'You better not have any other friends.'"

This is not to say that brothers from different fraternities can't socialize together. Indeed, casual friendships between Greek men are common at GU. They greet, joke, and banter with each other on campus, in class, and at parties, bars, and dances. But these relationships must not become significant or meaningful. A clear distinction must be maintained between the brothers and all others. Breaking this rule is tantamount to infidelity. To take a line from the Gammas' rush T-shirts: "NOTHING COMES BETWEEN THE FAMILY" (a Mafia reference).

Interfraternity Violence

Taken to extremes, this form of fraternal-centrism and isolation breeds a trigger-finger mentality that allows conflict to be resolved only through immediate violence. More peaceful means of resolution are perceived to be "girl stuff" or "pussy shit," as the Deltas John and Marcus put it. These young men are given a script that instructs them to never back down, to take everything personally, to fight as the first course of action, and to always remember that their actions (or the lack thereof) reflect on their chapter's masculine reputation. What do you do if a member of a rival fraternity talks shit about you? Hit him. What do you do if he talks shit about your fraternity? Hit him. What do you do if he eyeballs your girlfriend? Hit him.

The only way such inflammatory situations can be defused is for the transgressor to publicly apologize for his poor judgment—a very unmasculine, and, thus, unlikely, course of action in the world of fraternities. If this capitulation is perceived to be sincere, then, and only then, is it acceptable for the brother not to fight. Anything less than complete acquiescence, however, demands action.

Many times, however, brothers are dragged into fights not of their own making. It is quite common, for instance, for an isolated squabble between two men from rival fraternities to contaminate whole chapters. In March 2000, a disagreement between John, a Phi brother, and Kevin, a Nu brother, over an old high school girlfriend erupted into a mass rumble between their two fraternities. Peter, one of John's Phi brothers, detailed the fight's inception:

John hated this kid in the Nus, and he would see this kid out, and he would be with his brothers, and John was always with us. . . . One fight led to another. More of us kept getting involved until like six of us had been in fights with the Nus. So there was all that stuff just boiling on the surface. So, when the Nus fucked up our house [referring to an incident where golf balls were thrown through the Phi house windows, allegedly by the Nus], it was just on. By that time, we all hated those fucks, so it was easy. . . . But it started all over a fuckin' girl.

This Phi/Nu rumble, similar to the Alpha/Delta rumble discussed earlier, has taken on mythic proportions. As it has been retold to me (at least a dozen times), the two neighboring organizations met in the common parking lot behind their houses. As word spread, every brother within earshot sprinted to the battleground out of both curiosity and fraternal obligation. As Patrick claimed, "When the call comes, you have to go. It's brotherhood. You don't ask why; you just go."

As insults and threats were exchanged, a few isolated punches were thrown. "I say there were probably like five different fights, total," speculated Phi brother Justin. "A few were really intense." But, just as abruptly as the dispute began, it ended. Albert was, according to his brothers, "sucker punched in the face." He fell against the fence and was knocked unconscious. "We were like freaked because he was out, I mean cold. He was like shaking and shit," reported Charles, a Phi brother.

As the ambulance raced Albert to the university hospital, most of the participants on both sides expressed concern for the fallen warrior. "It was kinda weird, you know," Martin, a Nu brother, said. After that kid Al went down, we were all like really concerned. We wanted to fight, but, when he started convulsing or whatever, then it wasn't a game anymore. . . . At first I heard he died."

This collective concern lasted only until Albert was released from the hospital later that evening suffering from nothing more serious than a mild concussion. Once word got out that he was going to live—and, perhaps more important, that no one was going to be charged with second-degree murder—the mythmaking and spin-doctoring began. Each organization crafted its own history about the winners and losers, heroes and villains. Those brothers "lucky" enough to have attended the great Phi/Nu rumble of 2000 left with a lifetime of hypermasculine war stories:

> AD: Tell me about the mood at the Nu house after the fight.
> Pops: It's something that like both fraternities are kinda glad it happened. When I see some of the Phi brothers out, they love to joke about it too. It was kinda cool.
> Jason: You need to have a good fight once in your life.
> Jared: I remember after the fight, really once we heard that kid was OK, we all met, and everybody was still all drunk, and like, "Fuck them dudes," and everybody's hands were all bloody, and everybody's knuckles were all fucked up. Everybody was all hyped, and then a couple other guys were like, "Yeah, I just got here."
> Pops: Oh yeah, the guys that missed it were pissed. I don't think because they all wanted to really fight, but now they can't talk about it with us. You are left out of all those stories.
> Tim: I think it is also really important for everyone, men, to be in at least one big fight. It tests you as a man. You can see what you're made of.
> Jason: You know, it was a great night for us. We were so pumped with each other.
> Tim: It was cool to know that all your brothers will show up if they're needed. And afterwards we were all just laughing and talking. I don't know how to explain it.
> Jason: Brotherhood.

As this exchange illustrates, there are clear institutional require-ments for brotherhood. First and foremost is that all brothers are expected, as Jason, a Gamma brother, put it, to "be there" and to "have a brother's back no matter what" during a fight. What is not part of this ethics of fighting, however, is the traditional masculine rule that demands equal and balanced pairings during violent conflicts, that is, mano a mano.

When I was growing up in Tuckahoe, New Jersey, a white, blue-collar town, for example, it was inconceivable that any male with any self-respect would ever participate in a fight in which the numbers were not balanced and equal. Most of the time this meant that one male would fight another male while everyone else, including the participants' friends, watched. Intervention by a third party was permitted only to break up a fight that had become a lopsided victory. Thirty years later, according to most of my interviewees, this masculine axiom is still observed in most white, non-Greek communities across America. "I have to admit," Sam claimed, "that the idea of, you know, ganging up on people was weird. At first, I just was like, what?" Sam's brother Justin also thought that "it was a little fucked up. . . . In my high school, you were on your own. Everyone backed away, and two guys went at it. If more than one guy beat up another one, then we were like, 'What a pussy.'" Keith, an Omega brother, thinks, "That stuff is definitely a Greek thing. In my hometown in Connecticut, it was always, I mean always, one on one. It had to be fair." He remembers when "these two football players beat up this one kid for messing with a girl, and the whole school was like, 'What the fuck?' They lost all respect."

At GU, however, no such fairness rule exists. In fact, Greek men are taught that to passively observe from the sidelines is to neglect their fraternal obligation. Any fight, big or small, equal or unequal, demands their violent participation. When a group of Alphas found themselves outnumbering the Gammas a reported twenty-five to five at a tailgate party, for example, not a single Alpha claimed to have felt inclined to even the sides or guilt over their lopsided victory. "Fuck 'em," claimed Edward. "Talk trash to us, we will roll on you with numbers." Mark, an Alpha senior, matter-of-factly summarized the situation: "It was like this: the Gammas either had to back down or get beat down. They got beat down."

Similarly, when an isolated fight broke out at the Beta house between an outsider and Jack, a first-year brother, the outsider had to worry not just about Jack, his primary foe, but about Jack's sixty brothers. "This kid got the shit kicked out of him," Jack reported. "I tell you what, it made me feel really good knowing that I wasn't alone. I was punching the shit out of this kid, and he was being kicked in the head." After most of the brothers got their shots in, Jack told me, the outsider was unceremoniously "thrown out on his ass." "I think he was even fucked up even more after I left."

Fighting for Greek men, therefore, is not always an uncontrollable, testosterone-fueled reaction to conflict or a simple, less complicated means to an end. Fighting, especially alongside their brothers, also serves the purpose of allowing them to brag to all other men that they have been to battle and didn't back down—thus raising their rank in the masculine hierarchy. It gives them the ability to share meaningful stories with other members of their clan. It supplies them with a gender-appropriate means of expressing their loyalty toward and affection for other men. And it bolsters their self-esteem—especially if they are on the winning side of a fight. But, even for the losers, it is better to have fought and lost than not to have fought at all. "Nothing is worse than a pussy," argues Aaron. "I think we [referring to his fraternity] would all rather have a guy who doesn't back down and gets slammed than a dude who just won't fight."

Intrafraternity Competition and Aggression

Competition, aggression, and, to a lesser extent, violence are found not only between rival fraternities but also within fraternities. While not as intense or mean-spirited, intrafraterntiy competition is part of the everyday interactions between brothers. Walk into any house on GU's campus, for example, and you are sure to find some form of mano a mano contest being waged. Interestingly, many of the sports that these men pejoratively frame as *girl* and *stupid* when played against other fraternities are the very ones that they love to play with each other. At most houses, in fact, brothers organize chapter golf, bowling, pool, Nintendo/Play Station, and ping-pong (or beer-pong, the fraternity version) tournaments as diversions from their studies. Not only do such activities (called by some houses *brotherhood events*) serve to bond brothers; they also provide a context for nonviolent, but serious, in-house competition. As an added incentive to participation, winners earn bragging rights. As Neil, a Rho brother, reported: "We go bowling on brotherhood nights sometimes, and I'll tell you, we take it serious, I mean serious. We all want to win. . . . When I won last time, I talked shit like you wouldn't believe it. I was obnoxious. But that's all part of it, the fun of it."

But not all in-house competitions revolve around the so-called girl sports. Many activities take on a much more aggressive tone. The Rhos, for example, have a "juiced up version of dodgeball," as Patrick put it, that they play when they "are all fucked up." "We pound the hell out of each other," Patrick joked. "Broken fingers, bloody noses, you get it all." On most spring, summer, and fall afternoons, you can find the Gammas, Pis, Sigmas, and Nus on their basketball courts playing three on three or five on five "death matches." "Hell yeah, they're serious," laughs Jon, a Sigma. "Elbows are flying. No one wants to lose, especially not to a bunch of brothers you're going to have to listen to if they beat you." "There's been a couple times," Eban, a Nu, remembers, "that some hard games have ended up in fights. . . . These fuckers hate to lose—brothers or not."

The Chis prefer the more overtly aggressive activity of basement boxing or wrestling to test each other's mettle. Once in the ring, where one- to two-minute rounds "can get pretty heated and intense," according to Ray, boxing brothers literally try to knock each other out. While padded gloves and headgear are worn (most of the time), the clear objective is to win by a knockout. "It's great to go at each other," confesses Brad. "All is evened out on the mats. All is fair. You have a problem with a brother, two minutes with the gloves on, or just wrestling, will fix anything."

Remarkably, these activities do not produce long-term animosity between brothers. "I think that's the biggest difference between guys and girls," Janis speculates. "If a girl got into a fight with another girl, there would be drama for months. We would cry and talk about it; we would drag our sisters into it. . . . Guys just slap each other on the butt and drink a beer . . . as if nothing ever happened." While the getting-over-it process may not be as quick or as easy for these brothers as a slap and a beer, they claim to forgive and forget within a few hours, or at most a few days, of most altercations. As Lucas and his Iota brothers see it, "Only little girls hold on to grudges. Fuck, if we hated each other every time we were dicks, we'd never talk. It's just no big deal, really."

Turning Boys into Tough Guys

The preparation for this tough-skinned approach to fraternal competition begins for most freshman during the first week of pledging. In an effort to bond new pledge classes together, the older brothers pit their new initiates against the active chapter in myriad ways. Pledge classes are forced to compete in relay drinking races, bowling tournaments, wrestling matches, and softball, basketball, and tackle football games against their big brothers. And while these competitions are not optional—pledges who miss these events risk being blackballed—most brothers admit that they are the best part of pledging. Logan remembers the night, for instance, when he and his pledge brothers beat their older Omega brothers in laser tag: "We really didn't know each other at first. Then they [the older brothers] made us play laser tag. The [older] brothers were talking crap as if they were going to kill us. They didn't know what hit them. We were running through this big warehouse and just shooting the crap out of them. We beat them by, I don't know, two hundred points. . . . After that, we were like so tight. I think it was like, for all of us, our favorite night. We still talk about it."

Rick, the pledge trainer for the Mus, sees such activities as accomplishing a number of related tasks. First: "It is important to get those guys doing things together. To start acting, thinking you know, like a unit, brothers." Second: "The brothers also have fun fucking with the pledges. And I guess the pledges like it too. Some of the stuff at least." Third, and most important: "Those things are really good lessons for those guys. We teach them how to be tougher. . . . A lot of those guys leave high school, and they're pussies. Making them play football or wrestle or whatever makes them tougher—into men."

Along with using sports to make men out of boys, many fraternities also rely on a variety of noncompetitive hazing practices to toughen up their neophytes. On GU's campus, for instance, fraternities regularly impose a mandatory hell-week exercise regimen on their pledges—complete with boot-camp-style calisthenics and screaming drill sergeants. These workout programs are often supplemented with some form of sleep and/or food deprivation and excessive verbal abuse—both aimed at further accentuating the effects of physical exhaustion. And, while the stated primary goal of all these practices is to unify a pledge class, the secondary goal is to harden the next generation of Greek leaders. Robert, the outgoing Omega vice president, expands on this twofold goal: "I don't care what anyone says, hazing is a must. Otherwise you got a pledge class that doesn't know each other and are soft. Like I said, most of us still pledge [haze] because it builds brotherhood and it makes them tougher for life. Like I said, if you can get through pledging, you can get through anything. It definitely toughens you up." "You are a man when you get through—if you get through," he concludes, laughing humorously like Bela Lugosi.

Most pledges do, in fact, "get through," and they have the war stories to prove it. And most are more than willing to tell you—over a few beers—how they were toughened up through a sometimes humorous combination of verbal and physical abuse, menial labor, the forced consumption of alcohol, and the loss of personal freedom. Jason recalls being on call twenty-four hours a day, making late-night runs to Taco Bell, the liquor store, and Kroger's for potato chips. Lee and his brothers still laugh at having to clean the apartments of their older brothers while wearing children's Halloween costumes and singing to the Back Street Boys. When I asked Samuel what he had to do, he snickered and said, "Everything!" "I must've lit two thousand cigarettes, opened five hundred bottles of beer. . . . I even peeled grapes and clipped Bear's, this big stinky kid, clipped his toenails."

Many of these young men, however, have toughening-up stories that are not so benign. John and his pledge brothers, for example, were locked in their fraternity's attic, dressed in their best suits, "and had the heat turned up to, like, a hundred degrees." He continued: "We all had to sit there in the heat for hours and get yelled at for hours. They [the older brothers] also cranked radio static on like '10' [i.e., turned the volume as loud as it would go]. All you could do is sit there and go crazy and sweat the whole time." Next: "We had to go out in the hall and get on our hands and knees and balance on our chin and knees for, like, fifteen minutes. . . . Everybody's chin was bruised and scabbed and bleeding for like the next week."

When questioned about the logic behind such cruelty, the brothers consistently informed me that it is the "only way to turn pledges into brothers": "They all have to do it together, and it makes them tougher, stronger, you know?" The often-used war metaphor clarifies the point. "It's like going into battle. War sucks, but, when you come out of it, you are stronger, you know, you went to hell with each other," said Nathan, a Chi brother. When I asked John and his brothers whether they now inflict the same torture on new pledges, they all laughed. "Of course. Fuck, we went through it," John claimed. "Hell yes, they are going through it too," supported Michael.[3]

This "now-it's-my-turn" mentality is extremely prevalent among Greek men. In fact, it has been the one recurring obstacle that I have encountered when suggesting changes in fraternity pledge programs. While I have, I believe, convinced chapter leaders (e.g., student executive councils) that hazing is dangerous and unproductive, I have had little, if any, success among the rank-and-file brothers. While the first line of defense that most brothers throw up when questioned about hazing is the it's-good-for-brotherhood argument, even the most minimal of cross-examinations produces a ready admission like that of Jacob, then a new Xi initiate: "Oh come on now, yeah, hell yeah everybody wants their turn to bust ass. Hell yeah," he continues, laughing, "I want my turn."

Finally, it needs to be noted that having tough guys in your chapter is seen not only as a way to intimidate rival fraternities but also as a proven method of impressing elite sororities. "I don't care what they tell you, women love tough guys," argues Paul, a Rho. "Just watch—you know I'm right—look who gets the attention, who all the girls want. You know I'm right." As proof, Warren and his Alpha brothers told me of the night when they all went to a hockey game with the Sigma sisters. "You should've seen them," laughs Warren. "They were yelling and laughing, and I mean they were really getting into all of it." "They loved the fights the most," interjected James. "We were all like, 'OK, another fight, big deal.' The girls were like loving it. They kept talking about how hot the team was just 'cause they were sweaty and fighting, I guess."

Finding so many men articulating similar thoughts, I asked the women in the study whether there was any validity to such claims. Much to my surprise, many confessed that there was. While all claimed to be repulsed by bullies, most thought justified violence was attractive. Brooke remembers when her high school boyfriend was going to "beat the shit out of this guy" who hit her and she "was like, *Yeah!*" She thought: "It was way cool, you know, a guy that would fight for you." Similarly, June thinks that "it's cute because then it is like they are watching out for you." She is quick to remind me, however, that "you don't want some idiot to just beat up people for no reason, but, when he is protecting you, it is really cute." For Lori, having an aggressive man is more than just cool or cute. A traditional "tough guy," like her present boyfriend, makes her "feel safe and secure" in an unsafe world: "I want someone to make me feel safe. Like, if, well, if something is going on right now, I want someone I can come home to that is going to make me feel better about, you know, terrorism as far as that. You know, who will say, 'Well, it's OK. I'm going to take care of you.'" Being around tough guys, however, may not always be the safest place for women to be, as we shall see.

Women

Tough Guys and Sexual Assaults

The pairing of male aggression and female attraction to tough guys is a dangerous one. Much to my horror, many of the women I interviewed disclosed incidents of abuse by acquaintances, most of whom were fraternity friends and boyfriends. The sexual and physical abuse of women by intimates is not confined to Greek life or, for that matter, college life; it is an American epidemic:

- Twenty-five percent of women reported being raped and/or physically assaulted by a current or former boyfriend at some point in their lives (Tjaden & Thoennes, 2000).
- Three million women are physically abused by their husband or boyfriend each year (Greenfeld et al., 1998).
- Almost one in twelve women are stalked at least once in their lifetime (National Center for Victims of Crime, 2004).
- Fifty percent of the men who frequently assaulted their wives also frequently abused their children (Strauss, Gelles & Smith, 1990).
- Approximately one in five female high school students reported being physically and/or sexually abused by a dating partner (Silverman, Raj, Mucci & Hathaway, 2001).
- One in twelve college men admitted to forcing a woman to have sexual intercourse against her will (Koss, Gidycz & Wisniewski, 1987).
- One in five girls between the ages of fourteen and eighteen report having been hit, slapped, shoved, or forced to have sex by a date (Goode, 2001).

- Somewhere in the neighborhood of 300,000 women each year experience intimate-partner violence during pregnancy (Gazmararian et al., 2000).

Such statistics are disturbingly high, and many researchers believe that they rise even higher when the focus is narrowed to women in the Greek system. Bryan (1987), for example, has argued that over 70 percent of reported cases of gang rape have occurred at fraternity parties, and Copenhaver and Grauerholz (1991) found that almost half the sorority women they studied experienced some form of sexual coercion, 24 percent experienced attempted rape, and 17 percent were victims of completed rapes. "Almost half of the rapes occurred in a fraternity house," they concluded, "and over half occurred either during a fraternity function or was perpetrated by a fraternity member" (p. 31).[4]

Gwartney-Gibbs and Stockard (1989) and Kalof and Cargill (1991) found that Greeks are more likely to be more sexually aggressive, more likely to accept rape myths, consume larger amounts of alcohol and drugs, and place a higher value on social life at college than non-Greeks—all factors contributing to assaults on women. Boeringer, Sherhan, and Akers (1991) found that fraternity members are more likely than independents to use nonphysical coercion and drugs and alcohol as a sexual strategy. Not surprisingly, Martin and Hummer (1989), O'Sullivan (1991), and Sanday (1990) have all concluded that fraternities are places where rape is most likely to occur on college campuses.

After carefully delineating the specific contextual and behavioral characteristics leading to rape, Boswell and Spade (1996) have asserted that those fraternity parties marked by a gender ratio skewed in favor of men, gender segregation and fewer mixed-gender conversations, dirty bathrooms, louder music and less dancing, less friendly and sociable brothers, and greater alcohol consumption are considerably more dangerous for females attendees. In a similar line of research, Mohler-Kuo, Dowdall, Koss, and Wechsler (2004) discovered that college women who reside in sorority houses, are under twenty-one, drink heavily, are white, and frequent fraternity parties are at a higher risk of rape.

Disconcertingly, some of these contextual and behavioral factors are characteristic of many GU fraternity parties. When the women in this study discussed their social life within the Greek system, for example, many made direct reference to elite parties where excessive amounts of alcohol are consumed by both men and women, the music is so loud that conversation is impossible, and the entire fraternity house, including the bathrooms, is, as Kathy, an Omega, put it, "nasty and smelly, a pigsty." None, however, described the men as unfriendly or antisocial, and many described being treated with warmth and attention. The women do admit, however, that their reception is "cooler once brothers find out you're not available or easy." And the reception is even cooler for women considered physically unattractive. But, even given the occasional snub, most of the women in this study reported enjoying the time they spend in fraternity houses. "I have so many friends who are brothers in all these houses," reported Janice, "that I always have a great time. . . . People talk about how dangerous frats are, but they're not, I don't think so. I have never once felt uneasy, ever."

There is, of course, the occasional altercation in which a female visitor is pushed, verbally abused, and splashed with beer. But such events are taken very seriously by most chapters. The offending brother, more often than not, is not only sanctioned by the organization, for example, put on social probation or banned from subsequent parties, but also berated by his brothers. "I have no respect for any man," Kevin earnestly claims, "who would hit a woman. He should be blackballed. Period. I would ball a brother over that." Kevin is not alone in his chivalry. When I asked each organization to tell me what its taboos are, at the top of almost every list was the verbal, physical, or sexual abuse of female visitors. "You gotta be cool with the women," explained Mark. "If you get a bad rep, nobody [meaning women] will come over. The Phis are still trying to live their thing [the supposed date rape of an unidentified woman at the Phi house in 1994] down. People are still talking about it." The respectful treatment of women, therefore, is seen by most fraternities as both a moral and a practical imperative.

Nevertheless, physical and sexual abuse still occurs within the Greek system at an alarming rate. This state of affairs may shock those who consider college to be the last American bastion of enlightenment, but the women involved in this study were painfully aware of it as well as of the factors that contribute to it. "The Greek system is not always the safest place to be," asserts Jenny, a Pi. "It's like we spend all this time together, and we always party and are drunk. And a lot of those boys are, you know, rough." Jenny's sister Debora thinks the problem is that "guys don't know when to turn it off. . . . You know they are always like, 'I'm a bad ass,' and, when they get with girls, they forget to be different." Patricia attributes it to the rush process: "Guys love those other guys who are macho. . . . The more studs they get to pledge them, the happier they are. It's like, 'We got all the muscle heads.' So it's like, right, those guys are the dangerous ones, and they are Greek now."

Julie, a Kappa, believes, however, that it is more than just selective bidding that is to blame, that the culture of many elite fraternities encourages their members to think and act more aggressively. "I know so many, I mean at least a dozen kids from my high school who were so nice. Once they pledged—two are Alphas, like three are Sigmas, two or so are Chis—they just turned into jerks." When I asked her whether she thinks these "jerks" are more dangerous than typical college men, she responded unequivocally: "Let me say this, because there are a lot of really great guys out there, but, if you are talking about the typical frat boy, yes. They are just so cocky, as if no woman would ever turn them down. They are also, I mean a lot of them, are also just rude to women. So, yes, I think they would be more likely to take advantage of a girl, . . . not take no for an answer."

In the fall of 2003, Julie encountered one of those men who did not take no for an answer. Keith, a Rho, seemed to be a "nice boy." She had noticed him for a few semesters before their first date and thought he was "one of the good ones." That first date was fun—nothing too heavy, just some dancing and kissing at a pub. Their second date seemed much like the first—drinking, dancing, and kissing—until Julie asked Keith to walk her home. Once back at her house, they drank and kissed; he tried for more, she said no. The last thing she remembers before passing out on the couch was watching *Saturday Night Live*. "I had way too much to drink," she recalled, "and I could barely keep my eyes open." When she woke up the next morning, however, things were amiss, and not just because she was hungover. Her jeans were off, and she was "sore down there." It took her only minutes to fit the pieces together: "I passed out, and he had sex with me. That's it. He knew how drunk I was and did it anyway." "The funny thing is," she confessed, "I still talk to him like nothing happened. It's awkward, but we just act like nothing happened."

When I asked her why she has not confronted him or called the police, she, like so many women in her position, confessed to feeling partially responsible for the assault. "I guess I can't totally blame him," she claims. "I should have never gotten that drunk and brought him home. I mean, we were making out and everything. It was just stupid, stupid of me." As a result of that horrifying night, Julie and her closest friends developed a "pact to always look out for each other." They have come to realize that even white, middle-class, preppy women living in a white, middle-class preppy college town are not safe from aggressive masculinity.

Sadly, having friends looking out for you is no guarantee of safety. "I used to think that having great guy friends was great, you know," explained Nancy. "Like, he would be there to protect you from drunks, you know what I mean? Really, my parents thought it was great for me too." That trust was destroyed, however, one night after Nancy and Mark stumbled home from a Kappa party: "We had a really fun night. . . . So I kissed him. I mean, he ripped my pants and had his hands down there, and I was just screaming for him to get off me, and finally he did. . . . It was the worst night, experience, I've ever had in my life."

The morning did not mark the end of the horrifying experience. Like so many other women, Nancy continues to feel the residual effects of the attempted rape on her life. She admits that she is "still getting over it." Her sadness and fear are complicated by what she has identified as *guilt*. Wrestling with these myriad jumbled emotions, Nancy stoically—and understandably disjointedly—continued her story: "I'd be lying if I told you I was over it. I'm still getting over it. But it's been like—like when it's somebody you know and everybody else knows and he's a well-respected guy on campus, and you know, at times, I feel guilty because he's so nice to everybody. And I know I shouldn't feel guilty about it, but that's how it is."

Lisa, a Chi sister, experienced a similar betrayal. As she tells it, Stu, an Omega, was her trusted male confidant and protector. "He used to save me all the time. Like if I was at the bars and some guy would bother me, he would be like, 'Beat it.'" His role changed forever, however, after a Chi/Omega date party. Since she and Stu were both too drunk to drive, they were, as Lisa said, "just going to crash at his house." After some kissing and light petting, things began to spiral out of her control. "I said no about twelve times and stop, that he was hurting me. But he just kept after me. Pushing and digging."

Unlike Nancy, Lisa was unable to mask her sadness. As her sisters in the focus group consoled her, holding her hand and hugging her, she told of how she eventually confronted Stu about what had happened that night. "He felt terrible. He really did. He said he was drunk and horny and thought that I was just playing around." While they are no longer friends—in fact, she goes out of her way to avoid him—she had recently been asking around about his dating behavior. "I've talked to some girls at a party, and they're like, 'Yeah, he's really rough.' I guess that's how he is with girls." After finding this out, Lisa admitted to feeling less responsible about her role in the rape. "It sucks, you know, but at least I know that I am not crazy, you know? He's that way with everybody." However, like Nancy, Lisa expressed neither rage nor anger—only relief that she was blameless.

What most struck me about Julie, Nancy, and Lisa was their unarticulated anger. Clearly, they are pissed as hell that they are left to carry the burden of rape while their rapists get to walk around like Mr. Popular. But why aren't they articulating that anger? Why are they still talking to their assailants "like nothing happened"? One reason is the traditional gender roles in which they are trapped. Cultural expectations of appropriate female behavior leave women no option but to feel sadness and guilt, however undeserved. Nice girls don't get angry. Anger is for men.

There is, however, another consequence. Most date rapes go unreported. In fact, most of the women I interviewed told me flatly that they were "never" reported. "It's like ridiculous the amount of rapes that happen on campuses," asserted Nancy, the vice president of the Betas, "all the time, and it's, like, one out of, I don't even know how many, are reported. Never." Why? According to Beth, "People feel too guilty to speak out." "Its like *we*, I mean *they*, I didn't mean *me*," she says, laughing nervously, "aren't really sure what happened or if they said yes or what." Janis speculated: "Sometimes nothing is said because the girls feel like they were encouraging it or something. Like you can't go that far [making out with a guy] and then back down [say no to sex]."

Another reason much rape goes unreported is the inevitable public exposure. As Gina said, "Just look at what happened to that Kobe Bryant girl. They had her name and face on the Internet. She was getting death notices. . . . People sided with Kobe." Reporting a rape would, for Erica, simply be too traumatic: "Oh my God. I can't image it. It's like getting raped all over again. You have to tell everyone about it, and everyone is talking about you and pointing at you. Oh my God, no."

A final reason is the fear of social alienation. "There is this girl, well, she doesn't go here anymore," recalled Susana, "but she had this bad experience with this guy in a popular fraternity. . . . And all his brothers were calling her a liar and giving her a bad time. . . . She felt really bad all the time and then dropped out of school." Janis, a GU cheerleader, told a similar story: "I have a friend, I'm not going to give you her name, though, and she was raped by this jerk. He was like big man on campus, and everybody loved him. . . . At first she told me she was thinking how lucky she was for hooking up with him. Anyway, she got raped by this jerk, and she never did anything about it because he was too popular. And she wasn't a Greek, and he was, and she was afraid. I told her I would stand behind her because I know this guy is a big jerk."

What I found to be the most interesting aspect of these discussions of date rape is how eager most women were to talk about it and how fearful most men were to even acknowledge it. I asked both why. The women repeatedly told me that they wanted me to get the truth out and that, while people may not believe them, people would believe me, a male college professor. The men told me that even the rumor of rape can threaten a fraternity's very existence. "It's something you don't even joke about," said Patrick. "It is the worst thing that can be said about you. Sororities would never talk to you. . . . No one would pledge you. It's like having AIDS."

Many men also suggested that accusations of date rape are often exaggerated. As Kenneth put it, "Most of the time anymore, it's not true." He continued to explain this *very* popular male perspective: "I am sure that it happens. But, come on, everybody says they were raped. I think most of the time it's a girl that feels guilty for having sex so they say they were raped . . . [or] they end up saying no *during* sex. And, you know, you can't just stop and turn it off just like that. That's kind of bullshit." When I informed him that what he described fell under the legal definition of *date rape*, he looked bewildered. "Well, yes, I guess, but, if it is, then that's kind of bullshit, you know. What, you can do everything, let him go down on you, and then just tell him he has to go home?" While he assured me that

he knows it is "legally wrong" and that "he would never do anything" like that, he still "think[s] it's bullshit." Disturbingly, while I
was interviewing Kenneth, I noticed that his fraternity T-shirt proclaimed his organization to be "ABOVE THE LAW, BELOW THE PANTIES."
The accompanying cartoon showed a crazed brother ripping the
panties off a defensive and shocked sorority sister.

It should be pointed out that not all fraternities attract the same
type of hypersexual, hyperaggressive brothers. Suzie reported that
"what people call loser [struggler] fraternities have some of the nicest, sweetest guys on campus. These guys would not hurt a fly." But:
"No one—I hate to say it—even us—we don't really want to party
with those guys. I know it is terrible, but they are just like your uncool little brothers at home."

The Nurturing Female

Just as aggression and violence are central to these students' conception of masculinity, sensitivity and caring are central to their conception of femininity. As Susan puts it, "Women are just different. We
are more sensitive, and we are better listeners." Confirming this,
James rhetorically asked his focus group whom they ran to when
they were hurt. "I always called for my mom. So did my three brothers. Moms are just better at it. It's that whole maternal thing." "My
dad," he concluded, eliciting laughter, "would have told us to shut
up." Many of the students I interviewed also felt that the "maternal
thing" also makes women better and more natural caregivers than
men. No wonder so many of these Greek women pursue careers in
such culturally prescribed occupations as elementary school teachers, nurses, social workers, and, of course, wives and mothers.[5]

This essentialist perspective on women is obviously not unique
to GU's Greek men and women. According to myriad studies of the
relation between gender and occupation (see, e.g., Delamont, 2001;
Gerson, 2004; Hochschild with Machung, 2003), women do the
overwhelming majority of all the caregiving in the United States.
This is understandable, according to Wood (2005), because girls

and women have been told that they are supposed to "care about and for others" and to be nice, responsive, supportive, and friendly. "It's part of their role as defined by culture" (p. 164).

But what do GU's Greek women feel about this cultural imperative? Many, while acknowledging its importance to their idea of femininity, reported feeling stifled and silenced by it. "I sometimes feel like I can't say anything without being a bitch," admits Julie. At her Delta house, "if you don't always volunteer," or if you "get mad at somebody," then "you're a bitch." For Lori, life at the Omega house is similarly repressive. "In high school, I was really competitive. I played sports since I was like born. If we had a problem, we just dealt with it." Once inside the Greek community, however, this direct approach to conflict resolution changed. Instead of openly addressing a grievance, "you have to like always avoid it, even if someone really makes you mad." "I have a real problem with the sorority stuff like that," she says.

When open and public conflict does arise, Alice, a Gamma, says, "it is a long process with sisters because someone's feelings get hurt and you have to go and sit and discuss why their feelings were hurt and how you fix that." She pauses a long while, then concludes: "It's just a lot." The women in the Zeta house, according to Janice, are also "drama queens" when it comes to conflict. "Oh my God, girls in my house are such babies," she confirms. "If anybody gets their feelings hurt, it's like a soap opera. All the girls run around and talk about it." As bad as the initial fight is, however, Barb at the Gamma house thinks that the aftermath is even worse. "Girls hold grudges," she asserts. "I mean, guys will just fight, and they are friends again; girls will hold grudges for years. It gets so stupid." Barb's sister Caroline chimes in: "Here's a story that shows it. I was over at the Beta house last weekend, and the guys were all mad at this friend of theirs, so they all like trashed his room and stuff, and it was really fun, but if we [her sorority sisters] like did that to a girl, she would never forgive us. But the guy was fine with it, you know; he just did something back to them, and it's just like a fun game."

The cultural expectations of women extend even to the class-room. Nice girls don't argue, challenge, or debate. Kiki, the scholarship chair for the Chis, told me that she knows that she "freaks some people out in her classes" when she challenges her professor. "But I pay good money, and I have every right to do the same things that men do." Natalie expresses a similar frustration with the cultural prejudice against smart women. She believes that, in most of her classes, "intelligence for women is not necessarily a good quality, and it sucks that that's the case." "If you raise your hand and you have a comment to make," she thinks, "a guy is not going to be as attracted [to you] as [he is to] the girl who is sitting next to him who may be cute and says nothing." Jackie, however, is not so sympathetic to women of Kiki and Natalie's ilk. "I can't blame boys for not being interested in girls [who are too aggressive in class]," she says. "Who wants to ask a girl out who's always arguing?"

Notwithstanding such assertions, my experience at GU has taught me that it is the Jackies, and not the Kikis and Natalies, who are the anamolies. Of the over twelve hundred students I teach each year in my Introduction to Communication Theory course, a mass lecture, it is the sorority women who are always the most active and interesting participants in class. The same holds true in my much smaller upper-division seminars. While there are always two or three men who express their opinions more aggressively and dogmatically, it is on the whole Greek women who dominate thoughtful discussion. This observation is not meant to counter the claims or invalidate the experiences of my female subjects, who do, I believe, feel pressure to remain quiet and cute. But it *is* meant to complicate a simplistic notion of gender and highlight the many incongruencies that exist between ideological expectations and actual human behavior.

The Competitive Woman

The pressure to be kind and nurturing is only half the story of sorority row. Many Greek women who claim to have maternal features of their identities are also highly competitive—and proud of it.

The most obvious arena in which these women display their competitive nature is the annual sorority rush.[6] All the sororities devote a great deal of time, money, and effort to developing recruitment strategies, rehearsing skits, and aggressively courting the cutest and most popular women on campus. While rush can seem silly to non-Greeks, it is serious business to those involved. "Rush is very, very serious," explained Kaylee, rush chair for the Nus. "It is really the most important thing we do, no question. It is how we are judged."

Jessica believes that, because of the importance placed on rush, "the pressure on the girls to meet quota [the number of initiates you are expected to recruit as determined by the university] is crazy. We really stress, and like all the girls yell at each other if things are going bad, like, 'We are going to miss quota if we don't start working!'" "This year the Thetas [an elite sorority known for attractive sisters] missed quota," Nichole, a Gamma, explained, "and everyone just loved it. I hate them, hate. I have to admit, I was loving it." Given the intense competition, it is no wonder that Madison sees rush as a never-ending struggle that takes its toll on membership: "You have to keep proving yourself, every year. I'll tell you, it is why I think so many seniors get burnt out and move out of the house. A bad year, just one, and you can fall way back. Like the Gammas, remember? They never made it back. They just shut down."

But the competition for the best and cutest women on campus is not the only battle being waged on sorority row. Also continuously raging is the competition for the highest GPA. "The Alphas have always won the scholarship award [for the highest GPA]," reported Megan. "But we [the Omegas] got it this year; we beat them bad. And they were pissed." "We just loved it," she concluded, her sisters in the focus group laughing and cheering. "We can outdrink them and outsmart them," Virginia added humorously.

Other outlets for the competitive spirit of Greek women are found in sports. Nancy, a tomboyish anomaly in her hyperfeminine organization, bragged about her three goals and the Iotas' intramural soccer championship last semester. Julie was also really "proud" of how her sisters won the flag football championship game against their dreaded Omega rivals. "I don't play—I'm too girly," she says with a giggle. "But we kicked their butts. Our girls were like brutes out there." Generally speaking, however, most sorority members, regardless of affiliation, do not compete in athletics or prize athletic accomplishments. According to a disappointed Bailey, they see sports as "too unladylike":

> Bailey: I just get frustrated with the girls in my house because they're not competitive and you don't really have anyone to be competitive with like when I was in high school. They're all like, "I'll break a nail," or whatever.
> AD: Why do you think they feel like that?
> Bailey: Because they avoid conflict. . . . I don't know, they just say they hate competition and it scares them.

While many of these sisters may not enjoy athletic competition, most openly admit to being very competitive when it comes to talent contests. After all, dancing and singing are far more culturally acceptable for women than sliding into home or throwing a touchdown pass. The most coveted of these contests is Greek Sing, an annual competition in which groups from all the sororities are given eight to ten minutes to dance and sing for thousands of screaming Greek onlookers, including a panel of five judges. In preparation for the big night, as many as fifty to one hundred hours will be devoted to rehearsal, and auditions will be held to determine who will be the spotlight performers, who will be hidden in the back row, and who will be working behind the scenes, operating the lights and the sound. This latter job almost always goes to the unattractive and overweight women.[7]

"Oh yeah, Greek Sing is serious," a fired-up Hannah explained. "We practice for three months before . . . we hire a choreographer . . . we go for it." "We don't mess around," claimed the Omega president. "This is like the most important thing we do each year. No, it's no joke." As a professor who has both emceed and judged this event on numerous occasions, I can attest to these organizations' professionalism, preparedness, and pride. Some of the better acts, in fact, are as good as most NFL and NBA half-time shows.

But who are these women performing for? Is it for the judges, the men in the audience, or other sororities? "Absolutely, other sororities," says Jasmine, a Xi sister. "We like it when the boys yell and scream, and you know we want to look hot, but we want to shove it in their faces." "Oh, other sororities," concurred Hannah. "We want to win and blow them away." A more humorous Anna sees it as "kind of a war, but with music and leotards": "Everybody shows what they have been up to. . . . It is the one time a year that everybody shows off their stuff to each other."

It is worth noting that, traditionally, fraternities have seen Greek Sing as nothing more than an occasion for public buffoonery, binge drinking, and phallic humor. To take the event too seriously, in fact, would have been to call into question your organization's masculinity. After all, only pretty boys and fags sing and dance together onstage. The only exception was when a group of brothers was able to put together a rock band. While such acts broke from the spirit of the night, they did at least give a small number of men the opportunity to take the performing arts seriously. Recently, however, more and more fraternities are beginning to take Greek Sing seriously. They are working with sororities to choreograph their skits, practicing long hours on their public presentations, and even banning alcohol consumption the night of the show.

There are other, similar competitions, however, where impressing the men in the audience is the primary goal. In any given year, fraternities will sponsor three or four so-called fund-raisers where sororities are invited to perform for the critical eyes of the brothers. As discussed in chapter 2, these competitions are about selling sexuality, not highlighting the performing arts. The women who take part in them dress more provocatively, dance more suggestively, and are less concerned with winning or impressing other sororities than with "driving the boys crazy." "Some of these sororities can get downright raunchy. We have been bad a few times, but it is just fun to get the boys to act like idiots," admits Emily, a Phi. Julia puts it more succinctly when she says that it is all about being "loved the most": "We all want to be the most popular, . . . the sorority that the fraternities wants to do things with."

Competition does not, however, always come from a rival sorority. Often it comes from within a woman's own house. Sadly, the issues rarely involve challenging the status quo and expanding women's opportunities. Instead, they concern such matters as who's the most attractive, who's the thinnest, and who's the most popular with the boys, ultimately doing nothing more than confirming and reinforcing gender stereotypes.

The most often cited point of contention was over "how cute you are." "I mean, it is not a mean type of competition," explained Megan, an Eta, "but you would be surprised how much we all think about it." Nicole similarly tells me that women in her house "really dress for each other": "You like really want to look cute and have the girls say how cute you are." When I asked whether the emphasis on looking cute was for the benefit of a male audience, I was told, "Most of the time, it really isn't." "I know that's hard to believe," Hannah continued. "Don't get me wrong, we all want attention, the good kind, but we spend all that time getting ready because it is like, you don't want to be the worst one."

In this endless competition to look good for each other, nothing is more important than being thin (see chapter 4). When I asked what makes a sister attractive, for example, approximately eight of ten women isolated body shape and size as the key variable. While most acknowledged the importance of having a pretty face, nice hair, and fashionable clothing, these were all secondary concerns. Receiving external validation from your sisters, and, by extension, feeling good about yourself, was primarily an issue of not being fat.

In one very typical exchange, I asked the Delta sisters about competition at their house:

> AD: Tell me about competition and competitiveness at the Delta house.
> Emily: Being skinnier. [*Group laughter and affirmation.*]
> AD: What?
> Emily: Yeah, who is the skinniest. [*The group affirms her claim again.*] We all want to be the thinnest one.
> Alyssa: Who's funnier too. [*No support from the group.*]
> Jenna: Who has the best body, I think. That is really important.
> Mary: Yeah. Definitely.
> AD: What makes a "best body"? Is it being skinny?
> Mary: Most of the time, but not always. Girls check out other girls more than guys check out girls.
> Ann: Curves are good on a skinny frame. I mean, if you have that . . . [*Trails off.*]
> AD: So body size is what you guys are most competitive over?
> Emily: Yeah. [*Pensive pause.*] That sounds terrible. But I think that is what we think and, like, envy in a way.
> Jenna and Alyssa [*overlapping*]: It's true.
> Jenna: That's life in our house. [*Everyone laughs.*]

Like Jenna, most of the women I interviewed agreed that the competitive pressure to be thin, especially in elite houses, is oppressive. With "fifty girls living in one place," as Jennifer explained, "it's hard not to always be thinking about it and comparing yourself to everyone you see." But this concern is not solely the making of the Greek system. While many sisters reported that their fixation on their appearance dramatically intensified after they pledged (see chapter 4), most also acknowledged that they had been on that trajectory since grade school. A very thoughtful Kaitlyn elaborated on her journey into womanhood and her rethinking of the notion of competition: "I don't think it's just sorority life [that causes the concern with appearance and size] because when I was younger, like when we were in elementary school, all the girls were like competitive gradewise, and all the boys were like dumb asses, and then as things evolved the girls were like still in all the accelerated classes, but more than like, 'How did you do on that test?' it turned into like, 'Look, oh, she's so skinny. I have to lose weight now too.'"

Weight loss, however, is not just meant to impress other women; it is a proven strategy to win the attention of contested men. "There are only so many good men out there, so we fight for the good ones," explains Madison, provoking nervous laughter. "I'm serious. There are so many beautiful girls here, and the men have a field day. . . . The good ones are like hot property." Losing the fight for "the good ones" can also affect a women's self-esteem. "Nothing is worse than to be out in a bar with a friend," explains Sara, "and have guys perpetually come and talk to her. And you stand there, and you stand there like, 'What's up?'" Sara's sister, Gabby, chimes in: "Yeah, he is leaving with your friend, you're like, Why isn't he leaving with me? You just feel terrible about yourself like, What's the matter with me? Why her?"

This jealously is also directed toward sisters in steady relationships who have taken themselves out of the dating game. In theory, women are supposed to be kind and supportive, especially in their interpersonal relationships with other women, but many of the women I interviewed reported being envious of sisters with serious boyfriends. As Hailey put it, "Girls may say they are really happy for other girls when they are really happy, but I don't think we really are. It is kind of like, they have theirs, and it just makes you feel bad because you still don't." "'Oh, she has everything, Little Miss Perfect who has her whole life set,'" she mocks. "I know it's terrible to say." Chloe elaborates. She thinks that this envy is directed, not toward all sisters in relationships, only the ones in great relationships. "Some of the guys that my sisters are dating are weak. So it's not like any of us really want them. But like Carry here," she says, pointing across the table to her sister, "she has Mr. Wonderful. Law school, cute. . . . She's the type we hate." Laughter fills the room at this point, acknowledging the truth of what Chloe said. With further probing, the Lambda sisters told me that, unlike men, who frame their competitions in terms of attracting the most women, women tend to frame their competitions in terms of attracting the best men. "Ideally," confessed Jen, "I want a really nice guy. And if we see a girl that has that, we get kind of sad." "Or jealous," Carry interjects. "Or, OK, jealous," Jen admits.

The most striking aspect of these interviews is that many of the women acknowledged how illogical it is to vie for the attention of men or to lose weight to impress other women. Far from being duped by their culture's ideology, they recognized the absurdity of gender scripts that pit women against women in vacuous competitions that serve only to retard their advancement. Nonetheless, they also seemed unwilling or unable to act against the established system.

We are left to question, therefore, whether recognition is enough to liberate these students. In the end, peer groups, limiting conceptions of gender, and GU's deeply entrenched Greek culture were far more persuasive than was rational awareness of the power and effect of the patriarchy.

4. Her Laxatives, His Steroids

At alarming rates, members of elite sororities at GU have been injuriously starving themselves to get smaller, and members of elite fraternities have been obsessively exercising to get larger. These are the women and men who have defined ideal masculinity and femininity in terms of physical characteristics: the perfect woman is thin, white, and cute; the perfect man is muscular, white, and handsome. These developments are intriguing for two reasons.

First, the emphasis has long been on the female body in defining white heterosexual femininity—from the full figures of Mae West and Marilyn Monroe to the emaciated forms of Twiggy and Kate Moss (see Cancian, 1989; Riessman, 1990; and Wood, 1993)—there has not been a corresponding emphasis on the male body in defining white heterosexual masculinity (Bordo, 1999). Historically, men have never had to worry about being attractive, toned, young, or fashionable (Connell, 1990; Trujillo, 1991). Today, however, GU's fraternity men are reporting ever-increasing pressure to measure up.

Second, while the rest of the nation finds itself in the throws of what *Time* magazine has called an *obesity epidemic* (e.g., "Overcoming Obesity," 2004), Greeks at GU seem to be immune. The United States may be letting itself go, but not GU's Greeks, who are preoccupied with body shape, diet, and exercise.

This chapter details how GU students conceptualize and actualize their physical ideals and how those ideals affect their understanding of masculinity, femininity, and the self.

Women

Before They Pledged

Long before most women ever take their first steps on a college campus, they have received a steady barrage of cultural messages

115

about the appropriate shape and size of their bodies. As early as their tenth birthday, for example, 81 percent of American girls are already afraid of being fat. Of these, 51 percent claim to feel better about themselves when they are dieting (McNutt et al., 1997). Not surprisingly, roughly one of every two (or 46 percent of) nine- to eleven-year-old girls is "sometimes" or "very often" regulating what, and how often, she eats (Gustafson-Larson & Terry, 1992).

By the time these girls make it to high school, the pressure to be attractive is omnipresent. Lisa, a third-year Gamma, remembers the day she did not put on makeup before leaving the house. "My boyfriend and all my friends were like, 'My God, what happened?' He told me not to ever do that again, or he would dump me." Similarly, Deborah would "not be caught dead going to high school if she hadn't gotten up two hours earlier to shower, curl her hair, and do her makeup." The fear of alienation was "absolutely overwhelming." Jenny and her Sigma sisters even remember leaving high school over such traumatic events as "getting a pimple, a big one," "feeling ugly," "retaining water," or "wearing the same outfit that a friend had on." Maggie even snuck home once because someone told her she had greasy hair.

But bad makeup and hair were the least of their worries. The fear of being perceived as fat caused far more anxiety and depression in their adolescent lives. "If you were fat," Monica told me, "kids hated you, I mean hated." Her Delta sister Rachel "couldn't count all the girls in [her] high school with eating disorders, who were sent away, who went for summers to eating-disorder clinics." By her senior year, she remembers sitting with her female classmates "making fun of the sophomores in their 'anorexic stage'": "We would look down at the other end of the table at the sophomores, and they would all be there with only a water bottle and an apple." This is not to imply, however, that seniors have moved beyond feeling the effects of criticism. Gina painfully recalls the demands of dancing for a weight-conscious coach during her last year of high school:

Like, I was a dancer, and I didn't eat. Like, it wasn't accept-able. If you came into dance practice with a bag of chips in your hand, my dance instructor would say, "And you think you are going to perform on Friday, you are wrong." Like, it wasn't something you did. I can remember my best friend that danced with me, that summer before college, religiously, every day, we ate only yogurt for breakfast, we would go work out, we would have cottage cheese, we would go run, we would come back and have a small salad. That is literally probably what we did everyday.

If this sounds like a matter of life and death, that's because it is. Wooley and Wooley (1984) report that, of thirty-three thousand high school girls surveyed, 42 percent responded that losing weight was more important and would make them happier than success in any other aspect of their lives. Tavris and Baumgartner (1983) asked two thousand children ranging in age from the third grade through the twelfth how they think their lives would change if they woke up one morning as the opposite sex. Girls as young as nine noted how nice it would be "not to worry about looks all the time." The boys, on the other hand, singled out the importance of being "pretty." Most by their tenth birthday already understood the isolation and abuse that awaits unattractive girls (Wood 2005, p. 163).

By the time girls make it to college, most have already been so brainwashed by cultural stereotypes that they would be willing to make almost any sacrifice to attain the ideal body. For the last ten years, I have been asking my female students how many of them would make the Faustian trade and sacrifice one year of life to be effortlessly thin and beautiful until the age of sixty. On average, ap-proximately 85 percent say they would. Over 20 percent say they would sacrifice five years to vanity. Interestingly, when I ask how many would sacrifice one year to be highly intelligent, less than 1 percent respond affirmatively.[1]

The Price of Pledging

As bad as things were for these women in high school, the pressure to be thin and attractive only got worse once they entered GU's Greek community. Almost unanimously they told of the anxiety of being isolated in a population that is uniformly cute, thin, and white. In high school, Jen claims, "you were around a lot of different people—fat, thin, pretty, black, Chinese, normal, you know?" When she entered the Chi house, however, she found herself "surrounded by the prettiest girls on campus." For Lori, a small-town farm girl, "it was like being around a bunch of Miss Americas all the time. . . . They are always beautiful. So you find yourself thinking a lot more about how you look." The transformation to extreme body consciousness varied from sister to sister, but most of the stories mirrored Susan's journey from relatively happy high schooler to neurotic sorority sister. "When I was in high school," Susan said, "Lisa and I would eat McDonald's three meals a day. And, when we moved into the Tri-Gamma house, we were like, 'We can't do this anymore.' During rush this year—I never heard her say this before—she was like, 'I'm fat,' 'I feel fat.' And I was starting to feel the same way. Now we both are working out all the time just to keep up, just to stay normal with everyone." "It's the comparison that gets you all the time," Brook claims. "Everyone you're around is thinner, prettier, and they are all trying to get prettier and thinner all the time." "It's like a race," she concludes, "that I'll never win."

Angie believes that this unhealthy relationship with food is engendered by the very nature of the rush process. "The Greek system," she said, "rushes the pretty, popular people who are concerned about their looks and being liked by boys and being in that world." Consequently, as Angie told me, "the really cute girls look for the really good sororities on campus, like us, but we also look for those types of pledges. Cute girls make us look good, and we make them look great in return." After a pensive pause, Angie wondered whether that statement sounded "too shallow."

Another painfully honest sister, Martha, the rush chair at the Nu house, disclosed her sorority's criteria for selecting new members:

It is sad to say, and I hate to say it, but the cycle just perpetuates itself. We see a girl's picture, and we want her because she's cute. . . . To be the top sororities, you want the most girls, and you get the most girls by being the sorority that guys want to go out with, which means you get the cute girls. . . . It is very rare that a big girl leaves the house during rush and everyone is like, "We like her." We like the skinny, cute girls. We love them; we are like, "Let's get them." Big girls really don't even have a chance.

Not only is it unlikely that heavier women will be invited to pledge, but, as Dora observed, it is rare to even see an overweight girl involved in the rush process. Last semester, Dora vividly recalls seeing this "fat girl" walking from house to house looking for an invitation to pledge. "I thought, Wow, I can't believe she is here. . . . No house wants big girls. If you get that reputation, everything falls apart [i.e., no fraternities will party with you; no cute girls will pledge you]. It's terrible to say, but . . ."

At the Zeta house—an up-and-coming aspirer sorority—the older and cooler sisters have even developed a series of strategies for surreptitiously keeping the "big girls" out. These maneuvers, which Nancy and Lisa described in an e-mail message, are not publicly discussed, especially not in front of the sorority's youngest members, but they are regularly used by the organization's leaders to assure Zeta's continued ascension in the sorority hierarchy. The message in its entirety reads as follows:

Dr. DeSantis,

After the [interviewing] session was over, Nancy and I remembered something that we thought you would get a kick out of. Here is the info on ORT and DUFFs. Maybe you can use it in your book?

First of all, during Rush, you try to get rid of ugly girls. You can do this by floating in on them and bringing their score down (we can't really explain our voting process, though . . . ooo, sorority secrets!). We call this "ORT" or operation remove tool. A tool is any girl that is fat, ugly, unattractive, or just generally has an annoying personality.

Once ORT is going on, you also need to watch out for DUFFs. A DUFF is a designated ugly fat friend. Some girls love DUFFs. This is because they will hang out with them because these fat, ugly girls make them feel skinnier and prettier. It also makes them look like they are a nicer person because they are lowering themselves to hang out with some ugly fat girls. The key to a DUFF is that you only have one. If you are surrounded by DUFFs, guys think that you cannot make attractive friends and the DUFF policy backfires. It is a very shallow process.

See ya,
Nancy and Lisa

Another personal story of elitism and discrimination came from Alyssa, a Zeta sister who saw her brother's girlfriend, Beth, rejected because of her size. "She is wonderful. If she lost sixty pounds, she would be a Zeta in a second." Alyssa's support and personal testimony in favor of Beth, however, was to no avail. "On the last day of rush, Beth was cut from our list." When I asked whether it was Beth's size, Alyssa indisputably told me that she knew it was "only her weight."

Interestingly, the terms *overweight, fat, unattractive,* and *ugly* are rarely used in formal rush debates. They are seen as unproductive adjectives that are superficial, tacky, and crude. Certain houses have even prohibited their utterance in rush meetings. Instead, euphemisms that have been passed down through the generations, and that speak volumes in terms of subtext, are employed. More often than not, the ubiquitous *cute* signifies that a candidate meets a house's physical criteria. The Iotas, for example, consider a girl cute if she is thin, white, pretty, and perky and comes from a middle- to upper-class family. The Gammas, Kappas, and Mus reject unsightly candidates by using code phrases such as *the girl is not sorority material, the girl would not fit in here,* or *the girl would not be happy with us.* Regardless of the language employed, however, the end result remains the same: larger girls are discriminated against, either by small-minded women embarrassed by association with physical pariahs or by small-minded chapters afraid of social isolation from fraternities. However you cut it, the message is clear: "NO FAT CHICKS INVITED" (as a popular Chi fraternity party T-shirt puts it).

Not All Sororities Measure Up

Not all sororities are alike. GU's Greek organizations, like those on every other campus with which I am familiar, can, as we have seen, be divided into three castes: the elites, the aspirers, and the strugglers. The elites have the prettiest, thinnest, and most popular women on campus. The aspirers are more diversified in terms of type, weight, popularity, reputation, and attractiveness. This is not because they are more self-aware and self-actualized—after all, they do ultimately aspire to be elites—but because they are forced to be more lenient in their selection criteria. The strugglers break almost every stereotype the average student has about sororities. As one of my non-Greek students observed, they are the sororities "where all the misfits go." Their ranks are almost solely composed of women who are too ethnic, heavy, assertive, unattractive, or unpopular for the elites or the aspirers.

Differences other than the physical and the socioeconomic separate the elites from the aspirers from the strugglers. The evidence from both the interview process and observation overwhelmingly suggests that the women in the elite sororities are more obsessed with their weight, enjoy the process of eating less, engage in social comparisons more, and exercise more often.

When I asked the elite Alphas whether there was a price to pay for their popularity, most readily acknowledged that there was. Nicole, for instance, conceded that being an Alpha is a trade-off. "Don't get me wrong, I love my sisters, but it is tough being an Alpha. A lot is expected of you." In comparison, Nicole sees the sisters in the Tau house [a struggler sorority] as "probably being happier": "I think life must be nice over there." When I asked her why she did not pledge the Taus, she apologetically smiled and said that they were "not her type of girls."

In fairness, I also asked the Tau sisters whether they thought there was a difference between the two houses. Lisa told me, "The [elite] Alphas are great. I mean, I have some friends over there, but they are always so made up. They are always concerned about how they look for the boys." In comparison, she continued, "we sit around in sweats, eat pizza out of the box . . . we are slobs . . . it is great that way." I wondered, then, what were the disadvantages of being a Tau. Lowering her voice, Taylor admitted: "The fraternities really don't pick us to do things. We know that they make fun of us." Shrugging her shoulders, she confessed that the Taus are not "the beautiful ones": "It would be nice to be like that, but we are getting better."

In my capacity as professor and faculty adviser for over twenty Greek organizations, I have had the opportunity to attend dinners, social events, meetings, and charity fund-raisers at most of the houses on GU's campus. Past the obvious differences in chapter size (the Alphas, e.g., have 170 members, the Taus only 35), house and decor (the elites have the oldest, nicest, and biggest houses on campus), and operating budget (because of their size, influential alumni, and higher dues, many of the elites are quite wealthy), the cultural climate within houses is also noticeably different. Dinner at the Alpha, Chi, and Omega houses, for instance, is marked by controlled eating, diet-minded menus, smaller portions, no desserts, and a general lack of culinary joy. Indicative of this mind-set is Catherine's description of mealtime at the Omega house: "You come downstairs, there's never ever, ever, ever a meal that's not too greasy, too fat, too sweet. We have been telling our cooks for months what to do, but it is obvious that they don't listen." When I asked Catherine whether they ever eat dessert, she continued to complain about the lack of compliance from the hired help. "We tell them, Don't make cookies because I will be tempted to eat them. People will come downstairs, and, if cookies are made, it's like, Why, why did you do this?" The problem with cookies, as revealed later in the interview, is that, "if you eat one, then you will have to go to the gym later."

At the struggler sororities, however, dinner is far more enjoyable. At the Tau, Epsilon, and Rho houses, for instance, mealtime sees larger portions, balanced menus, desserts, second helpings, and laughter. A cookie at the Rho house is not followed by exercise; it *is* accompanied by a glass of milk. As the Epsilon president told me during my first dinner visit: "We like to eat over here."

There is one other significant difference between the elites, the aspires, and the strugglers. The strugglers, ironically, have a better esprit de corps, spend more time together, and know each other better (partly because the organizations are much smaller). Unfortunately, at this stage in their postadolescent lives, where external validation, boys, popularity, and thinness are still so important, the strugglers do not know how lucky they are. Instead of embracing their differences, diversity, sisterhood, and health, most misguidedly hope to become aspirers and dream of being elites.

This dream in its most perverse manifestation can turn sister against sister in the quest for Greek prestige. In one of the most disturbing events to happen at GU in the last decade, the national officers of the Zetas came to campus to reorganize their struggling chapter, headquarters having decided that the Zeta house was not elite, profitable, or large enough. After assessing the situation, the national officers determined that their GU sisters had initiated too many overweight, unattractive, and ethnic women and were now unable to compete with the larger, richer, more attractive elite sororities on campus. Consequently, chapter operations were temporarily suspended, current Zeta sisters relegated to alumna status (even though many were still in their first or second year of college), and the chapter then reopened with an aggressive rush strategy targeting cute, thin women who would, it was assumed, themselves rush cute, thin women. The plan seems to have worked. Today, the Zetas are considered to be one of the most attractive aspirer sororities on campus, likely soon to move into the ranks of the elites.

While such events often go unnoticed outside the Greek community, the reorganizing efforts of the Delta Zeta sorority at DePauw University in Greencastle, Indiana, made the *New York Times*. Evidently, the national officers of Delta Zeta were unhappy with the quantity and quality of their sisters at DePauw. After evaluating the merits of each of the chapter's members, they determined that twenty-three of the women were "insufficiently committed," forced those women into alumna status, and told them to vacate the sorority house. According to the *Times* report, "The 23 members included every woman who was overweight. They also included the only Korean and Vietnamese members. The dozen students allowed to stay were slender and popular with fraternity men—conventionally pretty women the sorority hoped could attract new recruits." One senior Delta Zeta sister reported: "Virtually everyone who didn't fit a certain sorority member archetype was told to leave." Sadly, DePauw lost a chapter that had become home to a diverse group of sisters, "partly because," as the *Times* concluded, "it has attracted brainy women, including many science and math majors, as well as talented disabled women, without focusing as exclusively as some sororities on potential recruits' sex appeal" (Dillon, 2007a). Shortly thereafter, the *Times* reported that DePauw had severed its ties with Delta Zeta (Dillon, 2007b).

By Any Means Necessary?

Since being thin is so important to so many sorority women, a great deal of time, effort, and creativity is devoted to weight control. By far, the most popular and often used method of weight loss in any sorority house is dieting. Almost all the women in elite sororities, more than three-quarters of the women in aspirer sororities, and more than half the women in struggler sororities unabashedly confess to watching what they eat. These figures do not tell the whole story, however. To truly understand the complex role that dieting plays in, and the degree to which it takes over, these women's live, one must conceive of the act of dieting as existing on a continuum.

At one end of the continuum, there are the relaxed dieters, mainly strugglers, who sporadically watch what they eat and often cheat. For them, dieting is not so much a way of life as an activity periodically undertaken that imposes no great hardship or demands no great sacrifice. Nancy, for example, tells me that she will "sometimes eat a salad for lunch" if she is feeling heavy. Similarly, Mary tries "not to eat after eight at night" and buys "fat-free cookies at the grocery."

At the other end of this continuum, there are the extreme dieters, primarily elites and, to a lesser extent, aspirers, who constantly monitor their food intake and obsessively count calories, carbs, and fat. For these women, dieting is a serious, ongoing battle against their bodies. Among the elites, Megan, for instance, eats only "a salad with fat-free Catalina for lunch and one for dinner," while sister Jen has "completely cut out breakfasts altogether." At the Omega house, according to Katie, "everybody is doing Weight Watchers or Atkins like a religion." Other elites confessed to "eating only [fat-free] pretzels for days," "filling up on Diet Coke," "living on Slim-fast," and "eating only lettuce, tomatoes, and spicy mustard."

During the fall 2002 semester, GU's administration became so concerned about extreme dieting that it initiated a series of in-house programs aimed at education and prevention. The elite Kappas could not have been happier. The sisters learn myriad new and innovative ways to lose weight and hide the evidence. "We watched this one girl on the video," Nancy recalls, "and she was talking about how she would guzzle three glasses of water before mealtime so she would only take like two bites of food, and we were all like, 'Great idea!'" "Honestly," Susan reiterated, "before dinner, we sometimes guzzle two glasses of water so we won't eat." "It is a great idea if you think about it," Judy, another Kappa sister, concluded.

There are occasions, however, when these elite women overdo it. They "go off their diet," "eat a big holiday dinner," or "wolf down a pizza," "cookies," or "McDonald's." Such lapses in judgment, I am told, are easily rectified. Many freely admitted to throwing up a big meal or junk food shortly after eating it. "It's like an undo button on a computer," Morgan humorously confessed. "Whoops, I shouldn't have done that." Jessica "really [doesn't] think it is that bad to do as long as you are not like doing it all the time. Sometimes it is a lot easier than dieting." Rebecca, a self-reported recovering anorexic, bragged that she can even think herself into a state of nausea. "If I eat too much—pig out—I don't even have to stick my finger down my throat. I can just think about it." "If I don't do it," claimed Tiffani, "I just feel terrible. I feel physically sick, really. And I also just feel better, like less guilty. You just don't want to do it all the time."

Along with extreme dieting, water consumption, and vomiting, many sorority women also employ exercise as a means of weight control. At the elite houses, for instance, sisters estimated that an average of 75 percent of the sisters exercise regularly, that is, five to six days per week, an hour and a half to three hours per session. At the Delta house, which has a private exercise room in the basement, all but an estimated three girls (of the 174 members) work out. "We're talking everyday, religiously," said Lauren. "Most of us," claimed Kathy, "work out six days a week. About, I would say, 40 percent of us work out twice a day, especially before spring break."

When I asked why so many devote so much time and energy to this painful regimen, most sisters initially insisted that it was for their health. After a few probing questions, however, most confessed that it was to lose weight or maintain their size. In fact, quite a few even confessed that the amount of exercising they were doing was probably not healthy. "There were days that I could not walk without being in pain," claimed Laurie. Susan remembers "having shin splits so bad that I was taking twelve Nuprin a day." Andrea has run so hard that she has had to "sit down for fifteen minutes before [she] could even move again." And Kim has "thrown up a lot after overexercising": "I think most of us probably overdo it, but it is like an addiction once you start. Yeah, it is like that."

For many, however, extreme dieting and obsessive exercise were either too physically demanding or not effective enough. Consequently, some sisters searched for new and less strenuous ways of cutting their weight. The Gammas, Thetas, Deltas, and Alphas, for example, discovered that cigarette smoking is helpful. "Along with the buzz they give you," Janice claims, "they really zap your hunger pains." Being a bit more subtle in her support of the strategy, Katie, a senior Theta sister, told me, "Rumor around the mill is that it increases your metabolism." While she did not admit to smoking herself, she did confess that she knew "a lot of girls who smoked to increase their metabolism." This is not an isolated phenomenon. White men are smoking less while white women are smoking more (U.S. Surgeon General, 2001; CDC, 2003). Of these new female smokers, it has been estimated that 40–50 percent are lighting up to control their weight (see WHO, 2003).

As risky as smoking may seem to some, many sisters searched for even more extreme means of weight loss. Alcohol, in conjunction with starvation, for example, was discovered to be a fun and effortless way to keep one's girlish figure. Jan from the Phi house, for instance, told me that a lot of her sisters purposely drink on an empty stomach so that the calories they consume can easily be "thrown back up before bed." "You get really drunk fast and cheap, but you also don't have to worry about screwing your diet." For Brenda at the Epsilon house, drinking and vomiting is simply a way to "feel a little less guilty in the morning." "You get drunk, you get it out of your system and stay thin, you know what I mean?"

While purposely throwing up may be a bit extreme for most, the use of over-the-counter drugs is far more acceptable. Diet pills, caffeine tablets, and even laxatives are used by many of the women I talked to. These "safe" and "legal" means of weight loss, I was told, are especially useful for emergency situations, "Like when you have a [fraternity] formal," "can't fit into a dress," or are "leaving for spring break." "There are a lot of times," confesses Savannah, "that we need to lose five or ten pounds quickly. I don't do it every day, but every once in a while I'll take Xenadrine or Hydroxycut. No big deal." And, according to Liza, a fourth-year Phi sister, "Hydroxycut also keeps you up" so that you can study. It's a win/win situation. "You lose weight and get better grades."

While all the methods covered above are proven and time tested in most elite houses, some women began thinking outside the box—searching for newer and more innovative ways to lose weight. The most disturbing of these came from Suzie and her Gamma sisters, who were contemplating the feasibility of using illegal narcotics. "Those people [addicted junkies] never want to eat. They're always thin. Can you imagine, never even wanting to eat and being thin?" While, after noticing the look of horror on my face, they assured me that they would "never really try it," they did say that, if they ever did, "it would be cocaine or heroin because it makes you the skinniest." Suzie concluded the session by joking that the Gammas could be known as "those girls that look like Calvin Klein models"—a reference to Klein's early-1990 advertising campaign where the strung out look was used to sell jeans.

How Thin Is Too Thin?

It is important to keep in mind that most of these young women who are obsessing over their weight are not obese. They do not weigh three hundred pounds, and they have not been ordered by their doctors to lose weight or risk diabetes, heart failure, and stroke. They are, by any reasonable criteria of health or beauty, attractive and lean. Many, in fact, would be perceived as being too thin by the average observer.

So how thin is too thin? As Megan, a Delta sister, told me, "Everybody wants to be the tiniest girl. Everyone wants to be able to share the size 2 clothes, right?" Girls may say that they "don't want to lose too much weight or get too skinny, blah, blah, blah, blah, but they are all lying. I mean we want to be that little."

For Emily, it is prepubescent girls who possess the ideal body. She recalls a recent trip back home during which she attended a high school party. While she and her girlfriends were waiting in line for a beer, they noticed the new group of incoming high school freshman girls: "These girls were so hot. They don't have any hips; they don't have any boobs. They are like this big around. And I'm like that is so cool." Her friend Danielle continued the explanation: "We strive to be twelve again. When you are twelve, you can't wait to finally be curvy, and get boobs, and look like a woman. And, as soon as you do, oh my gosh, I want my twelve-year-old body back. I want no hips, no anything."

Others strive for a different look. Kayla proudly told me of the time her boyfriend's mother asked her whether she had an eating disorder. "To me," she recalls, "that was like the biggest compliment I have ever heard, like man, I am that skinny." Similarly, Emma remembers being approached by one of her sisters at the Eta house. "One of the younger girls who is in our chapter asked me whether I was bulimic. She asked me, 'How do you make yourself throw up?'" She confessed, "At the time, I took it as a compliment. Looking back on it now, I think it is pretty disturbing."

But not everyone thinks that having an eating disorder is disturbing. At the Theta house, where the sisters estimate that 10 percent of their chapter has anorexia or bulimia, some think that it is an effective way to get attention. As Emily sees it, "A lot of girls who have problems get a lot of attention from their friends. You know, people talk about you and talk to you about it." These girls, she argues, "are kinda like celebrities." And, in a house with over 180 sisters, being recognized is no small feat.

Robin, a sister at the Beta house, has seen eating disorders unify and bond members. She told me how a group of older sisters all "go to the Chinese buffet and just eat and eat and eat. . . . They would stuff themselves, and then they would all go to the bathroom and throw up. Then they would all go out to the bars." And since all these women are very popular, "all the younger girls want to hang out with them. They are like the really cool older girls that all the boys love. . . . It is like their cool little club."

When I asked whether anyone ever intervened in the lives of these eating-disordered women, most confessed that they didn't. Some avoided the problem in order to avoid interpersonal conflict. Others said nothing, according to Janis, "because you don't really know whether the girls *really* have a problem or not. I mean, we're not doctors." Most disturbingly, some did not approach their sisters because they did not see the harm or danger in being thin. As Janice, a senior Lambda sister, put it: "There are never really any interventions. It's really sad to say. I'm sorry if you guys [referring to her sisters sitting around her at the interview] disagree with me. . . . It is kind of like this across all sororities. Yeah, someone is really skinny. You may hear she's got problems, but she's skinny. I hate to say it. If she's skinny, what difference does it make? What's the harm? Most sisters don't see the problem, so why would they intervene."

There were other sisters, however, who did view these disorders as the disturbing and life-threatening diseases that they are. Amanda knew that her roommate Lisa had a serious problem when she could no longer "sit in church because her bones ached so bad when she sat in the wooden pews." Danielle discovered her pledge sister Hannah's problem "from the remains" left in an isolated shower stall. Then there was the case of Alexis, who was so experienced at identifying eating disorders that she claimed she was "better than a psychiatrist." During her junior year, she and six of her sisters—all of whom suffered from an unhealthy relationship with food—moved out of the Xi house because of its destructive eating climate. In their new apartment, they established ground rules: "You are not allowed to discuss food, you are not allowed to discuss exercising, you were never allowed to discuss how long you had been at the gym." Even with such rules, however, Bailey, the youngest in the house, "started to get really thin": "The minute Bailey started getting an eating disorder, we all knew immediately. She started lying about her food; she disappeared for a long time after she ate anything, which wasn't often. She spent tons of time in the kitchen cooking things for other people. I saw the pattern and was like, 'Boom.'"

In each of these cases, sisters wisely intervened. Amanda accompanied Lisa to her appointment with a dietary specialist at the student health center. Danielle called Hannah's mother. And Alexis and her roommates collectively approached Bailey in "an in-house sitdown" where they "confronted her" and disclosed their own battles with eating.

In one of the more moving and surprising encounters that occurred during the course of my research, Emma, a recovering anorexic, bravely shared with me and her sisters her private story of how she is regaining her health and taking back her life, one day at a time: "There are lots of people that have problems that just don't talk about it. I did last year because I still suffer from it. But I learned that you've gotta learn to love yourself. If you don't love yourself, then, yeah, you're going to feel the pressure. You learn to respect yourself. If other people don't respect you, then that is their problem. But I wake up every day, and there is always some pressure to be thin because there is always something on TV, or in magazines, or other beautiful girls." During a debriefing session after the interview, Emma told me that that was the first time she had ever discussed her struggle in front of her sisters. "I'm really glad I did it. It helped me a lot just to say it, and maybe it will help one of the younger girls in there. You know, they will know that they are not alone and that I'm there if they want to talk."

There's More Than Enough Blame to Go Around

Using elite sororities as the lone cultural scapegoat is not only overly simplistic and naive; it also deflects the critical eye away from other individuals and institutions equally responsible for the battered self-esteem of these women. There is, for example, no greater villain than the mass media and its irresponsible presentation of computer-enhanced, airbrushed images of impossibly beautiful and thin fashion models as normal. Over the last decade, empirical research has irrefutably demonstrated the deleterious effect of such images on young women:

- The average American woman is five foot four and weighs 140 pounds, but the average American fashion model is five foot eleven and weighs 117 pounds, thinner than only 2 percent of the general population (Smolak, 1996).
- A comparison of the most popular women's and men's magazines found ten times more articles relating to dieting and weight loss in women's magazines than in men's (Andersen & DiDomenico, 1992).
- Whereas 69 percent of female television characters are thin, only 5 percent are overweight (Silverstein, Peterson & Perdue, 1986).
- Exposure to idealized images of impossibly thin fashion models results in depression, shame, guilt, body dissatisfaction, and stress (Richins, 1991; Stice and Shaw, 1994).
- There is a direct relation between media exposure and eating disorders (Stice, Shupak-Neuberg, Shaw & Stein, 1994).[2]

Villains, however, come in many forms. They are not just billionaire media moguls, music-video directors, sexist hip-hop artists, and advertising executives. They are also sometimes the people in our lives whom we love and trust. For many of the women in this study, it was their parents—and in particular their mothers—who did as much (if not more) harm than MTV and *Cosmopolitan* combined.

This connection between parents' attitudes about weight and their daughters' body satisfaction has been well documented. Thelen and Cormier (1995), for example, observed that parents' encouragement to lose weight was positively correlated with their daughter's body weight, desire to be thinner, and dieting efforts. Similarly, Pike and Rodin (1991) found that mothers whose daughters were eating disordered were themselves more likely to be eating disordered and to think that their daughters should lose more weight than were the mothers of non-eating-disordered girls.

Courtney, a third-year Gamma, has experienced firsthand such a dysfunctional mother/daughter relationship. "My mother has always told me that she hasn't gained more than five pounds since she got married, and she expects me to be like the same." During her freshman year at college, however, Courtney committed the unforgivable sin of gaining fifteen pounds. "As soon as I walked in the door over Christmas break," she remembered, "my mother started saying things like, 'You are really filling out,' and, 'You need to make sure that you don't get any fatter.'" To this day, Courtney still hears how her "ass looks big in those jeans, honey," or how, "if she's not careful," her sister (the chubby one in the family) will be able to wear her clothes. Courtney assures me, however, that her mother "only says those things because she wants me to be happy."

Then there is the heartbreaking story of Olivia, whose mother started calling her "fat" and "chubby" in the second grade. Under the relentless pressure of her mother's abusive love, Olivia developed an eating disorder and, as she puts it, "basically stopped eating." One day during a high school cheerleading event, she passed out. "I basically hadn't eaten since seventh grade, you know, and I would get light-headed a lot." Her mother was so mortified by her daughter's unseemly public display—and, of course, by the gossip that circulated around the neighborhood about "Olivia's condition"—that she forced Olivia to transfer to a different school in the middle of the year. Her transgression, Olivia speculated, was not that she was starving herself to death but that she let others know that her thinness was not effortless.

Even worse off was Kathleen. In one of the last interviews that I conducted, I invited her and five of her Omega sisters out for pizza. I thought that it would be a nice way to thank them for devoting their time and energy to the project and also that they would find the casual atmosphere a welcome change from the formal interview room. While the topic of that day's interview was supposed to be dating and long-term relationships, the discussion surprisingly moved to mothers and food. Kathleen solemnly interjected: "My mom wasn't verbally abusive but was very skinny and couldn't understand why I wasn't and kind of took it out on me." Triumphantly she announced, however, that she had "learned to accept" herself and that she didn't "have a problem with food anymore." As the seven of us waited for the large pepperoni pizza to arrive at our table, Kathleen continued: "I mean, I know I probably shouldn't eat this pizza coming, but I'm going to."

Once the pizza arrived, we all dug in—except for Kathleen, who never touched a crumb. As the rest of us ate, she ordered glass after glass of water. While chewing on ice at an increasingly rapid rate, she concluded her story:

> It's not as much as I feel pressure even from my family, but when I go home and I go to the fridge, or something like that, I guess because my mother was the one that when I did gain the weight my freshman year, she was the one who got on me about it constantly. "You've really put on weight, you can't afford to gain anymore weight, and da da da da da." When I go home I feel like, if I'm walking towards the refrigerator, she's basically asking me, "What are you getting? What are you getting? You shouldn't eat that. You don't eat that." So I almost feel like I hear her voice in my head every time I grab something I shouldn't be eating.

A more predictable, but no less benign, villain in the lives of these women is men. Gabby's obsession with thinness, for instance, began when her boyfriend broke up with her because she was too fat. "After he told me I did not turn him on and that I was too heavy," she recalls, "I started working out to try to get him back, and I just became obsessed with it." Others starved themselves in the hopes of finding a boyfriend. "All the guys that I know," reported Katelyn, "are only attracted to really hot girls with great bodies, those types. I have had guys actually ask me why don't I look like that." She admits that, although she is already "thin and cute," she still thinks "being a size 0 or losing another five pounds" would get her more attention from guys: "I think, and I know I'm crazy, that the guys will drool over me too."

But are men really that critical of body size and thinness? According to Anna and her Beta sisters, "they definitely are." As Anna says, "I've heard it":

Brianna: Anna is right. Like on spring break guys who themselves don't have perfect bodies would sit and criticize girls. "She should not be in a bathing suit, the pig."

Kelly: I've already had this happen. I gained a bit of weight at the end of last semester, and I came home for the summer, and my guy friends were like, "Wow, you have been drinking a lot." I said I was, but I really wasn't. I just gained weight. They all noticed.

Rebecca: Yeah, I have a friend who went away to Georgetown. She was always cute and little. But she came home after her first year and had gained a little weight. All the guys joked, like, "Is she Georgetown's new linebacker?" I was like, please, she still has the same personality, but that did not matter to them.

Anna: Guys definitely notice, and they let you know that they notice too.

But not every woman in this study thought that men wanted ultraskinny girlfriends. Becky, a senior Mu sister, has "given this lots of thought" and thinks that, "at a certain point, they start getting grossed out." She remembers one day, for example, "this fraternity guy approached me in class and said, 'Oh my God, I think that girl has anorexia or something. That's so fuckin' gross.'" Similarly, Erin remembers when "my best friend was hugged by this guy at a bar, and he was like disgusted. 'My God, you are all skin and bones.'" Grace from the Theta house thinks that, today, "guys see really skinny as associated with having some kind of eating problem." Becky, Erin, and Grace concede, however, that the average man will be "grossed out" only by "really extreme thinness." Regular skinny, I was informed, is still hot.

Some of the women I talked to, however, think that men want more than regular skinny. "Girls may think that 'thin is in,' but guys want curves," said Emma. "I have this friend who is insanely skinny," Lauren told me, "and, when we go to bars, my other friends who are curvy get many more guys than she does. Simply skinny isn't pretty to them." Nicole further refines this theory: "I think that men want skinny with giant tits. She is supposed to have a waist this big [connecting her thumb and forefinger to make a small circle] but have boobs catapulting out of her top." After hearing Nicole's description of the perfect female, the other sisters at the session unanimously agreed. They all humorously screamed, "She's right!" And, from what the men in this study have told about their ideal female, she is, indeed, right.

It should be noted, however, that many of the women I spoke with acknowledge racial differences in taste. White men may prefer thin, big-chested women, but black men, according to Christine, "love bigger women." Laughing as she elaborated, Jenny told me that "brothers like big butts." "My ass," she says, "is too big for white guys, but black guys love it." Sierra observed, "Any time you see a black guy with a white woman, she will always be a big girl. It is like that every time." When I asked why black and white men use different criteria in selecting a mate, the responses fell into one of three categories: the *culinary hypothesis,* which asserts that food and the process of eating are more important in black society; the *cultural hypothesis,* which argues that black men are taught by their culture that larger women are sexier and more desirable; and the classic *Oedipus hypothesis,* which contends, as Zoey, a Pi sister, put it, that "since men have bigger mothers, they are naturally drawn to bigger women." Whatever the reason, however, the women I spoke with claimed to feel less anxious about their body shape and size when around African American men.

Men

The days of a man's man rolling out of bed, pulling on a pair of worn-out jeans, and splashing cold water on his face are fast becoming only a memory. Today, many young men—especially young, affluent white men—are spending as much time and money on their appearance as their female counterparts are. Urged on by clothing manufacturers, hair and tanning salons, body-shaping gyms, men's lifestyle magazines, and fashion-conscious girlfriends, a new generation of men has embraced a new definition of *masculinity.*

The result is the rise of the *metrosexual,* first identified by the journalist Mark Simpson in 1994. According to most definitions, a metrosexual is a young urban man with a heightened aesthetic sense who spends a great deal of time and money on his appearance. As *The Age* has observed, these men "go to hairdressers rather than barbers; avoid using soap because it's too harsh for their skin; visit the gym instead of playing sports and even have difficulty deciding what to wear" ("Rise of the Metrosexual," 2003). Even ESPN has gotten into the act, posting tongue-in-cheek warning signs of metrosexuality on its Web site: looking in the mirror more than five times a day, using hair-care products and facial moisturizers, tweezing, waxing, or trimming body hair, wearing designer boxer shorts, enjoying shopping, and spending more than twenty dollars on a haircut ("Are you a metrosexual?" 2003).

This is not to say that fashion consciousness is new to men. A "sense of style," according to Bordo (1999), has always been a staple in America's homosexual communities. What *is* new is that *straight* men are now getting into the act. "Twenty years ago," according to *The Age,* "male fashion, skin care and vanity in general were identified with gay men. Now sexuality is irrelevant. . . . Brad Pitt, Tom Cruise, Pat Rafter, . . . and footballers such as Craig Wing are manicuring their appearance" ("Rise of the Metrosexual," 2003).

The change in men, however, is more than just outward and superficial. It is inward and substantive as well. This new breed of man is emotionally softer and more sensitive, caring, and nurturing than his grandfather. According to Alexa Hackbarth (2003) of the *Washington Post,* these new men are "not afraid to embrace their feminine side" and describe themselves as "sensitive and romantic." Still, as complex as the new man may appear, the satirist Jeanette Scherrer (2004) believes that he can be summed up in two words: "male pussy."

The Birth of the Greco-Sexual

Like most other popular trends in America, metrosexuality has gone to college. And, since most fraternity men are young, affluent, heterosexual, and white, they have been extremely receptive (and ideally vulnerable) to the metrosexual message. Surprisingly, however, they have not adopted it wholesale. Instead, they have taken elements of the new masculinity (fashion and body consciousness) and merged them with remnants of the old (individualism, competitiveness, emotional stoicism), adopting as it were the worst of both worlds. Consequently, a moniker other than *metrosexual* would seem to be in order. Perhaps *Greco-sexual* would be more accurate.

This change in GU's men has not been lost on GU's women. When I asked them to tell me the one thing about the men that would shock my readers the most, 90 percent said it was how much time and effort they spend on their appearance. "They care a lot more about their appearance then they care to admit," claimed Alice. Janice agreed that, contrary to what most people think, "men really care about how they look. They spend as much time getting ready as girls do." Lennie's boyfriend even shaves his body, plucks his eyebrows, and goes to a tanning bed. "He is like a girl anymore."

As essential as such activities are to Greco-sexuality, however, it is the vanity—as manifested in weight lifting and body shaping—that most women saw as the great male secret.[3] "The thing that would shock people is how much time these guys now spend on their bodies at the gym," Lori asserted. "They are like nuts about it, unhealthy nuts." Gina reported that her boyfriend "goes to the gym every day. It's like part of his life. He freaks if he misses a day, ever." Suzanne thought that men were "far worse than girls" when it came to obsession with physical appearance: "It is part of their lives, and, if they miss [a day of lifting], they think they are out of shape and flabby." Margaret described this new male obsession this way: "Imagine a guy with anorexia, but, instead of thinking he is too fat, he thinks he is too skinny. I mean, they look great to me, but they think that they have to go to the gym every day, like religion. It is all they think about." "And sex," she adds, laughing lightheartedly.

The women are right. The primary physical attribute defining Greco-sexuality is not hair gel, shoes, or waxed eyebrows; it is a muscular body. Lifting has become an obsession at most elite fraternity houses. It has been estimated by most of the men I interviewed that, in GU's top fraternity houses, at least half of the brothers lift regularly, with another quarter working out less frequently and with less verve. The regular lifters go to the gym five or six times a week for for two- to three-hour sessions. Not surprisingly, the already high number of lifters increases dramatically right before spring break and summer vacation as the young men prepare to take their shirts off in front of young women.

Truth be told, these young men devote more time to lifting than they do to anything else, save sleeping. Whereas, during the average week, they spend twelve hours each doing homework and surfing the Internet, fourteen hours each attending class and watching television, and fifteen hours drinking/partying, they spend sixteen hours lifting.

Just as all sororities are not equally body obsessed, however, neither are all fraternities. Only a quarter of male aspirers and a fifth of male strugglers spend time at the gym. But, as Brian, a junior Alpha, puts it, in the elite houses, where the big men on campus reside, "lifting is a way of life."

"Chicks Dig Muscles!"

As I began asking these young men why lifting had become so important in their lives, I received a variety of explanations. For a few, lifting was a way to "feel good about yourself." As Robert explained, "When you come back from the gym, you know, you worked hard and did it. You feel good like you accomplished something." Similarly, Elton believed that "even if the rest of the day is bad, you can go work out and feel good. You have control over that, at least." Robert found the feeling produced by working out similar to that produced by dressing up. "You know when you put on really nice clothes and you look in the mirror and you feel really good—dressing up and stuff—well, that's what it's like. You just feel good about yourself."

Some claimed to lift for the health advantages. Lewis said that he has "always been really concerned about what I eat and how I take care of myself. Lifting is part of being healthy for me." Larry, Lewis's biological brother, similarly reported that lifting "releases these endorphins that get you high, really. I just feel really good— healthy—after I lift." Finally, Al, who openly admitted to having a "violent temper," confessed that, after lifting, he "loses a lot of the unhealthy aggression." "I don't feel like punching people," he told me, "but, if I miss a day at Gold's [his gym], it does start to build up."

Many also commented on the confidence that lifting gives them. "When you lift, you feel like you are 'on,' you know. I walk around feeling confident," reported Marcos, a Beta. John remembered how "shitty" he felt about himself before he began lifting. "In high school I was a slob, you know what I mean, and I never really did anything. I wouldn't really talk to new people or girls." Once he started lifting, however, "everything changed": "Now I go up to people and start conversations. I feel good walking around. I'll tell you, lifting has made me happier about myself."

Lifting has supplied Mark, a senior Chi, with the confidence to be more aggressive and less deferential in volatile situations: "When you go somewhere and there's a bunch of outsiders or guys looking to give you shit, you are just more confident that, if something happens, you can handle it. I don't back away. I used to. But now I'm more confident, so I don't. If I have to beat somebody down, I will, and can. I guess lifting has given me the power to be more confident so I can protect myself." Similarly, Kevin also highlighted the confidence that lifting has given him around other men: "It's not that I am looking to fight, but, when you walk into places, if you lift, you have a different walk; people notice it. Your confidence tells people that you have the guns so don't even think about it." "I love that feeling," he concludes, "I gotta be honest."

For others, it is not so much about intimidating other men as it is about impressing them. "In the house," Joshua admitted, "it's cool to have the guys notice. They respect it, you know? They respect you more." At the Gamma house, Jacob told me, "everybody lifts": "So we all kind of compete with each other. When another guy tells you 'you look good,' it means a lot more than some joe off the streets." For Daniel, it is the combination of both impressing and intimidating his brothers that is seductive: "For me, when another guy comes up to me and says, 'Dan, you look wider,' whatever kind of compliment he throws at me, it's just you know what I mean? This fucker wants to make fun of me, you know? I know he's goofing around, but I know part of him thinks that I'm getting slightly a little bit bigger. And I see him in the gym too, and he's huge you know, but you know what I'm saying?" For men like Joshua, Jacob, and Daniel, therefore, lifting has become a modern-day alpha-male contest. They employ it in the struggle to establish their place in the hierarchy—making sure that they not only impress but also intimidate. This kind of intimidation is not like traditional browbeating. It is more like siblings or friends jockeying for position in the pack—serious, but still ultimately friendly.

When it comes to nonbrothers, however, the competition is much less friendly. On numerous occasions, I was told of the tacit battles that take place at the gym. "Everybody watches everybody else when you are at the gym," Daniel admitted. "Every guy is looking to see how much the guy next to him is lifting." Gabriel believed that such surveillance is "one of the reasons everybody pushes so hard. You don't want to be the guy that's a puss; you want to be talked about, you know?" Nick, Gabriel's Nu brother, concurred and described the gym "as kind of a stage in a way. I mean, when you are lifting, especially if you are serious about it, people like watch you perform. So, hell yeah, we really push ourselves for other men, but not in a fag way."

Impressing other men, however, is far less important to most than impressing women—the primary motivation for most of these brothers. "We all lift for the bitches," joked Christopher. "If anyone tells you different, they're fuckin' bullshitting you." And, as Jack, a senior Alpha, puts it, "The women love it, I mean crave it." Dylan, a senior Gamma, reported, "When you're at parties, they'll come up and rub on your arms and rub on your stomach." Noah, a junior at the Delta house, had had similar experiences: "Girls [will] come up and be like, 'Take your shirt off! Pull up your shirt a little bit, let me see your abs.'" Similarly, Greg told of "girls just sitting there, intoxicated, and they're a little more truthful, saying like, 'Yeah, you've got a nice body.'" Jordan from the Omega house has even had a graduate teaching assistant he once had "come up and say, 'You look like you have been lifting,' real flirtation and shit."

A nice body gets you more than compliments, however. "Girls will fuck you if you got the package," Dylan claimed. "Oh yeah, they want to see what it is like to have you." Jacob agreed and said that he considers the gym the best thing to have ever happened to his sex life. "They love hard arms, abs, you know, a cut chest." In the hands of an expert player like Kyle, women don't stand a chance: "At parties they'll come up, kinda just like mess around and grab your arm and be like, 'Oh, that's nice,' and their clothes come off. You have the ability to play that card, and some guys don't, like because they don't do shit. Like, I'm not gonna name names, but there are guys around here that just don't do dick, they just sit around, and they, you know, they just fuck off. You have the ability, you can play that card because you feel confident in yourself."

The Pressure of Nonconformity

For the nonlifting brothers, life is getting tougher. To begin with, as Dennis claimed, "the brothers that do lift kinda look down on you like you are a slacker and stuff. I mean, I just don't have time or money to do that shit." Tony at the Beta house saw lifting as creating new divisions "between the lifters and slackers" in a one-time unified fraternity. "All the brothers that lift together hang out together now. When they all go to the gym, you feel bad about yourself, sometimes, like those guys are doing something and you're not." "All the fat fucks stay at home with each other," Tony humorously concludes, "and we feel bad about how we all look."

Such comparisons also demoralized Michael. "It sucks always being around these guys that have these bodies," he confessed. "I could do it if I wanted to, but you start to feel a little bad about yourself like you're the only guy that looks, you know, normal." For Sam, the worst moments came when the shirts are off: "I hate it, fuckin' hate it. We just got back from spring break, and those guys loved taking off their shirts. . . . Or, when we play ball out back, those guys always take their shirts off, and especially if girls are watching." After a long pause, he admitted that "it is embarrassing, you know. You feel like the skinny kid on the schoolyard again."

Shopping for clothes is another humbling activity in the world of the nonlifter. "Trying to find something to wear sucks," a frustrated

Allen reported. "I mean, everything is tight. If you don't lift, you look like skinny in all that shit." Ben, a senior Gamma brother, remembered the good old days when "clothes at A&F [Abercrombie & Fitch] were baggy. Then like last spring or something, I guess, everything was 'muscle fit.' I don't look good in any of these new clothes."

Even worse, however, for nonlifters are flirting and dating. Women are beginning to expect their men to be muscle-bound—in much the same way that men expect their women to be model thin. "I can tell a difference already in girls and what they like and talk about," claimed Dave. "Even my girlfriend tells me that she and all her [Alpha] sisters love guys that lift. Just watch them at parties." Concurring, Justin said he saw "these girls all the time just rubbing on those guys. I swear, I have seen girls come up and just rub on those guys, under their shirts. It happens all the fucking time." Evan and Nick, nonlifting best friends and brothers at the Sigma house, have even been asked by women why they don't lift, "like it is expected of everybody." "Yeah, you get pressure," Nick claimed. "You feel it." Evan humorously interrupted: "Fuck 'em, we'll start dating fat chicks."

By Any Means Necessary

With so much at stake—self-esteem, confidence, health, the respect of men, and the desire of women—it is no wonder that these men will go to extreme measures for the perfect Greco-sexual body. Along with spending sixteen hours a week at the gym, they also carefully plan what and how they eat. Kevin, who reads *Men's Health,* told me he eats only natural foods "and things high in protein . . . eggs, tuna, stuff like that." Similarly, Jack reported eating "a lot of chicken breasts. Tuna is really big, steak. Really, anything with a lot of protein. And I stay away from the carbs." David thinks of his body "as a machine." "You need to put good stuff in if you expect to get the results you want," he said. "You can't eat McDonald's all the time and wonder why you're a fat ass." Morgan went so far as moving out of the fraternity house because the meals were not conducive to his lifting regimen: "I care. I mean, I hated to move, but I was just wasting money—I would never eat there and have to go buy my own food."

For the vast majority of the lifters, however, simply monitoring their diet is too passive and ineffective an approach. They have turned instead to over-the-counter oral supplements that assist and expedite their body shaping. And they are unapologetic about it. "Supplements are great, man," said Justin, an Alpha. "If you want to get big and you are not using them, you are a fool." Connor and his Epsilon brothers told me that "creatine [methyl guanidine-acetic acid][4] is the big one that everyone uses." But they have all tried others: Nitro tech, Phosphagen, VPX Sports, Biotest MAG-10, CytoSport Muscle Milk, Cytodyne Xenadrine EFX, Cytodyne Myo-Blast CSP3, Ripped Fuel, Xenedrine.

Of course the type of supplement you take depends on your body type. "There are two types of guys," Jordan, an Epsilon, informed me. The first type is "fat and wants to lose weight." "These guys take diet pills like Xenedrine." Most of the guys, however, "take protein supplements to put on weight," weight that will then be turned into muscle at the gym. But, even within these two classifications, brothers vary greatly in terms of what they use and how often they use it. The key, I was told, is to mix and match for the right effect. Kevin's supplemental regimen, for instance, starts with "a couple Ripped Fuel pills" before going to the gym—these are legal amphetamines that supply a jolt of energy, allowing him to lift longer and harder. Once at the gym, he will drink "some type of sports drink with creatine in it." He will then go home and eat a high-protein dinner with a "weight gainer protein shake for dessert."

Not surprisingly, this seven-day-a-week supplemental regimen is not cheap. Most of these young, financially struggling college men spend forty to sixty dollars a month on it—above and beyond the dues to their private gyms. According to some of the Greek alumni I have interviewed, however, there may be an even higher price to pay for supplement use. Matthew and some of his Gamma brothers reported really struggling with their weight now that they are off supplements. While they admit that they are "no longer working out as hard as we did while in college," they feel that supplements "really screwed up our metabolism." Twenty-three-year-old Kevin said, "I should not have to be fighting my weight like this. I know it is because my body has not readjusted itself to act naturally." "You can't fool your body into doing one thing for years," Jackson asserted, "and then expect it to be balanced when you stop. We all artificially put on weight; now our metabolism is out of whack."

While the long-term effects of supplement use have yet to be scientifically determined, steroids have for decades been considered harmful and, thus, their use criminalized. Nonetheless, the perfect body is so coveted that many of these young men will risk the threat of heart damage, a reduced sex drive, uncontrollable rage, shrinking testicles, a reduced sperm count, infertility, baldness, prostate cancer, body acne, gynecomastia (abnormally large breasts), increased body hair, and liver damage.

Given the negative publicity that steroids have received over the last twenty years, I was not surprised that no one openly admitted to their use. I was publicly told that they were too unpredictable, expensive, and difficult to acquire. Interestingly, when I asked who would use them if they were made freely available, more than three-quarters said they would, especially if they could "cycle them." Cycling, I came to find out, is the process where you inject yourself with steroids for three months, then stop for nine. This process is repeated until the desired effect is achieved. Proponents of cycling believe that it minimizes the harmful consequences of steriods while maximizing the positive effects.

The morning after an interview with the Zetas focusing on lifting, Robert, a senior Zeta brother and a trusted student, stopped by to give me the "real story" on steroids. The reason no one talked about steroids, I was informed, is because there is a cabal of lifters who have tacitly agreed to "cover for each other." According to Robert, the conspiracy of silence is necessitated by the stigma attached to steroid use. "If word got out that you are using, some would think you are psycho." Others, I was told, view users as sexually dysfunctional, emotionally unpredictable, and irresponsibly vain.

Because of this stigma, "even a guy's own brothers may not know he's using." But, according to Robert, there is an increasing number joining the ranks of steroid users. "You would not believe," he claimed, "how many guys are really using Deca." Deca (Deca Durabolin)[5] is believed by its proponents to be safe, especially when cycled. How do you know who is using? "Just look for the guy who is larger than everyone else" or find out who recently had a "growth spurt" in the gym.

Other Elements to Greco-Sexuality

Simply achieving the chiseled body of the lifter is not the Greco-sexual's only concern. Having achieved it, he must learn how to properly frame and accentuate it.

The first step is the removal of body hair. It's not just that body hair is considered disgusting. Hairlessness makes a body look bigger and enhances muscularly definition. And everything goes, even pubic hair (yes, everything looks bigger).

Next, a tan is essential for maximum impact. Consequently, going to a tanning bed is a must. Just don't overdo it. Nothing is more of a turnoff, I was informed, than looking artificially brown.

As tragic as it may seem, the next step is putting clothes on the perfectly chiseled, perfectly smooth, perfectly tanned body. Feeling the same pressure that the women reported, Greco-sexuals spend a great deal of money on their wardrobes. Having the right clothes from the right designers is crucial if they are to be popular with the men and desired by the women.

Thus, the transformation from high school boy to Greco-sexual fraternity stud is an expensive one. Those young men without very generous parents must either take part-time jobs (usually as waiters, bartenders, or retail salesmen) or rack up the credit card debt.

Four young Delta brothers sat down with me to discuss their recent transformation and the cost of "looking good":

> Brian: One thing, like before I came to this place [the Delta house], I didn't own one pair of dress pants, one pair of dress shoes, or a dress shirt, 'cause I wore jeans all the time, and now weekends we're all decked up in nice clothes. Everybody does it.
>
> Justin: Shit. I bought a $100 pair of dress pants, and I was like, What the fuck was I thinking? But it was like what Brian was saying, you know, you have to have the right clothes.
>
> AD: So everybody is concerned about fashion in your house?
>
> Dylan: Oh yeah. It is part of our look. We have a certain look. We had a pledge that one of our actives took him to the mall and made him buy like $250 of new clothes 'cause we didn't want, he was a cool guy, but we didn't want him dressing like he was dressing, so we made him go to the mall and spend $250.
>
> Eric: Yeah, jean shorts. [*Group laughter.*] It is not like it was in high school. It is expensive. I just bought a Banana Republic shirt yesterday for $70 for Friday's party with the Kappas. I better get laid! [*More group laughter.*]

Don't be deceived into thinking, however, that Brian, Justin, Dylan, and Eric were ugly losers before being tutored in the ways of metropolitan fashion by their older brothers. All four young men are clean-cut, physically attractive guys. Only such raw physical material is invited to pledge any of the nation's elite fraternities.

A Homophobic "Rush Crush"?

After spending over twenty-five years of my life working with fraternities, I am still shocked by how important physical appearance is in determining who receives bids from elite chapters. On the one hand, the brothers of these homophobic organizations "hate fags" and would never accept a "homo" into their house. The very idea of men being attracted to other men "grosses" and "weirds" them out. On the other hand, they want every cute (read: noneffeminate) boy who comes through the door to pledge their house. And, the more attractive the prospective pledge, the more attention he receives. It is not uncommon, if fact, for really cute boys to be *courted* (the brothers prefer the term *rushed hard*). Sororities, being more honest about the attraction, have labeled this particular brother-pledge relationship a *rush crush*. The pledge being courted may be taken to private parties and cookouts, given cigars, T-shirts, and hats, treated to dinner, and verbally schmoozed for weeks. If the coveted boy finally commits, the house is elated. If he is lost to a rival fraternity, the brothers are more than jealous; they are heartbroken. After all, nothing hurts like unrequited love.

Like sororities, however, fraternities use code words to refer to a rushee's physical appearance during rush meetings. The offer of a bid will be supported, not because John is "cute" and "adorable," but because he is a "stud" and "good with the women." Everyone in the room knows, however, that the reason John is going to receive a bid is because he will make the chapter and all the brothers look better to outside observers, especially sororities. It is no coincidence that the fraternities with the most physically attractive brothers are also the most popular with the sororities.

Interestingly, however, when I asked sorority sisters which fraternities had the *nicest* guys, the elite chapters were never mentioned. The strugglers and, to a less extent, the aspirers were always credited with being the most respectful, polite, and gentlemanly. The elites, on the other hand, were characterized as "assholes," "cocky jerks," "arrogant," and "rude." Nonetheless, the struggler and aspirer fraternities are consistently excluded from social gatherings by the very elite sororities that praise them for their kindness. As Mark, a Rho brother, observed, "Everybody says we are the nicest guys—the type you want to marry—but we never get called for parties by the Betas, Alphas, Chis, Deltas [four elite sororities], almost never." "Maybe it is true what they say," speculated Michael. "Women like guys that abuse them."

Conclusion

A focus on body shape and size clearly illustrates the symmetical nature of gender relationships in our society: men want to get bigger to impress women; women want to get smaller to impress men. Of course, as in all symmetrical relationships, when one party changes, the other must change as well. But who is the culprit here? Is it men pushing women to get smaller? Is it women pushing men to get bigger? Or is the agent of change something else?

Some, like Susan Faludi (1992), argue that men are becoming physically larger and acting more aggressively to compensate for their diminished power in the public sector, lashing back as more and more women take on roles (provider, boss, leader) previously reserved only for men. Others, like Jean Kilbourne (1999), believe that corporate advertising is responsible for convincing both sexes that only by spending a significant portion of their income on beauty aids can they be acceptable aesthetically. Still others, like Jean-Marc Carriol (quoted in "Rise of the Metrosexual," 2003), see the influence of the feminist movement behind this new trend in body shaping, women simply demanding that men care about their appearance too.

The fact is that there is some truth to all three positions. The battle over the human form has been waged by many interdependent cultural forces, including the patriarchy, the media, and empowered women, making it difficult, if not impossible, to single out any one villain. Identifying the victims, however, is a far easier task. The losers in the "body war" are both the men and the women who are investing their time, money, energy, and self-esteem in the effort to attain the unattainable, the perfect body. Both have been equally exploited, tricked into sacrificing their human potential for the barren pursuit of vanity.

These emaciated young women and muscular young men have other things in common than victimization. Despite the size differential, they are two sides of the same unhealthy coin. They both obsess over body size and physical appearance, devoting a great deal of time and money to the pursuit of perfection, yet remaining unhappy with the way they look; sacrifice their health to their vanity; and judge people, individually or in groups, on the basis of physical appearance alone. Tragically, this may be the only instance where true gender equality exists on GU's campus.

5. Bros before Hos

Michael and Jenny met at an Omega fraternity/Theta sorority Super Bowl party when they were both sophomores. While both had been involved in previous relationships, neither had been in love before. As Jenny recalls, "We weren't looking for it, but, when it happens, you can't do anything about it." And, according to both, "it" happened almost immediately. Michael thinks it was "love at first sight": "Everybody at the party knew it. . . . They were all talking about it the next morning. We knew it too."

Two and a half years later, Michael and Jenny's premonitions proved accurate. In the spring of their senior year, they were engaged to be married—much to the surprise of no one. Initially, both tried to keep the big news a secret: Jenny to *ensure* a successful and surprising candlelight ceremony at her sorority, Michael to *avoid* a successful and surprising treeing ceremony at his fraternity.

The next morning, Jenny, bursting with anticipation, called Lisa, the Theta president, to tell her the good news and to initiate the candlelight process. Lisa, thrilled to be the inside confidante, immediately started preparing for that night's secret ritual. By dinner, all the sisters at the Theta house had been informed of the "candlelight" scheduled for 6:00 that evening.

In the Theta living room, the sisters excitedly gathered in the traditional oversized circle and awaited instructions. Lisa informed the new members of the protocol for that evening's event. "For you new girls," she began, "this is a candlelight ceremony. One of our sisters has some great news for us." She continued her instructions: "I will light a candle and begin passing it around the circle. The sister that blows out the flame is the girl that is engaged. Then we all hug and cry."[1]

The sisters speculated as to the identity of the "lucky girl" as they nervously passed the flame. Finally, as the candle reached Jenny's hand, she hesitated, made eye contact with her sisters, and blew it out. After a half hour of hugging and crying, the sisters gathered around her as she retold every detail of her special night. For that evening, at least, Jenny felt like a princess.

Things, unfortunately, were not going so smoothly for Michael. His Omega brothers found out the *bad news*. "I knew they would eventually," Michael told me, "but, after only one day, I was sold out by somebody." His brothers planned the kidnapping perfectly. As Michael naively stepped out of the front door at his apartment, seven of his brothers tackled him, duct-taped him, and transported him back to the fraternity house. He was stripped naked, tied to the biggest tree in the Omega front yard (ideal for pubic humiliation), and covered with food—a contemporary version of being tarred and feathered. After Michael had suffered twenty minutes or so of mortification, Jenny was called by the brothers and informed of his unfortunate predicament. As scripted, she arrived with a good sense of humor and freed her betrothed from public display. "How humiliating," Michael remembers, "having to have your girlfriend rescue you."

At the end of the evening, both Jenny and Michael felt bonded to their brothers and sisters in ways they had not before the enactment of these time-honored rituals. They both admitted to feeling more loved, connected, and important. Even as Jenny dried her tears and Michael picked cornflakes out of his ears, they both knew that that night's events would be warmly retold countless times throughout their life together. "This is the stuff that memories are made of," Michael proudly professed.

As both Michael and Jenny testify, such time-honored fraternity and sorority rituals bond one generation to the next. They are, according to Eric, the Omega president, "the things that makes Greeks different from the marching band or chess club," linking brother to brother, sister to sister.

Equally important, however, are the lessons embedded in these rituals. Viewed from this perspective, treeing and candlelighting become more than just meaningless, juvenile traditions. They are, instead, powerful teaching devices that highlight the importance to both men and women of masculine independence and feminine dependence. Both learn, for example, that for a man to lose his individuality to a woman is emasculating and something to be ridiculed (after all, he has ignored the cultural imperative to be independent) and that for a woman to lose her individuality to a man is ennobling and something to be celebrated (after all, she has fulfilled the cultural imperative to be dependent). In short, what is learned is that men are better off without women and that women are better off with men.

But these lessons are not unique to the Greek system. They are, in fact, two of the dominant motifs of masculinity and femininity in American culture. How many of us have experienced similar rituals at bachelor parties and bridal showers? Still, as we shall see, such notions are not always accepted without question by GU's Greeks. Sometimes they are challenged.

Men

As Wood (2005) puts it, American men "are expected to be confident, independent, autonomous. . . . A 'real man' doesn't need others" (p. 161). He especially doesn't need women. Like the prototypical Marlboro Man, he is, according to Doyle (1995), a self-reliant loner, at peace only when freed from the restraints imposed by human contact. Hollywood's nineteenth-century Shane, twentieth-century James Bond, and twenty-first-century Terminator have all helped teach generations of American men that emotional connection should be tolerated only for short periods of time—primarily to save women before riding off into the sunset, alone. The worst thing that can happen to a man, in fact, is to be tied down by the proverbial ball and chain. Like a wild stallion, a real man needs to avoid being "whipped," getting "hitched," or being "saddled" with a family. Given such cultural expectations, it is no wonder that Michael was so mercilessly hazed for committing to and caring for Jenny.

Opposite-Sex Relationships

Women are not completely unwelcome in the lives of Greek men. As discussed in chapter 2, these men—like most of the men I have known in my life—want to have sex with as many beautiful woman as possible. This intercourse they fantasize about is at its most arousing when it is emotionally meaningless and, thus, psychologically inconsequential. A sentimental or spiritual connection would only complicate and de-eroticize the liaison.

There is another side to most of these men, however. Battling their urge to have meaningless sex with anonymous women is their desire to make a meaningful, romantic connection with one woman. While it is not always clear which side of this tug-of-war is winning, these young men are certainly not as emotionally empty as their bravado at first implies.

Most dream, in fact, of settling down, falling in love, and getting married—sometime after the fun and laughs have ended at the frat house. And surprisingly, the women they envision themselves with are not "millionaire nymphomaniacs who own liquor stores," as the old joke goes. Mrs. Right is significantly more substantial. Of the hundreds of fraternity men I interviewed, most were in agreement on the six qualities they were looking for in a mate: she should be attractive, intelligent, sophisticated/classy, kind/maternal, cool/fun, and have a good sense of humor (representative samples of their views on desirable female attributes appear below).

Physical Attractiveness
"OK, she needs to be hot, obviously."

"Big titties."

"She is hot. Not slutty hot, but classy hot."

"She will have a nice body, not fat. She cares about how she looks."

"Looks are important. I mean she has to *do it* for you, you know. She doesn't have to be a 10, but, you know, an 8 or 9."

Sense of Humor

"I like girls that can laugh at things. At themselves."

"She has to be able to make me laugh."

"Can she get silly and not be so serious all the time."

"If she is going to be with me, she'll have to have a good sense of humor, or she won't make it."

Intelligent

"You may not care if a piece of ass can carry on a conversation, but I want my wife to be smart—be able to talk about the world."

"I think I would like to have a professional wife who is smart and has a good head on her shoulders."

"If you are going to spend the rest of your life with her, she better be intelligent. I mean, she doesn't have to be Einstein, but she should be able to keep up with you."

Sophisticated/Classy

"She will have to be classy. She'll have to dress nice. Know what clothes to wear. Speak right."

"The ideal woman is high-class. Not too hard to keep, you know, but sophisticated. Like Princess Di."

"My mom is a perfect woman. She never curses. She is always polite, Miss Manners like. She would have to be some of that."

"She has to have a good reputation. I can't be with her if she was trashy before."

Kind/Maternal

"I think I would really like to find a wife who is really good-hearted."

"She'd have to be a good mother. She has to love kids and doing that whole thing."

"The feminazis don't like it, but I want a woman who can take care of her family . . . a sweet woman."

"She would have to be really nice. I hate bitches. She's kind, you know what I mean?"

Cool/Fun

"The only way I can see myself married is if I can find a girl who is cool. If I want to go out with the guys, she has to be cool with it."

"She can't be catty. I hate the gossipy, backstabbing shit that girls do."

"I'm looking for a woman who can hang out with the brothers, who is not telling me to stop hanging with the brothers. She has to be cool. Cool with the brothers."

"I want a girl that I can get shit-faced with and the next day take her home to my parents."

What is striking about these men's conception of the perfect mate is not only how it deviates from traditional definitions of femininity but also how it highlights the desire for friendships with women. There are, of course, the predictable attributes on the list: they want someone who is attractive, kind, and sophisticated. But some are unexpected: they want someone who is funny, smart, and fun. What these men claim to be looking for is a wife who is also a friend— "hot" and "cool" at the same time. They also want a wife who is their equal, not the "little woman" to cook and clean for them, but a partner, a confidant, and a kindred soul—albeit one who earns less than they do.

Interestingly, while these men envision *themselves* in happy, healthy relationships, they are intolerant of their brothers in such relationships—at least while they are still in college. Such male-female connections are viewed as anathema to independence and freedom. Mark, a junior Kappa, sees such connections as "cancers in a house": "You start to get too many brothers who spend all their time with chicks, and everything falls apart." Similarly, Elton, the Epsilon social chair, believes that "steady girlfriends are the worst thing that can happen to a fraternity. None of the brothers want to go out; none of the brothers are *allowed* to go out." Warren remembers such "dark days" at the Chi house: "During my sophomore year, all the seniors . . . started settling down. Talk about shitty times. Our parties sucked. . . . Our weekends sucked. Thank God we got through it and most of those guys broke up or graduated."

The main problem with relationships, however, is the loss of brotherhood and camaraderie. "Girls," as Jacob succinctly put, "take guys away from their brothers." After assuring me that there is "nothing gay about it," John described the conflict between women and brothers this way: "Pussy is pussy. It comes and goes, but brotherhood is for life. Just think about it. How many girlfriends, one-night lays you have had? They come and go, but your brothers are your brothers for life. So it is not like a fag thing; it is just that you got to know what is real, you know. Brotherhood is real. Pussy comes and goes. . . . It's always 'bros before hos'; that's what we all say."

John is not alone in his sentiments. Most brothers I have talked to proudly admit that they have either had brothers try to break up their relationships or tried to break up brothers' relationships themselves. "It's part of the game," laughed David. "I have this brother, Rob, and, for the last three months, all he's told me to do—every time I see him—is to drop my girlfriend. He'll say, 'Drop that dumb cunt.'" In all honesty, however, David admits the he would "probably do the same thing to him if he had a girlfriend."

The women in these men's lives are acutely aware of the threat that they pose to brotherhood. Most, by their sophomore year, learn that, as Kaitlyn put it: "If you date a frat jerk, you date his whole damn fraternity." The key, as Nicole saw it, is to remain unthreatening: "If you don't, if the girl gets more important than the fraternity, all the other brothers gang up on him, and you, sometimes. You can't win that battle."

There are, of course, strategies woman can use to attenuate the fraternal backlash—bringing their cute sisters with them, giving their boyfriends a lot of free time, not spending too many nights at the frat house, befriending their boyfriend's friends. But the effort is not always worth it since, in the end, as Alexis, a junior Gamma, like other ex-girlfriends, admitted, "You will almost always come in second place."

Most interesting about the drive for independence from women, however, is that it demonstrates, not the traditional notion of masculine independence, which eschews relationships of any sort with both men and women, but a new kind of masculine interdependence. Brothers' romantic relationships with women are discouraged because they pose the greatest threat to their fraternal relationships with other men.

Same-Sex Relationships

MALE INTERDEPENDENCE

On most counts, fraternities are one of the most traditional institutions in America. They reproduce many of the conventional themes of masculine identity. But, while the brothers can, unfortunately, be patriarchal, misogynistic, aggressive, violent, and homophobic, they can also be fiercely loyal, selfless, supportive, and dedicated to each other's welfare—all traditional attributes of femininity. And it is this aspect of Greek life—not beer or women—that brings alumni brothers back, year after year, searching for that connection with other men that is often sadly absent in their postcollege lives. As one Alpha alumni brother recently confessed to me: "You can't trust or depend on other guys in the real world. There's no brotherhood out there, that's for sure."

But what is brotherhood—this thing that every member claims is the essence of the fraternity experience? According to Markus, a senior Lambda, "Brotherhood is always knowing someone has got your back. They will always be there if you need them." For Bill, it's about having comrades "to always talk with and listen to. . . . They know everything about me, everything." "It's about being able to trust these guys with your life," David, a third-year Phi, thought. "I mean, we are not going to war, but anytime I need them—for the rest of my life—I can count on most of them." Finally, for Ray, the vice president at the Iota house, brotherhood is something more than just mere friendship: "It is so much more. Friends don't have a commitment to each other; brothers do. I will be there for them, all of them, even the brothers that I don't spend a lot of time with or even like that much. Friends don't think like that."

For Markus, Bill, David, Ray, and thousands of others, *brotherhood* is not a nebulous, abstract concept; it is a human bond, actualized in daily life. There are three independent component parts to the notion of brotherhood. First is meaningful self-disclosure and confidential communication, which are essential in establishing trust and an emotional connection among brothers. "We really know each other," Joshua asserted, "everything about each other . . . good and bad." Second is self-sacrifice for a brother in a time of need. "Anyone can be there when times are good," claimed Ray, "but a real brother will be there when hell breaks loose." Third is unconditional loyalty and devotion. "No matter what—whether he is wrong or right—I have his fuckin' back. That's brotherhood," proclaimed Eric. "That's what it's all about."

Surprisingly, the men I interviewed never mentioned drinking, womanizing, drug use, partying, or participating in panty raids as salient features of the fraternal experience. This is not to say that such things don't go on. But it is to say that they are not what keeps these young men coming back to each other. As my old fraternity adviser, John Williams, used to say: "Beer gets the boys in the door during rush, but brotherhood keeps them in for life."

The next obvious question, then, is, How is brotherhood formed? With so many in our society searching in vain for this type of human connection, how are these young, often crude and hedonistic men able to attain it? I have discovered at least four key factors that contribute to the formation of this interpersonal bond of brotherhood.

The Fraternity as Family. First, the use of the metaphor of fraternity brothers as family members within these organizations in framing their union with each other is crucial. There are, of course, "big brothers" and "little brothers"—the most sacred of "fraternal" bonds. There are also, however, "house mothers" (women who live in the house as caretakers), "pledge dads" (older brothers in charge of the pledging program), "founding fathers" (the founding members of the chapter), "little sisters" (women made honorary members),[2] "sister sororities" (organizations made honorary members), and "grandfathers" (big brothers who are at least one generation removed from little brothers). These family members congregate in a "house," not a complex, a unit, or a dorm. Alumni are encouraged to "come back home" every year for "reunions" where they share "family secrets" and discuss "black sheep" relatives. In short, there are all the linguistic ingredients needed for a healthy and happy extended family.

These appellations, however, are not just empty metaphors. As Lakoff and Johnson (2003) have convincingly argued, metaphors create and frame social reality. They supply the perspectives with which we view ourselves and others. For example, since argument is conceived of as war, it becomes war: when we argue, we "fight," we try to "win at all costs," we take "cheap shots," we "hit below the belt," we "shoot down" main points. Such language would be inconceivable if we conceived of argument as dance. Instead, we would be forced to "move together," "listen to the common music," and "coordinate our turns." *Argue* would become a verb meaning "two parties sacrificing individual desires to reach a mutually pleasing outcome." Considered in this light, the act of becoming a "brother" transforms a young man into a family member, and, as a family member, he deserves the unconditional support, trust, and lifelong devotion of the men who are not mere friends but his "brothers."

The power of the metaphor of fraternity brothers as family members is apparent, for example, in the loyalty these men demonstrate for brothers they personally dislike. As we often find in biological families, relatives may not always get along, but, in troubled times, they put their grievances aside for the good of the clan. So it goes with brotherhood. Last May, for instance, Derek, one of the least popular brothers at the Omega house, instigated a fight with some Psi brothers. Within two minutes, every one of Derek's brothers in the vicinity showed up ready to fight for their (often annoying and selfish) brother. Marshall, a senior Omega brother, explained: "With a fraternity as big as ours [there are eighty-five brothers], you are bound to get some guys you don't get along with. I'll be honest—Derek is a pain in the ass. But I'll tell you what. I would be there for each and every one of them if they need me. That's why I showed up to the fight. It is what being a brother is about. It's family. It's different than friendships. That is the responsibility you undertake, accept. 'Blood is thicker than water,' or something like that, as they say."[3]

Discovering Self-Disclosure and Intimate Friendships. Men in our culture generally self-disclose less, have fewer intimate friendships, are more reticent when it comes to expressing affection, touch less, and stand farther away during interpersonal encounters. This pattern of emotional isolation begins early in a boy's life. As Wood (1999) has argued, any young boy "who shows sensitivity or vulnerability is ridiculed as a sissy, a crybaby, a mama's boy or a whip" (p. 182), both in the classroom and on the playground. Consequently, as Kindlon and Thompson (2000) put it, men rarely develop an "emotional vocabulary that expands their ability to express themselves in ways other than anger or aggression" (p. 7).

By the time these boys become men, their relational isolation widens. Stein (1986) suggests that this is in part due to male competition, the lack of affective role models, and a need for control. Also, as Herek (1987), Lehne (1989), and Nardi (1992) argue, the stigma attached to homosexuality further leads many to become more reserved and isolated, denying the real importance of friendship with other men. The cumulative effect of all these factors is that, as Stewart, Cooper, Stewart, and Friedley (1998) argue, adult men struggle to develop "the qualities necessary to maintain meaningful relationships with other adult men" (p. 103).

This does not mean, however, that men do not desire meaningful interpersonal relationships. Men, "no less than [women], still need to feel emotional connection" (Kindlon & Thompson, 2000, p. 7). The problem is that our society offers them so few acceptable outlets for emotional expression. This is the main reason, I believe, why so many young boys participate in organized team sports, adolescents join street gangs and Internet chat rooms, and older men search out fraternal lodges (e.g., the Masons, the Shriners, the Elks) and philanthropic clubs (e.g., the Lions, the Knights of Columbus, Kiwanis) and join bowling and softball teams. We all want human connection.

It is this same desire to connect with others that draws so many young men to college fraternities. Once inside the safe and familial confines of their house, brothers—perhaps for the first and last time in their lives—begin to share, self-disclose, and listen to each other's stories. Such communicative activities are not just tolerated by Greeks; they are encouraged through both daily practices and sacred rituals.

Almost every daily practice that takes place in a fraternity revolves around talking. By their very nature, houses arrange large numbers of men in close proximity to one another. "When you are in our house, there is just no escaping each other," explained the Gamma brother Joseph. "Forget about privacy. There is someone always in your face." In virtually all these domiciles, the brothers are forced to eat together, shower together, and, on many campuses, even sleep together in one giant room, often the house's attic level, where bunk beds are lined up in military formation. These houses also have common living rooms, family/TV rooms, game rooms, libraries, computer rooms, and study rooms. And, as if this were not enough contact, many brothers admit that they often e-mail, instant message, and cell phone each other during their rare moments of privacy. As I have often joked, a fraternity house is ergonomically designed to force people to communicate. If a young man is not extroverted or social when he arrives, he will be when he leaves.

Not everyone, however, is thrilled with all the talking or what gets talked about. Allison, John's girlfriend, has come to realize that her love life is public knowledge at the Epsilon house. While she is impressed with the love the brothers share, she wishes that there were "some things that were still private" about their relationship: "They are very, very protective of each other. They talk about things that I would say normal guys would never discuss. John's brothers know everything about me, I would say. I mean everything about me. To the disturbing point that they share everything. Normal guys have locker-room talk, but these guys will sit down and talk about fear of commitment, sweet stuff that girls talk about with girlfriends."

Many fraternity rituals and structured activities also encourage self-disclosure and communicative vulnerability. For example, many chapters devote segments of their weekly meetings to the retelling of humorous stories or the airing of complaints, criticisms, and concerns. At the Alpha house, for example, brothers participate in a rap session called "For the Good of the Chapter." Each member is obligated to express what he feels is going right, going wrong, or needs improvement in the family. In my chapter, we similarly "Pass the Bone" after Monday-night dinners to highlight the weekend's more embarrassing, but always humorous, events.

There are, however, other more serious opportunities for communication. In one of the more moving rituals at the Kappa house, new pledge brothers are summoned at midnight by their big brothers. Once there, they are led into the ritual room, where the entire active chapter awaits. Much to their surprise, they are not hazed but talked to. Each person in the room, starting with the seniors, tells the group something deeply personal or painful about his life. Brothers share losses, defeats, deaths, heartbreaks, and humiliations they have never disclosed to any other man before. There are tears, hugs, lives, and love shared on that night. No one leaves unchanged.

The Beta brothers share a similar experience at their annual overnight retreat:

AD: So tell me about your retreats.
Nick: Each year—for years—we go away to a national park to talk. The brothers and pledges have to show up.
AD: What do you talk about?
Nick: Things that you did as kids that made you who you are now.
Mike: Family things and shit like that.
Josh: This year we had a brother talk about his religious commitment and how he is wrestling with that and the partying at the house.
Nick: A brother talked about having cancer.
Keith: Yeah, one of our brothers had testicular cancer. He's OK, had to get one of his balls removed or whatever [*nervous laughter*]. During the retreat, we all prayed with him for about thirty seconds. He's all right now, thank God.
Kevin: We had Joe talk about, he broke up with his girlfriend after five years. They were to be engaged, and he found out she was cheating on him the whole time.
Nick: It gets really heavy at times. But in a really great way.
Josh: Really heavy. I will never forget it, never. Heavy.

The quantity and quality of talking at fraternity houses is integral to the cultivation of brotherhood. These men are afforded four or five uninterrupted years of talking time in a safe, nonjudgmental, familial, and nurturing environment. Sadly, however, this type of meaningful communication will end after graduation for most of these young men. In the real world, they will be expected to act like the traditional American man, stoic, reticent, and self-sufficient. Their conversations will be reduced to the emotionally and spiritually vacant topics of sports, politics, and tits and ass. It is no wonder so many fraternity alumni look back on their days as active brothers as the best days of their lives.

Alcohol as Communicative Lubricant. Since these young men have been raised in a culture where personal disclosure is frowned on, they enter college without the linguistic or emotional repertoire needed for interpersonal intimacy. As Wood (2005) has argued, "Masculine socialization constrains men's comfort in verbally expressing some feelings and, further, . . . limits men's opportunities to practice emotional talk" (p. 171).

Once these young men move into their fraternity houses, however, these rules change. They are now asked to talk to other men about their internal lives. While many are excited to finally have this opportunity, they are also apprehensive at the thought of such personal risk taking. Not surprisingly, then, the vast majority claimed to rely on alcohol's lubricating effects to make them "less self-conscious" and "more talkative." "I think it just lets you let your guard down," theorized Coop. "You don't worry so much about the images that you're putting off to people. You just open up." "Yeah, me and Coop never use to talk about serious shit," Justin chimed in. "But we kept finding ourselves the last two drunks up at every party. We pull up two chairs by the door and sit all night and drink and talk. He is like my best friend now." According to David and his brothers, "Beers relax you. You don't stress about shit, so we start talking more. If you are just sitting around sober, no one really ever opens up, but, after a few beers, you can't shut any of us up." Johnson further expanded on the necessity of alcohol: "It's not like we haven't tried to do it without drinks. A few times, these sororities would invite us to these dry events. They sucked. No one talked, interacted. Everyone just left. It was gay."

Of course no one wants a gay event. So alcohol is used to facilitate communication and interaction. The Deltas, for example, always bring beer to their chapter retreats to guarantee both attendance and bonding. "The first thing we did this year," the Delta pledge trainer told me, "was to get our pledges and go down to [a small rural town] for a brotherhood thing. It was great. We all got to know each other a lot better. We had a couple of kegs, sat around all night and got shit-faced and just shot the shit. It worked!" And booze does seem to work. I have been told hundreds of times how alcohol "loosens you up," "makes you less controlled," "frees you to be more honest," "blocks everything else out," "helps you focus and talk," and "lets you be more affectionate." "I hug everyone when I'm drunk," confessed Mark.

This is not to imply that Greek men drink only to reinforce the bonds of brotherhood. Many proudly admitted to drinking three or four times a week for the sole purpose of "getting shit-faced," "picking up babes," "letting off some steam," or just "having fun." Alcohol has essentially become a constant at Greek gatherings, whether the event is a party, a sporting event (watching or playing), a charity fund-raiser, a formal dance, a retreat, an alumni reunion, founder's day, parents' day, or a stay-at-home TV night. In fact, most houses now sponsor "predrinking" gatherings to guarantee that no one shows up to anything sober.

This is also not to imply that the amount of drinking that goes on in fraternities is not a serious social problem. In my twenty-five years of involvement with the Greek system, the vast majority of all deaths, accidents, date rapes, fights, arrests, incidents of property damage, injuries, and academic failures that I have had to deal with have involved alcohol abuse. Unfortunately, GU is not an anomaly. The National Advisory Council on Alcohol Abuse and Alcoholism has found that most college campuses are breeding grounds for binge drinking, the consequences of which can be devastating, if not deadly. For example, one study (Hingson, Heeren, Zakocs, Kopstein & Wechsler, 2002) reported that, each year, among college students between the ages of eighteen and twenty-four:

- 1,400 die from alcohol-related injuries (including automobile accidents);
- 500,000 are injured while under the influence of alcohol;

- more than 600,000 are assaulted by another student who has been drinking;
- more than 70,000 are the victims of alcohol-related sexual assault;
- 400,000 have unprotected sex while under the influence of alcohol; and
- 100,000 report being too intoxicated to know whether they have had sex at all.

Other studies (Engs, Diebold & Hansen, 1996; Presley, Meilman & Cashin, 1996; Wechsler et al., 2002) reported:

- about 25 percent of college students missing class, falling behind, doing poorly on exams or papers, and receiving lower grades overall because of their drinking.

And one study (Knight et al., 2002) reported:

- 31 percent of college students meeting the criteria for a diagnosis of alcohol abuse, and 6 percent meeting the criteria for a diagnosis of alcohol dependence, in the past twelve months.[4]

As disturbing as these finding are, every significant study conducted in the last thirty years has found that drinking by Greeks is even more excessive and produces more deleterious effects than the drinking done by the non-Greek college population. As Cashin, Presley, and Meilman (1998) found in their analysis of the drinking habits of over twenty-five thousand students on sixty-one different campuses, "Students in the Greek system averaged significantly more drinks per week, engaged in heavy drinking more often and, with minor exceptions, suffered more negative consequences than non-Greeks" (p. 63). This is no mere coincidence. For, as Eagly (1978) and Moos (1979), have argued, groups (such as fraternities) that reinforce and reward traditional masculinity typically abuse alcohol more often. After all, real men always pound back the beers before raising hell and getting laid. The lyrics of some of the more popular Greek drinking songs highlight the connection between alcohol consumption, antisocial behavior, and misogyny:[5]

The Drinking Song (a.k.a. *The Raise Hell Song*)
Drink beer, drink beer
Oh, come drink beer with me.
For I don't give a damn for any old man,
who won't drink beer with me.
Bring out the old golden goblet
with the Sig Ep heart upon it,
and we'll all have another keg of beer!
For it's not for knowledge
that we come to college,
but to raise hell while we're
raise hell while we're
raise hell while we're here.
Oh, we will drink, drink, drink to Epsilon
and we will raise our glasses high;
And we'll drink to our fraternity,
and we'll be loyal 'til we die, until we die.
Oh, how we love our sacred brotherhood,
and we will laud it to the sky.
And when the day is done we'll drink just one,
to Sigma Phi Epsilon!

The Virgin Song
She was a virgin in her freshman year
She was a virgin with her conscience clear
She never smoked nor drank nor necked nor petted
She was the sweetheart of the campus you can bet!
Until she met that guy from Sigma Chi

Who took away her virginity.
So let's drink, drink, drink, drink, Sigma Chi![6]

Pledging and Hazing. Without exception, every one of the thousands of brothers I have known across America has identified the fraternity hazing process as *the* key to brotherhood. "Take pledging away," I was told, "and fraternities will die. They will be nothing more than a club, a sorority, a bunch of strangers sharing a house."

But what constitutes hazing? According to the Kappa Alpha Order, one of the oldest and largest international fraternities in the country, *illegal hazing* is defined as "any conduct, activities or action . . . causing . . . physical or mental discomfort, chagrin, embarrassment, ridicule, or personal displeasure" (KA Laws, Title 9-261). Supplying a more detailed description, the North American Interfraternity Council (the governing board for the nation's 350,000 active fraternity members) identified twenty-four of the most historically popular and dangerous hazing practices, everyone of which I have witnessed, sometimes on numerous occasions, as a younger brother:

- Forced or required consumption of alcoholic or non-alcoholic beverages or substances.
- Forced or required consumption of spoiled foods, raw onions, goldfish, or any unpalatable foods which an individual refuses to eat.
- Dropping food such as eggs, grapes, liver, etc. in mouths.
- Tying individuals to chairs, poles, or other objects.
- Simulated or actual branding of individuals against their will.
- Causing excessive fatigue through physical or psychological shocks, such as forced participation in extreme exercise beyond normal ability.
- Paddling new members.

- Pushing, shoving, tackling, or any other kind of physical abuse not associated with events of an athletic nature.
- Throwing any toxic or otherwise harmful substance at an individual.
- Line-ups, any form of verbal abuse, or any other activity which serves no constructive purpose.
- Deception of new members prior to the ritual which is designed to convince a pledge/associate member that he will not be initiated or that he will be injured during the ritual ceremony.
- Any individual or group interrogations of a negative nature.
- Creating areas that are extremely uncomfortable due to temperature, noise, size, or air quality.
- Assigning or endorsing pranks such as panty-raids, harassing another organization, etc.
- Assigning or endorsing an activity that is illegal or unlawful, that would constitute theft, burglary, or trespassing, or that would be morally objectionable to an individual.
- Conducting quests, treasure hunts, scavenger hunts, paddle hunts, big sister hunts, or little sister hunts that include illegal activity, physical abuse, or psychological abuse.
- Requiring pledge/associate members to march in formation.
- Carrying useless items such as coconuts, helmets, swords, burlap bags, shields, paddles, rocks, dog collars, bricks, etc.
- Assigning or endorsing the wearing of apparel in public which is conspicuous and not normally in good taste.
- Requiring or endorsing the pledge/associate members to yell or chant when entering or leaving the chapter house.
- Requiring memorization of non-fraternity and non-academic related materials.
- Assigning or endorsing public stunts or buffoonery.
- Requiring or encouraging pledge/associate members to act like animals or other objects.
- Requiring pledge/associate members to participate in the act of flouring and/or showering other members.[7]

The Kappa Alpha Fraternity and the North American Interfraternity Council, however, are not alone in their public condemnation of hazing. Every college, university, and national fraternity in America has also publicly denounced hazing—a legal necessity given the litigious nature of contemporary society. Privately, however, most administrators admit that it is still practiced—and those who claim that it is not are either duplicitously cautious or woefully removed from the lives of their students. And a number of nationally prominent fraternity leaders and university officials have confessed to me that hazing will, they believe, be around as long as fraternities are around—it is part of the Greek culture—and that the best they can do is to implore chapters practicing it to do so more safely, less cruelly and abusively, and, above all, as inconspicuously as possible.

Ironically, the only stakeholders who seem not to condemn hazing are the people who have actually been hazed. Jacob, a senior Lambda brother, for instance, saw the process as not just a useful but a necessary teaching tool: "What we do really is show them that they have to rely on each other, trust each other, no matter what. You need to pledge [i.e., haze], there is no substitute. They can't read a book and learn it." For many, this process is analogous to military training. "Yeah it's tough," confessed Warren, "but it has to be. When they come out the other end, they are brothers. Like the HBO movie *Band of Brothers* [a miniseries about soldiers in World War II]. Those guys in war are bonded together forever."

Others see pledging as military boot camp, the preparation for war, not war itself. The Gammas, Alphas, and Sigmas even take their "pukes" to a local military training area and have them run through actual U.S. Army obstacle courses. Keith, the pledge trainer for the Sigmas, conceived of himself as the chapter's drill sergeant, "trying to bring a bunch of maggots together and make them brothers": "Yes, there is a lot of humiliation and yelling and shit, but it is like what the army does. We have to break them down as individuals before we build them up as a group. There is a lot of psychological shit." He later elaborated on the process: "We line them up, yell in their faces that they are scum and that they are not making the cut. Sometimes they have to eat nasty shit: Cow stomach, hot sauce, pigs' feet, raw fish, Limburger cheese. We also run them through a lot of exercising—like the military. They start throwing up. They think they are going to die. But it is through stuff like this, they learn—become brothers. I know it sounds fucked up, but, if you have never gone through it, you just don't get it."

Not every house, however, uses such extreme measures. The Nu brothers primarily focus on group activities. "We are a little different," asserted Christopher. "We got in big trouble years ago for hazing, so we really don't any more. When we see a pledge class start to break apart, we make them spend the night together in the chapter room." He tells me, "The pledges do fun things, little leadership activities and stuff." We make them "wrestle each other," "go on scavenger hunts," "serenade sororities," "play sports together."

But not everyone is convinced that brotherhood can be formed through such benign and fun activities. "The Nus are pussies," I was told by Robert, a confessed "old-school" Gamma. "If pledging is fun and you are never tested to see what you are worth or what you are really made of, you will never be a man." The Xi brother Anthony also believes that pledging has to be "tough work or it's a waste. People only take pride in the things they work for, you know? You have to feel like you accomplished something that others didn't."

The perceived benefits of such arduous initiation practices do not end after graduation. Many that I talked to, like the Rho brothers, believed that it will continue to pay dividends long after they leave school. "If you can make it through pledging, you can do anything, just about anything in life," said Thomas. "You may think that's a bold statement," interjected Nathan, "but I think that it's piece of mind you earn. You did something big, so the next big thing that comes in front of you, you're like, 'Been there, done that.'" "It's confidence in yourself," concluded Brain. "Pledging is something no one can ever take away from you. It is something that you and your brothers did together."

It is the rare American experience of masculine intimacy—produced by the framing of the fraternity as a family, the intimate self-disclosure, the alcohol consumption, and the hazing—that more than any other phenomenon of Greek life fascinates me. Even given the dysfunction that characterizes many fraternities, the camaraderie and the unconditional love found within them have the power to turn emotionally disconnected boys into caring and loving brothers. How paradoxical. One of the last bastions of traditional American masculinity practices—indeed, embraces—the best qualities of traditional American femininity.

Women

Opposite-Sex Relationships

One of the primary cultural imperatives is that a woman be relationally linked to a man and a family (Stewart et al., 1998, p. 45; Wood, 2005, pp. 140–142). As Betty Friedan (1963) observed over forty years ago, nothing disturbs our society more than seeing an unmarried, childless woman. She is linguistically framed as an *old maid,* a *spinster,* a *dyke, godforsaken,* and *barren,* unlike a single man without children, who is rhetorically rewarded by being framed as a *playboy,* a *stud,* a *bachelor,* a *gigolo,* or a *player.* Responding to such social pressure, generations of affluent American women have attended college hoping to find educated, wealthy husbands.

To listen to GU's white, middle-class sorority women tell it, however, life is, not a quest to find a man, but a journey rife with opportunities. Like their male counterparts, most admit that they would like to get married someday, but, before settling down, they want to have careers and enjoy the single life. According to the U.S. Bureau of the Census (2004), this trend of waiting longer before marriage has spread nationwide. When Friedan wrote *The Feminine Mystique* in 1963, the average age at marriage was twenty for women (twenty-four for men). In 2006, the average bride is twenty-five (the average groom twenty-seven).

Why are women waiting longer, and what are they waiting for? To find out, I asked some of the best and brightest women in America to discuss the relational pressures of being young, female, and educated.

THE IDEAL MAN

When asking these women how they conceived of ideal femininity, the vast majority responded by discussing the importance of marriage and family. "Life as a woman," Janet remarked, "would be terrible, lonely without a family. So, of course, I think that being a woman means being a mom and a wife. But we all have to choose what we want." Rachel viewed the connection between femininity and motherhood as no mere choice but, rather, a sacred contract with God: "I think that women were made to have children. We are not only physically able, but I think God gave us all a maternal drive. Some women may not pay attention to it, but it is why I think we are here on earth." For Alice, being a wife and mother is the only really important thing in life. "If I die and I am not a millionaire, or if my house isn't the biggest, so what? But, if I die and I am not surrounded by my husband and family, lots of grandkids, well, that must be the saddest thing."

The men they envision themselves with in this happily-ever-after scenario, however, are not the horny, drunken brothers of their college years. They are traditional, masculine, and romantic men. Most of the hundreds of women I interviewed agreed on the five most important attributes that they are looking for in a mate: he should be physically attractive, a gentleman and a romantic, not *too* emotional, a good father and provider, and macho (representative samples of their views on desirable male attributes appear below).

Physical Attractiveness

"Yes, I want my man to be hot!"

"Muscles and a nice ass."

"Brad Pitt would be nice."

"He does not have to be beautiful, but I have to be attracted to him. He has to be cute. Not fat or hairy. Not bald."

Gentlemanly/Romantic

"He has to be a gentleman too. I don't want a husband who sits on the couch and farts and watches football all day—classier and romantic."

"I want someone who will hold the door open for me. Buy me flowers. Spoil me."

"My dad is a great guy. I want him [the man I marry] to be polite, respectful, a real gentleman like my dad."

"I guess a guy who is a little old-fashioned. You know, he does all those things that boys don't do anymore . . . hold the door open, surprise me with gifts, be polite."

Not Too Emotional

"I want him to be sensitive, but not a crybaby or anything."

"I have a boyfriend who is like emotional, telling me everything he's thinking. Like, No, stop it, don't cry. And it's just, he's like right there borderline to the point of being too emotionally expressive."

"I want a man who is willing to show emotion. I saw my dad cry one time, and it was when my mom didn't think she was going to live. I mean, I want my husband to do that. If I'm about to die."

Good Father and Provider

"I tell you what I don't want. I don't want to be the only one to take care of the kids and the house. I want a husband who will do his share of the work."

"If I can find a man who will love me and his kids, a family guy that loves that, that's key."

"Money is not the most important, but he has to have a good future. We won't want to struggle."

"He has to be a good provider. I'll work too, but, when the kids come, he has to be able to make enough for all of us. OK, how about a doctor or lawyer [*laughing*]."

Macho

"He has to be nice, and kind. But he still has to act like a man. Contrary to what you men think, we still want our men to act like men."

"My boyfriend is like really buff. He's a man's man. Everyone loves him. All the men love him because he plays ball and stuff. But he doesn't have *Playboy* magazines in his room."

"This is terrible to say, but I am never attracted to those nice boys. I like my man to be kinda macho. I want him to sweat, play sports, have muscles. I love that male thing. Like Brad Pitt in *Fight Club* . . . or Russell Crowe in that gladiator movie."

What is most striking about this list is how traditional it reads. These women want a Prince Charming on steroids who will provide for, care for, and intrigue them. Interestingly, what they do *not* seem to be looking for is a man who can be a friend, a companion, a kindred spirit. Unlike the men in this study, who are, in fact, looking for kindred spirits in their mates, the women seem not to prioritize such a connection so highly. They prefer the strong, silent type, the father figure.

These findings are consistent with the gender differences uncovered in much recent research on friendship and marriage. Studies have found, for example, that men are more likely to consider their wives to be their best friends (Brehm, 1992) and eight times more likely to commit suicide after divorce (Kposowa, 2000). Women, on the other hand, are more likely to marry for reasons other than love (Cancian, 1987), have a less romantic notion of marriage (Brehm, 1992), and are more likely to confide in their female friends than in their husbands (Rubin, 1985).

Would these women agree that there are such gender differences? Surprisingly, many did. In a series of follow-up interviews further exploring this question, I was told that, as important as men are in their lives, strong female friendships are irreplaceable. Alice, for instance, thought, "Women just know each other better. It just makes sense that we understand each other in ways men can't [understand us]. . . . Men and women are just different." For Maggie, it was the woman's need for conversation and connection that makes other women invaluable: "One thing that I learned living in the house is that women, like, need to talk a lot more. Most men don't; they hate it. They would rather go drinking or play sports than talk. . . . So that's why girlfriends are so important."

Deborah saw this relational pattern already forming among the young, unmarried women she knows. Her sisters may have boyfriends, she argued, but they are not their best friends: "OK, I know a lot of girls that like have boyfriends, but they don't hang out with them, or it's like they really don't like each other. I mean, they like or love each other, but I am not sure most of them would pick each other as the one person they want on the desert island with them. I think most enjoy the company of their sisters more. . . . And I am sure the guys would say the same thing. Guys just have more in common with their buds." It appears, therefore, that the sorority sisters I interviewed view same-sex friendships and opposite-sex romantic relationships in much the same way as the majority of women in America do. Men are necessary to fulfill specific roles in a woman's romantic life, but female friends retain their primary interpersonal importance, long after the marriage vows have been taken.

Most of these sisters also feel no immediate pressure to get married and have children. They all seem to agree that there will be more than enough time later on to worry about settling down. "I really don't see myself getting married," admitted Anne Marie, "until I am in a job and can support myself, maybe twenty-seven, twenty-eight." As for Becky: "Marriage will probably come in five years, or more. I don't think our generation feels that pressure the way our moms did." "Our moms were all married so early," agreed Susanna. "Mine was married and pregnant by eighteen years old. Today we all see what went wrong, you know, women getting married when they haven't even lived yet. No wonder there are so many divorces." For Allison, however, it was not the *women's* immaturity that is the problem: "Men are just five years behind us. The reason that more of us aren't engaged is because these *boys* are just still idiots." She catches me laughing and responds, "You know I'm right, you know it!"

So if these young women are not looking for husbands right now, what *are* they looking for? Roughly half claimed to want a boyfriend, not because they need a man to complete them or to give them a sense of worth, but simply because life is nicer with one around. "I am not looking for a husband," claimed Robin. "I just like having a boyfriend to talk with . . . to play with . . . to kiss." Lauren's take on things was that a boy gives her things her sisters can't: "I can't go on dates with Lisa, here [*pointing to her sorority sister*]. I can't curl up on the couch and snuggle with her. . . . Boys are fun in different ways, that's all." Erin considered having a boyfriend simply less complicated than dating around: "Having a steady is just easier. Guys are shady, you know. It just is easier having a steady guy you can count on. I guess it's comfortable."

Almost as many claimed to want nothing more than "a simple date." "Is that asking too much?" an exasperated Katie asked. "We don't want a husband—*calm down guys*—we just want to go on a date." Time after time, I heard the same thing. If Mr. Right comes along, fine. But what many of these bright, personable young women want is to have a good time, to be treated decently by men, and to go on an old-fashioned date. They are tired of hooking up at bars, going out en masse, hanging out, and worrying about whether they will have an escort to the next sorority date party. The Kappa Jessica, an English major, even poetically offered her "'kingdom for a date.' That's not too much to ask, is it now?"

Along with finding the independent-minded Katies and Jessicas of GU, I also discovered a less independent group of women who wanted more than an occasional date or a boyfriend to have fun with. These "chronic daters," as many of their sisters have labeled them, *need* to be in a relationship. Their numbers are small, probably no more than a fifth of the Greek population, but their reputations are well known. In fact, almost every focus group had stories of such addicted sisters. "It's like that's the only thing that's important to them," claimed Devon. "They're miserable unless they have a boy. And, when they do, we never see them anymore." A good example is the infamous Jackie from the Theta house, whose habitual dating had become the target of sorority humor: "Question: What does Jackie bring on a first date? Answer: Her suitcase." There is also Elizabeth from the Pi house, who had had five boyfriends in her life, each relationship lasting two years. Her sisters were positive that she had "never spent a night or weekend alone." "I don't think she even keeps a toothbrush at her house," her Pi sisters playfully razzed.

Less humorous are the sisters who are so desperate for male companionship that they allow themselves to be "shit on" by their boyfriends. I heard too many stories of young women who remain in unhealthy, destructive relationships just to be in relationships. "Everyone knows when a guy is stepping out," explained Wanda. "The Greek community is a pretty tight-knit group. We all know." The only ones who didn't know, it seems, were the girlfriends. "It's like they don't want to know," elaborated Kim. "I can't tell you how many times I have told some of my sisters about the dogs [cheaters] they date, and they always make excuses for them." "I think deep down inside they know," speculated Donna, "but they rationalize.

Like they need that boy so bad that they look the other way or say it's just gossip. . . . All he needs to say is, 'No baby,' and she believes him."

Perhaps the most interesting finding to surface, however, is that steady boyfriends are *not* institutionally prized or rewarded, regardless of the occasional candlelighting ritual. Similar to the sentiments echoed by fraternity brothers—but not as protective, jealous, or severe—were sorority sisters' views of most long-term relationships as anathema to sisterhood. "I hate it," announced Beth. "These sisters get boyfriends and forget all about everything else. They make terrible sisters." Mary took it more personally: "When a sister finds a guy and drops off the face of the earth, it's a slap in the face, like she was just using us until something better shows up." There are strategies, however, that can be employed to deflect such sisterly criticism. First and foremost, a dating sister must make sure to balance her time. "If a sister makes sure not to forget her girls," Sissy explained, "then most of us are cool about it." But spend every night at his house, and "you are going to get shit for it." Aware of the importance of this balancing act, Erin made it a point to "never spend more than one night in a row at Michael's house. No matter what, I go home and eat and hang with my sisters."

When it comes to the cultural imperative that women be dependent, most sorority houses (with the exception of two very conservative groups that earnestly recruit marriage-minded women) seem to be places of refuge from the unwanted pressure to marry that these women will face in their postcollege lives. Most sorority women are far more concerned with their grades, their social lives, and their weight than they are with getting married and starting a family. This does not mean, however, that Friedan's thesis is obsolete. Women are simply free to wait longer before the pressure to marry kicks in. I have talked to far too many unmarried alumnae over the past few decades who testify to the looks of horror and judgmental questions (e.g., "Why aren't you married yet?") they receive daily to believe that there has been any significant change in society's expectations of women. They are still seen, first and foremost, as wives and mothers.

Same-Sex Relationships

SISTERHOOD IS NOT LIKE BROTHERHOOD

That "sisterhood is not like brotherhood," as Elisa put it, may come as something of a surprise to some people. In fact, the overwhelming majority of sisters I interviewed agreed that the bonds between brothers are significantly richer and more emotional than those between sisters.[8] "I guarantee you," argued Patricia, a senior Gamma, "that you pull a guy from one of the top fraternities on campus, and they can name everyone in the fraternity. And that is not true with us." For Jessica, a junior Omega sister, it is more than just knowing names that makes fraternities "better"; it is their commitment to each other: "I mean, I love my sisters, but it is different. I mean, we know each other, but we don't know each other the way these boys do. My boyfriend is a Psi brother, and he is crazy. I mean, I know he will keep in touch with all his brothers. We won't. We won't even try after graduation. It just means something more to them. We're like girlfriends. But they're like family. Yeah, I hate to admit it, but fraternities are better. Everyone knows it." What makes this discovery most surprising is that the overwhelming majority of research on female-female non-Greek friendships has found just the opposite (e.g., Campbell, 2002; Taylor, 2002). Female friends are more communicative (Aries & Johnson, 1983), share more details of their lives with each other (Rubin, 1985; Schaef, 1981), and maintain intimacy over time better (Becker, 1987) than male-male relationships.

How, then, can the comparative lack of connection in sororities be explained? The interview and focus group evidence suggest that there are at least four contributing factors:

Size Matters. Part of the explanation of why fraternities are more bonded than sororities is the size of the organizations. Across the nation, elite sororities are significantly larger than elite fraternities. At GU, for instance, the top seven sororities average 130 members, with the largest three numbering over 170 sisters each. The top seven fraternities, on the other hand, average only 65 members, with only one numbering over 100 brothers.

This discrepancy in size is due to two factors. First, there are more incoming first-year women than first-year men interested in joining Greek organizations. It is not uncommon to have over eight hundred potential pledges visit GU's twenty sororities during the first week of fall semester. The nineteen fraternities usually get less than half that number and are ecstatic to get four hundred potential pledges.

Second, sororities put a great deal of energy and effort into expanding their membership. Spurring this drive for growth, the university assigns each sorority a "target quota" that is based on size and past performance. Not "making quota," as it is commonly referred to, is both publicly humiliating and a source of mean-spirited humor on the part of other sororities. Consequently, each house works diligently throughout the summer preparing for rush week. As for the fraternities, quality seems to be far more important than quantity. Not only does the administration not assign quotas to the fraternities, but there is also far less competition among fraternities over size. In fact, those fraternities perceived as having too many members are accused of lowering their standards or being dumping grounds for misfits. Most freely admit that they would rather have twenty studs than fifty losers. For a fraternity's reputation is based, not on size, but on the selective criteria used in determining membership.

The Formation of Cliques: Smaller May Be Better. In their classic 1982 study, Maltz and Borker argue that children's schoolyard play prepares the genders for adulthood differently. Boys' play is marked by larger groups and is driven by clearly delineated rules and roles (e.g., baseball, football), while girls' play is marked by smaller groups and conducted without clear-cut goals or rules (e.g., playing house, vet, store). It stands to reason, then, that, since Greek organizations are nothing if not structured and rule driven, young men entering college are ideally prepared to manage fraternity life and young women ill prepared to manage sorority life.

This may explain why so many of GU's sororities tend to segment into smaller, more intimate cliques. As I have witnessed often over the years, many of the women find the sisterhood that exists between smaller groups of sisters who share common beliefs, backgrounds, and experiences more meaningful than the sisterhood that embraces the entire chapter regardless of personal differences. And it is *these* friendships that withstand the test of time. As alumna Audrey sees it, "Men may be tighter with more of their brothers, but I think the friendships that I have with my *best* sisters are just as strong, if not stronger."

Competition and Cattiness. When I first heard the critique leveled by the men in this study, I dismissed it as sexist. When I encountered it again in the research of Eichenbaum and Orbach (1987), Miller (1987), and Rubin (1985), I began to wonder whether it just might be true. And, when almost every sorority focus group and female interviewee echoed it, I was forced to take it seriously. The fact that sorority women are "so catty you wouldn't believe it," as Abby, a Pi, put it, may well be a barrier to the formation of true sisterhood. Janice, a Sigma, also found them "catty and backstabbing," Susan, an Omega, considered them "nasty gossipers about each other," and Elizabeth, a Beta, branded them "bitches." Michelle, another Sigma, characterized them as "competitive" and "jealous of each other," Karen, an Iota, felt that they were "envious of girls who are prettier than they are," and Josie, a Zeta, accused them of being "jealous when another sister is happier, skinner, more popular, whatever." They "fight each other for attention when boys are around," according to Lisa, a Mu, "hate it if someone is getting more attention at the bars," as Hannah, a Tau, reported, and are, in the opinion of Taylor, a Kappa, "always looking to see who is skinner or who is dressed better or is cuter." Erin, a Phi sister and a women's studies major, summarized the problem: "Women are their own worst enemy at times. They produce 95 percent of the bad drama in their own lives, and most of it is worrying about men. It breaks my heart to say, but it is true."

"Guys," Erin assured me, "do not act like that with each other. They are taught differently in pledging." "Brothers," a thoughtful Jessica remarked, "pull together, not apart. They don't fight with each other; they fight with other fraternities. It is like them against the world." Similarly, Margaret from the Rho house sees brothers championing each other far more often: "Guys seem to be happy for each other—you know, unless the brother is a real dick—when things happen for them." They are not like sorority sisters: "They don't seem to be so catty and hurtful. They're different. Less sneaking and gossipy like."

One possible explanation for this difference may be a matter of cultural scripts that encourage men to be direct, honest, and unambiguous, and women to be more nurturing and nonconfrontational, when disputes arise (Tannen, 1990, pp. 149–187). As John claimed, "Only little pussies talk behind your back. If we have a problem, we deal with it and move on." Women, however, are not given the liberty of openly and honestly confronting their sisters when problems arise; rather, they are pressured either to remain silent or to air their grievances to their friends behind closed doors. As Jenna, a senior Xi sister, saw it, "Guys are more honest. If they don't like you or what you did, they will tell you and get it out there and get over it. Girls won't do that. They will run around to each other and never confront the girl. I hate that."

What the gender differences in cultural scripts do not explain, however, is the source of the cattiness and backstabbing: the attention of men. Disputes among sisters are, sad to say, not over such substantive issues as reproductive rights, career options, politics, or racist attitudes. They are over who looks better, who gets more attention, who is thinner, who sleeps around. And, as absurd as it may seem, these disputes are rarely over a particular man; most often they are over acceptance among and popularity with men generally. "We all want to be liked," Jessie confessed. "We want to be the prettiest and the thinnest because we think that it will get us more attention. I know it is screwed up, but what can I say? Sorry."[9]

The Lack of Pledging. A final explanation for this lack of sisterhood is the absence of sorority hazing. While the practice can still be found on smaller campuses or within isolated pockets on larger campuses, the old rituals of abuse and humiliation have become history for most sororities. As a substitute, GU's sororities have introduced a new system that is the polar opposite of the old: pledges are now coddled and spoiled by their older sisters. Far from eating goldfish, dressing in trash bags, or getting paddled, today's pledges— now officially called *initiates*—receive weekly gift baskets filled with such items as clothes, cookies, candies, picture frames, gift certificates, and Greek paraphernalia. They are taken to lunches, dinners, movies, and parties and are indulged in every imaginable way throughout the course of their pledge semester.

While the new form of initiation may sound like a more effective way to inculcate the values of an organization, it does not result in the level of sisterhood and selflessness that are yielded by hazing. "What the hell does giving a picture frame do for sisterhood?" Vanessa sarcastically asked. "It's silly. Even worse, it's meaningless. No one gets anything out of it." "We need to start pledging again," argued Lisa, a senior Omega. "I know we would have less girls come out for rush, but pledging would be great. I think we would be much tighter, like the boys." Speaking from experience, Annemarie explained to her Kappa sisters how her high school sorority "did it right." She and her fellow pledges were made to "mud wrestle," "wear a shower curtain," and "dress like a bumblebee" at school. She admits that while it was humiliating—especially the day they "dumped big buckets of food" on her—"you become really tight with the girls, I mean really." "When you go through that stuff," she concluded, "you feel different with each other. Like you all did the same thing and made it."

Even responsible alumni sisters with families and careers want to see the female pledge program reinstated. Misty, an Alpha sister (class of 1984), could not believe how things have changed for the worse: "These girls are great, beautiful, blah, blah, blah, but they suck. Nobody pledges anymore, so sororities are nothing more than girls' clubs. They do nothing that makes them respect their chapter; there's nothing they have to do." Her sister Clarisse (class of 1987) agreed and thought that, without the hazing they both went through, "the [sorority] experience would be less important and meaningful" to them. "Misty and I probably wouldn't even be friends like we are today without what we went through together."

As much as I want to believe that there is a better way of form- ing human bonds than hazing, I am forced to agree with Annema- rie, Misty, Clarisse, and the American military. Pledging, with all its flaws, still produces an inexplicable connection between both the abusees and the abusers. And, as most of GU's Greeks, male or fe- male, would agree, it is the absence of sorority pledging that is the primary reason why "sisterhood is not like brotherhood."

Conclusion

Of the five gender themes identified as my focus of study in this book, only relational independence versus dependence proved not to be an accurate predictor of the behavior of the men and women in the GU Greek system. Rather, an interesting inversion of the culturally pre- scribed patterns of masculinity and femininity was uncovered. The men rejected individuality and embraced intimacy, confessing to the desire for a female lover to share their lives with, and demonstrating emotional ties to their brothers that are rare among men generally. The women embraced individuality and rejected intimacy, admit- ting to being too preoccupied with professional success and self-ac- tualization to be concerned with marriage and too judgmental and nonsupportive to form the kind of true friendships that constitute sisterhood.

These unexpected patterns, however, begin to fade soon after graduation. Of the hundreds of alumni brothers and sisters I've talked with over the last quarter century, most admitted to having lost touch with the majority of their Greek family. Many sadly confessed to exchanging only the occasional phone call or the obligatory Christmas card. And, while the men seemed more surprised by the failure to maintain their fraternal bonds, the women too were shocked that such meaningful friendships could be so quickly and easily severed after graduation. Lack of contact, however, should not be taken as a sign of indifference. Most alumni readily admit to thinking often and warmly of their brothers and sisters. "I miss them. I miss them all," claimed Alex (class of 1977). "Real life is just too crazy to do anything about it." For Mark, my own old fraternity roommate, it is the combination of family, work, and distance that makes the maintenance of old friendships seemingly impossible: "I thought I would be in touch with our brothers forever. Hell, I don't even talk to you anymore—what, once every few years? I'll tell you, I don't have enough time for Alice [his wife] and the kids. Where am I going to find time for anything else? It's definitely not the way we thought it was going to be. I thought we would all grow old together, didn't you?"

In the end, the old friendships of adult Greeks resemble most old friendships of adult independents. With the passage of time, we all seem to drift away from each other, and we all regret the lost connections and broken promises of lifelong ties. The only difference is that Greeks tend to set their sights higher than do independents, expecting to maintain their bonds with more people.

6. Soccer Moms and Corporate Dads

The dirty little college secret rarely discussed by professors in mixed company is that women generally outperform men in the classroom. They work harder, think more critically, are less dogmatic, approach school more seriously, score higher on exams, write better, and are more pleasant and collegial in class. In my classrooms over the last ten years, for example, women have earned 84 percent of the As in my upper-division courses. They also constitute 94 percent of my department's honor society and control thirty-one of the top thirty-five spots on the department's GPA ranking.[1] Across the GU campus, women similarly excel. The all-male GPA is 2.81, the all-female GPA 3.0. This gender gap in performance is even more pronounced in GU's Greek system. As table 3 illustrates, sorority sisters academically outperform fraternity brothers from their freshman year through graduation.

Table 3. Fraternity and Sorority GPA Distribution

	Fraternities	Sororities
Overall GPA	2.74	3.15
New members	2.62	3.06
Returning members	2.83	3.24

GU students are not anomalies. National statistics from elementary schools, high schools, and colleges testify to a gender gap in intelligence (statistics taken from Hacker, 2003, pp. 79–87):

- Among the high school seniors who took the SAT test in 2000, 43.7 percent of the girls had A averages, compared with 35.3 percent of the boys.
- Among high school seniors, 74.1 percent of the girls devote at least an hour each day to their homework, compared with 57.4 percent of the boys.

- Among high school seniors, 6.8 percent of girls devote an hour or more each day to video games, compared with 19.2 percent of boys.
- For every 100 boys now in an advanced placement course, there are 124 girls.
- For every 100 boys now in academic honor societies, there are 158 girls.
- Women now earn 57 percent of all B.A.'s awarded in America.
- Since 1970, female enrollment has steadily increased at Brown, Columbia, Cornell, Dartmouth, Harvard, Pennsylvania, Princeton, Stanford, and Yale. During the same period, male enrollment has decreased.

As unfair as it may seem, most of these more prepared, harder-working women will take the proverbial back seat in the public sphere to less learned men. According to Hacker (2003, pp. 165, 168), for instance, the earnings of women working full-time are 27 percent less than those of men working full-time. And, while men hold the majority of high-paying professional positions (e.g., 70.7 percent of lawyers and physicians, 76.5 percent of architects, and 80.1 percent of dentists are men), women still disproportionately dominate the poorer-paying, less prestigious occupations (e.g., 98.4 percent of secretaries, 93.1 percent of nurses, 85.7 percent librarians, and 82.5 percent of elementary school teachers are women).

These inequities are *not* lost on GU's Greeks. John, a third-year political science major, for example, was aware of it. He reported that, while that he "may not do that good in school," one day he will "have it made. I know it; I guess I have always known it." It is one reason, he confessed, "I don't break my ass in school." Debora, a fourth-year Spanish and business major, was also aware of it: "I know that I will have to do twice as good to get only half as far [as a man]." "It's not fair," she continued, "but that's the way it is."

Part of the explanation of this disturbing phenomenon lies in the sexist hiring and promotion practices that have been uncovered by researchers over the last four decades (see, e.g., Bartlett & Kennedy, 1991; Epstein, 1971; Holmstrom, 1972; Kanter, 1977; and Weitzman, 1985). Of equal importance in understanding the post-college lives of these woman, however, are the decisions they make about their own future and the pressure placed on them to behave like appropriate future wives and mothers.

Women

The Tennis Mom

Roughly a quarter of the women I interviewed claimed to want the traditional "wife life" once they leave college. Many of them could easily climb the corporate ladder, earn advanced degrees, or run for political office if they so desired. Instead, they dream of a life filled with PTA meetings, lunches and shopping trips with girlfriends, breadwinning husbands, and beautiful, healthy children.

Some, like Nancy, a Gamma English major, wanted to enter the domestic realm as soon as possible: "School has been fun, but, when I graduate, I really want that storybook life. I want a big house, a hot husband who makes a lot, beautiful kids, and credit cards." Susan, a senior Gamma sister, similarly dreamed of a life with "lots of babies" and a "minivan." Lisa, a Delta sister, wanted to "quit working as soon as she gets married . . . and be a great mom." She expected her husband, however, "to work and make money." She openly admitted that she had "certain expectations" of the man she will one day marry: "I want him to work longer because he will be the primary income. I won't be that wife that nags about him coming home at 5:00. I will support his drive to be successful. He'll be working for all of us."

Interestingly, most of the women who expressed such domestic goals either awkwardly apologized for them or acknowledged the social pressure they felt to do more with their lives. Katherine, an

Omicron sister, stumbled through her description of what it is like being a woman in college: "I think that it is hard for girls. It is embarrassing to say I want to get married in three years and have lots of babies and not work. I think a lot of girls. . . . I don't want that, but I think that girls feel bad about that. As girls we are taught that, but we are taught to be strong. Oh, never mind, I don't know what I am saying. But you understand it's hard being a girl."

Similarly, the Tau sister Janet tells of the backlash she feels for wanting the traditional domestic lifestyle: "When my mom was younger, you know, she felt pressure to be the perfect mom. Not anymore." "I hear it so much more [today]," she explained, "that women are looked down upon for staying at home. When I tell people what I want to do, I get looks like, 'You do?'" With tears welling up in her eyes and a growing sense of frustration in her voice, she told me that she is "looked down on." But, she angrily proclaimed, the people who look down on her "are not superior" to her: "So what if I want to be a stay-at-home mom?"

A less emotional Judy, a senior education major, did not care whether she was seen by "feminists" as "the anti-Christ." Her dream was to "quit working and get married": "I want to have babies and put dinner on the table at 6:00 and be a tennis mom. And, you know what, I am not going to apologize for it!" On hearing Judy's charge, Lauren, a sorority sister sitting to her left, attempted to console her by reassuring her that no one thought less of her. Lauren lost her supportive tone, however, when, in the very next sentence, she wondered "why women who want to *only* be moms go to college. I mean, you don't need a degree to be a mom." After an extended pause, Judy responded: "But the degree will make me a better mom." Lauren and Judy hugged.

There were also a surprising number of women who planned to work for only a few years and then become full-time wives and mothers. Some wanted, as Nancy put it, "to have a degree and work for a few years" so that they could, again in Nancy's words, "say I did it" and also "show others that I did it." Jessica similarly wanted her degree and a very short-lived career to show others that she was "not a freeloader":

My parents brought me up in a traditional sense of go to college and get a degree. But it kind of ends with a degree. I can say I did go to school. And the degree is also in case I don't meet him [i.e., her husband] in college. My parents stressed for my brother to go to college and get a job. But, for me, it's just get any degree. My parents may not like this, but I would also like to work part-time for a short while. That way I can show everybody I'm not just someone who lives off my husband's money. I could make a living for myself if I wanted.

Others, like Cynthia, were more pragmatic and wanted to make sure that they "have something to fall back on if something—God forbid—happens." Cynthia's mother was "caught after her divorce with no skills and no credit, nothing. She was screwed. That's not going to happen to me." Then there was Brenda, who saw work solely as a means to an ends. She planned to "work for a few years because it will make you look better for Prince Charming. You are more attractive if you are smart and intelligent and have a good job." After the right man comes along, however, she wants to "focus on her family."

While these sorority women had different dreams, they were united by the pressure they felt to "do more with" their lives. Some were embarrassed and apologetic, others attempted to deflect criticism by earning a degree or working part-time, and still others sought like-minded sisters, joining their sororities specifically in order to keep as much distance between themselves and what Judy called "those feminists." There are, for example, two popular sororities on campus that are known not only for recruiting "blue bloods" (wealthy girls from traditional families) but for also having an organizational climate that supports and encourages sisters who choose the domestic path after college. "The Deltas and the Mus," observed

Jenny, a Chi sister, "are the houses where girls go to earn a 'Mrs.' degree. We all joke about it, but everyone knows it's true." Even the Delta and Mu sisters openly admit it. "It is who we are," said Frannie, a fourth-year Delta. "We have a lot of girls from rich families that want a certain life," reported Sara, the Mu president. "Most will marry doctors or lawyers . . . have kids . . . work with charities. . . . Our girls also like to shop." And, indeed, Frannie and Sara were right. Many more women from the Delta and Mu houses whom I interviewed claimed to want a more traditional life than women from other sororities.

This is not to imply, however, that the Deltas and Mus serve only to shelter their members from the critical eyes of the more progressive minded. They also create an organizational culture that subtly rewards their members for choosing a traditional domestic life after graduation. A woman joining them becomes part of the group, one of the girls, a kindred spirit. As Lisa proudly told me, her Delta sisters helped her "make up" her mind about her life: "I was probably like most women after high school. I was not really sure what I wanted to do." After pledging her sorority, however, "it became easier" for her to "choose motherhood." Adopting a similar tone, Maggie from Mu reported: "It is comfortable knowing that your sisters don't think you're like nothing for not working." At another sorority—like the professionally minded Alphas—women, Maggie believed, "feel pressure to go out and work, even if you don't want to work."

The Working Mother

The majority of the women I interviewed, including quite a few Delta and Mu sisters, claimed to want a life both at home and at work. Being "just a mom" and being "married to your job" both sounded incomplete and imbalanced to most of these women. Their aspirations varied widely, however. Carol, the Xi vice president, eloquently described the problem of trying to oversimplify today's female students: "Most of the girls that I know don't fit neatly into any one category. Most want to be married and have children, and they also want a career. But some of my sisters want to work more or spend more time at home than others. I guess what I am saying is that it is all about degrees. You know, a ratio of home and work, you know, kids and a job. That seems to me to be where the difference is anymore. We want it all—just in different degrees is what I'm saying."

Many conceived of "having it all" as having a job that allowed them to privilege their families over their careers—a choice never discussed by any of the men in this study. Most of the women who sought such a balance strategically selected majors that facilitated their goals. Lindsey, a Phi sophomore, declared education so that she "could be home when [her] kids were home." Why was Gina going to be a teacher? "[So] I can spend my summers with my kids and watch them grow up." Robin thought "teaching was perfect" for her. She wanted to make sure that her "kids aren't latch-key kids, that someone is home for them." Many of these women also saw the "school schedule" as enabling them to be more attentive to their husbands." Anne, for example, said that she "loves to cook." She told me, "It's not that I want to be a 1950s wife, but I think it would be nice for my husband, and my kids, to have home-cooked meals at night."

Not all women who aspired to such a lifestyle majored in education. With technology radically redefining work as something one does, not someplace one goes, many women planned to work out of their homes. Andrea, a 4.0 business-major senior, wanted to "be an accountant." "Accounting is something that I could do at home," she felt, aided by laptops and the Internet. "You know, work in a firm for a few years. Then move everything at home so I can stay at home with my kids." Utilizing the advantages of technology, Stacy similarly planned on "working as a freelance journalist for a newspaper or magazine out of my living room." "It does not matter," she told me, "where I write my articles. You just send them in over e-mail when you are finished." Technology, she believed, will enable her to "have everything": "My job, my kids, my freedom."

Within this working-mother camp, there were also many women who wanted to equally balance their professional and domestic lives—not privilege their families over their careers. Jenny, a Theta marketing major, for instance, told me: "I think of myself, and I know I will need a balanced life. I need a family, but I also need my career." She drew inspiration by "looking at all the successful working women" she knew. Her favorite is a sorority alumna who "got her law degree. And she is a partner already. And she is pregnant. She is really aggressive; she don't take shit off of anyone."

Most of these women, however, drew on maternal role models for guidance. Some mothers served as a negative touchstone. Melissa, for example, told me that, after her parents divorced, her mother "started law school and was never around." Things got so bad, she said, "that my sister basically raised me most of the time." "I will work," Melissa had decided, "but never forget my kids." Similarly, Stephanie recalled growing up in a house without parents: "I want to be there. Growing up, I had parents who weren't. And I want to be there. And it wasn't really a bad thing. I don't remember much of it. I would rather my children come home and me be there. I will be successful, I know it, whatever I do, but I will make sure that I don't forget about my family. It was done to me, and I won't put my kids through that."

More often than not, however, mothers served as positive role models. At times, it was the strength they exhibited in the face of tragedy. After losing her husband in an automobile accident, Elizabeth's mother "held the family together": "She is working, taking care of my little brother, and me, making all the arrangements." Elizabeth wondered how she did it: "She is my hero. She handles it all." Other mothers inspired their daughters in less dramatic ways. "My mom rocks," proclaimed Andie. "She is beautiful, successful—she has a great job as a real estate agent, and a great mom. You know, in high school, she never missed any of my games . . . softball, track, basketball."

But it was not only mothers who inspired. Fathers also taught their daughters indelible life lessons. "My daddy is a wonderful man," remarked Whitney. "He always told me how great I was, how beautiful, how smart. I need to find a man as good as him." "He was there as much as my mom was," she told her sisters. "They have a great balance. Someone was always home, not always my mom, you know. It was a fifty-fifty split." For Whitney, therefore, a "balanced" life meant an equitable relationship with her husband. "You can't do it alone," she said, talking to her sisters. "Otherwise somebody gets cheated."

For some, however, a husband was not seen as a necessity for a balanced life. When I asked Laurie what her ideal life scenario would look like, she told me that she has "two": "If I don't get married, I'm gonna have a great job and a Mercedes, a big house, and really hot boyfriends. If I do get married, I'm gonna have a great job, a big house, a Mercedes, of course, two kids, and a really hot husband." She reassured me that "either way, I'll be happy—I'm gonna have it all."

In most cases, however, these women saw a husband as part of a complete and balanced life. When I asked Gail to elaborate about the importance of finding Mr. Right, she apologetically admitted that, for her and most of her sisters, "a man is part of the plan": "I would like to think that there are a lot of girls who don't give a shit about guys, who just want to get out there. I'm like that to a certain sense. I have all these dreams. But, you know what, I also want a guy, sorry. I want to meet a man that is supposed to make my life beautiful, whatever. I want it both. A career, a husband, kids, the whole package, sorry."

I've talked with hundreds of women in the course of researching this book, and throughout all those conversations an ambivalence was always present. On the one hand, they were apologetic about wanting to find "Mr. Right." On the other hand, they felt guilty for wanting a life outside the kitchen. These women struggled between opposing forces, being pulled by traditional ideas of the domestic life and pushed by modern ideas of the professional life. The sense of ambivalence was so strong, in fact, that I am led to believe that it is the unfortunate cross that women today, Greek or not, must bear.

The Working Woman

Not all the sorority women I talked to were worried about balance. Some—perhaps a fifth—had decided that, at least for the foreseeable future, work was going to take precedence over family. Anne, a junior psychology major, didn't "even want to think about settling down." After college, she wanted "to travel before having kids or getting married. . . . I see myself thirty or thirty-five years old before I want to slow down." "That's why I'm in college," she asserted, "so I can do those things."

Others, like the irrepressible Maggie, were less concerned about age and more concerned about who was wearing the proverbial pants in the relationship. Her boyfriend of three years wanted to get engaged, Maggie told me. "That's fine and great," she said as laughter filled the room, "but, as soon as I graduate, I am leaving. If he can handle it, he can follow me around." But she made it very clear that she was "not going to change for anybody."

Becky was another young woman who was not going to let a relationship deter her from career success. As she told the focus group, her boyfriend of two years had volunteered to be a "stay-at-home househusband" while she aggressively pursued her professional aspirations. Not that "being a mother" wasn't important to her. But "being a dad" was of "the utmost importance" to him: "I just want to be a corporate dean somewhere." Becky's other Xi sisters could only stare at her in bewilderment. Patty, her best friend, simply shrugged her shoulders and laughed with affectionate amusement: "Where did she come from?" It was clear that Becky was the outlier in her sorority.

As aberrant as Becky may appear, she was not alone. There was Allison, for example, who "never wants kids, ever," Laura, who "would be just as happy never getting married," Stephanie, who wants "to date and not get serious until she is old," and Sydney, who put the room in hysterics by confessing that all she "needs to be happy is a cat and a cucumber." "Men and babies," she huffed, "are too much work."

The Role of the Sorority in Preparing Tomorrow's Leaders

Maggie, Becky, and the other professionally oriented women I interviewed readily credited their sororities with preparing them for their postcollege professional lives. Many, in fact, said that, for women who were focused and driven, sororities were *the* best place to develop leadership skills on campus. Andrea, the Alpha president, told me, "Any girl who wants to learn about leadership can run for an office." Since taking over as president, she had "learned accounting skills, communication, leadership": "I spend so much time in meetings with really influential people, deans, the provost, the president, parents." After a semester of such training, Andrea assured me, she "could run a Fortune 500 company." I, for one, didn't doubt her.

Heidi, the treasurer of the Omegas, similarly sang the praise of her sorority and its concern with the professional development of its members: "We have tons of positions in our sorority that we can put girls in where they have to control something or lead something. I think that is something that Omega does pretty good—give girls plenty of chances to be a leader. That is one point that we stress during rush when we are talking to girls. Greek life will give them more leadership opportunities that will help them after graduation."

Some women addressed this issue of professional development from a more critical perspective. Erin, a Pi sister now in graduate school, believes that claims about sororities being excellent professional training grounds are, at best, overstatements. "Greek organizations," she asserted, "are very conservative and traditional institutions." Little changes from year to year, even from generation to generation, she felt. The primary responsibility of those assuming leadership roles in Greek organizations was to reproduce customs, rituals, practices, and beliefs—in short, maintain tradition. In the real world, she argued, corporations are not looking for people to simply reinvent a wheel that is already 150 years old. The truth of the matter, Erin concluded, was that Greek leaders do little more than decide whom to drink beer with at the next tailgate party.

With that point taken, however, I do believe that a woman's involvement in a sorority can, nonetheless, serve as an empowering experience for her. While she may not learn how to implement the latest human-resource strategy, she will be given, for perhaps the first time in her life, the opportunity to chose, make mistakes, implement strategic plans (albeit conservative ones), balance budgets, and reward, reprimand, encourage, and lead members. Such experiences are inevitably transformational. I have seen hundreds of reserved, disfranchised freshman women metamorphosed by their Greek experiences, possessed in the end of greater self-esteem, greater confidence, and the ability to think and act more independently.

This is not to imply that there are no casualties of the Greek system. Many young women also leave their sororities with eating disorders, wasted potential, drinking problems, and abusive boyfriends.

Men's Response to the Working Woman

Many of the women who spoke with me about their postcollege careers felt compelled to comment as well on some of their boyfriends' (and, in some cases, ex-boyfriends') reactions to their professional aspirations. These men felt so threatened, these women reported, that they became competitive and even abusive whenever the topic of their girlfriends' career goals was raised. "The male ego," Denise argued, "is a fucked up thing."

Nancy, who just ended a long-term relationship, described the ambivalence she felt about traditional masculinity: "I appreciate all those he-man qualities about him—I mean, he is a real man's man—but with those qualities comes a lack of respect for my characteristics and my desire to be successful." What Nancy thought most professional women were looking for was a new type of man, one who embraces a more contemporary masculinity: "I think we all want a man who aspires to be successful but, at the same time, someone who is also going to appreciate and encourage you as you do the same thing."

Echoing the same frustrations and desires, Bernie told me that she wanted "to have the freedom to get married and not have my husband *expect* me to stay home with the kids": "I want a husband who is going to be as excited about what I do and accomplish." Finding such a man, however, is not that easy, according to these woman. "Good modern—if that's the word—men are tough to find," Bernie continued. "Most have this ego that feels threatened by us," she said, pointing to her other sisters sitting around the conference table. She wondered how many "women just give up" to keep their husbands and society happy, "just not do anything, stay at home." Exasperated by the thought of such pressure, she exhales forcefully.

Similar sentiments were also evident in a conversation I had with Lauren about her relationship: "It's really hard because of social norms . . . especially when you're the one putting out the credit card. Like it happens to me now." Lauren works as an intern for a law firm in town and has far more money than her boyfriend, a typical struggling college student. "He feels very threatened, like it's a big issue because, if I want to go out to dinner, I'll invite him out to dinner, and I'll pay." He invariably turned the situation into a joke by "asking for his dick back" afterward.

But finding a modern, supportive man was not the only hurdle these young women faced. Many saw society as being just as traditional and stubborn as men. Janet, commenting on the social pressure men feel to provide, believed that "being a man is much tougher than before. There are all these really great women coming out of college, and it's harder for them to be like our fathers were." Society's expectations, she asserted, have refused to change with the times. Consequently, her culture made her "feel guilty for being too successful" and men "feel like wimps for not being the big breadwinner."

Kelli also saw society's intolerance posing serious problems for her and her boyfriend, Rob, as they planned their postcollege lives together. "It is not Rob's ego I worry about," she told me. "It is everyone else around us." "I want Rob to be as successful as I am, but I don't think he needs to be necessarily more successful than I am. I mean, I think that, as far as socially, people are going to look down on us, I mean, even if both of us are OK with it. I think that, if I am handling the credit card, other people are going to look at us funny, and that's going to make us uncomfortable even if both of us are OK with it."

Women on college campuses are not the only students worrying about employment, gender, and social expectations. These topics also dominated many of the discussions I had with the men in this study.

Men

It's Not Cool to Study

There is among Greek men a strange but telling disconnect between the idea of doing well in college and doing well in their postcollege careers. At GU, as at most colleges in America, not only do Greek men have lower GPAs (their average is 2.74) than their sorority sisters (their average is 3.15), but they are also outperformed by the general university population (its average is 2.95) and the non-Greek male population (its average is 2.82).

Still, this apathy in the classroom should not be taken as a sign of indifference to their postcollege careers. These men worry, sometimes to the point of obsession, about life after graduation. "The idea of not having a great job makes me sick," Eric confessed, "really sick. I will feel like such a loser if I can only find a shit job." The obvious follow-up question, then, is why so many fraternity men sleepwalk through school.

The answer to this confounding question, I argue, lies in the definition of masculinity that has been ingrained in, not just these young men, but all American men. Succinctly put, a man who per-forms too well academically runs the risk of being seen as effeminate, a bookworm, or a nerd. The brainwashing, argue Kindlon and Thompson (2000), starts long before college. The typical American father dreams of his son growing up to be, not valedictorian of his senior class, but the star quarterback on the football team. And, in most elementary, middle, and high schools, the message of anti-intellectualism has been institutionalized. After all, when was the last time a pep rally was held for the chess club, the captain of the math team landed the captain of the cheerleading squad, the cheerleaders performed at a band concert, or the debating team took the stage to a standing-room-only crowd?[2]

This dysfunctional prioritizing also takes place in most elite fraternity houses. While lip service to academic success may be given at formal meetings—*Okay, guys, let's get good grades this semester*—the everyday practice is to tolerate, if not encourage, academic underachievement. After all, as the joke goes, if you're on the dean's list, you must not be partying hard enough. And a fun-loving partier is always more valued in a fraternity house than a nerdy bookworm. I have witnessed on numerous occasions, for example, young men recently put on academic probation receiving high fives from their brothers for a semester successfully wasted in a bottle or a bong. Even as they flunk out of school—like John Belushi's Bluto in the 1978 film *Animal House*—their popularity and reputation grow; they are the brothers who infuse the house with life and laughter.

In certain crisis situations, however, a modicum of pressure is pragmatically applied to those brothers whose GPAs have fallen dangerously low. At GU, for example, pledges can be initiated only if they have a GPA of 2.0 or higher and no fraternity with three consecutive semesters of diminishing grades can register for a university-recognized social event (of course, unrecognized parties take place surreptitiously most nights of the week).

In such situations, the executive leadership council of a chapter will strongly encourage all brothers to raise their grades so that the chapter's average reaches an acceptable level. This pressure, however, is motivated, not by a chapter's desire to have academically astute and professionally prepared brothers in its ranks, but by its desire to be in good social standing with the university and to have all its pledges initiated in a timely fashion.

How to Study and Still Be Cool

Fraternities' anti-intellectual bias should not be surprising. They are, after all, traditionally conservative organizations. This is not to say that a brother will be blackballed for making the dean's list. But his academic drive must be tempered with a certain amount of socializing. "You can't stop having fun just because you're in college," Masson explained, "you know what I'm saying? Some guys forget that. They lose a lot of their friends. You can still go out, get drunk, party with the ladies, and do fine." While other more studious, less social students may have higher GPAs, Masson isn't worried about such competition. In the end, he rationalizes, his investment in socializing will pay dividends after graduation. "Since I did party and was normal," he expanded, "I'll be twice as good at interviewing, you know what I mean? I can shoot the shit about golf, basketball, stuff like that. The nerd who stayed in the stacks can't do that like me." For Mason, and many others like him, a college man must balance academics with a healthy dose of beer and ESPN or risk being an unemployed and emasculated social retard after graduation. His theory, of course, rests on the supposition that all interviewers will be, not just men, but men just like him, men who will talk about "golf, basketball, stuff like that," during job interviews.

Others in the study adopted the more refined strategy of time management to balance masculinity and scholarship. "It's about allocating your time, being normal, social," Michael claimed. "As long as you hang out and not just stay in the library all the time, the brothers are cool. But, if you are more concerned with grades and not with the brothers, you are not going to fit in." There are caveats to this rule, however. John thought: "If you have a test the next day, then staying in is OK, but, if you're just staying in to work on regular stuff every night, then you need to rethink why you're here." Finally, Joe offered it as his opinion that "studying—you know, unless you have an exam the next day—should be done before 10:00 P.M. It's weird to stay in your room when everyone else is partying and having a good time. I mean, if that's what you want to do, why the hell did you pledge?" For Michael, John, Joe, and many others of their ilk, therefore, studying is acceptable only in moderation, when there is an exam the next morning (cramming and pulling all-nighters are far more preferable—and masculine—than incremental preparation), or earlier in the day. With such guidelines dictating fraternal study habits, it is not hard to understand why GU's all-fraternity GPA is the lowest on campus.

While balance is crucial to most brothers' conception of the ideal college man, there are always the academically diligent few in each house who break this rule. In order to do so and still be liked and respected, however, a brother must create an identity as a hyper-driven professional who has precociously started on his adult career path. Far from being seen as an effeminate bookworm, then, he is seen as focused and competitive. It is crucial to remember, however, that a brother cannot study simply to gain knowledge or to be conscientious, both very feminine motivations. Real men are studious only insofar as being studious furthers some professional or financial end.

A number of studious exceptions readily come to mind. From his very first day on campus, for example, Brian let everyone know that he was on the fast track. Doing everything short of carrying a leather briefcase and wearing Brooks Brothers suits to class, he announced that he was taking no prisoners on his way to Wall Street. Consequently, his academic focus was not seen as effeminate or nerdy. Rather, it was part of the aggressive and assertive pursuit of his goals. He became, in short, the academic alpha male of his house.

Then there was John, a premed major who, with less macho bravado but with the same dedication, constructed a doctor-on-the-fast-track persona for himself. Far from being dismayed by how little John socialized, his brothers at the Omega house considered him a great public relations man for their organization. "It's cool to have someone like John," remarked his brother Phil. "We tell our pledges about him—you know, we have doctors here—and my parents think it's great."

There was also Lewis, a political science major in the Zeta house who, by his own pronouncement, was going to Harvard Law School after graduation. With such a lofty goal, of course, Lewis found that he could not "party at the fraternity house every night." His brothers were not just understanding; they were supportive. After all, he was going to be rich and famous one day.

The Pressure of Making It

In the past two years, Brian, John, and Lewis have all graduated from GU. Unfortunately, they have all encountered some disappointment in their postcollege lives. Brian, for instance, still waits in his college town for his Wall Street invitation. Disheartened, he is now considering law school as an option. John did get into med school, but not the East Coast Ivy League university of which he had dreamed. Finally, Lewis did so poorly on his LSATs that he is now considering any law school that will accept him. Living with his parents back home, he wishes that he "had not talked so much about it. It's kinda embarrassing. Everyone is always asking me about it."

These young men, sadly to say, are just a few of the heartbreaking casualties in a society that judges a man's worth by his occupational achievement. As Wood (2005) has argued, being a good provider with a socially prestigious and well-paying job is still the "primary requirement for manhood" (p. 160). And Faludi (1999) makes a similar case. The cruel reality, of course, is that the masculine standard of success is beyond the reach of most American men. Consequently, even college-educated, hardworking young men like Brian, John, and Lewis feel like losers.

Mark, a charming and personable Beta brother, recently talked with me in my office about his future and his fear of failure. Like many other young men I have talked with in the past two decades, he expressed his growing anxiety about not fulfilling social expectations. "It's killing me," he claimed. "I've already sent out bunches of resumes, and no one has given me an interview." He was proud of the effort that he put into college (he graduated with a 3.2 GPA). But he still found "the thought of going back home without a job . . . humiliating." Clay, another one of my advisees, was concerned about what his high school friends would think: "I have my five-year reunion coming up, and I always dreamed of showing up with a great job and a hot wife." As of now, he has neither. "It is probably not such a big deal for women," he speculated, "but, for me and my buddies back home, it's like you're a zero." Only half jokingly he told me, "It wasn't supposed to be like this." For many of my male students, unfortunately, that's the way it is.

With so many men anxiety ridden about not finding just the right job with just the right firm at just the right salary, I began wondering what the source of the oppressive and relentless pressure they felt was. I asked, for example, whether they felt "pushed" by their fraternity: most just laughed. "No, no, not from my brothers," James assured me. Mark similarly told me, "The brothers are cool. They are in the same place I am." It is "pressure I put on myself. I know what I want my life to be, and you get worried you're not getting there." Other times, there is external pressure from home. "My mom and dad, mostly my dad, want me to do good," claimed Jason. "He gets angry about my grades and tells me that I won't get a job. Now that I'm on the market, you know, he's like, 'You fucked around for four years, blah, blah, blah.'" The pressure from Jim's dad was more subtle but every bit as stressful. "My dad is a big-time lawyer," Jim told me, "and he is famous, and it's hard because everyone asks me—his friends—if I am going to take over for him. Isn't that a laugh?" Like Jim, Rob's family also produced external pressure: "Everyone in my family is wealthy. My dad and his brothers have this business, and their sons are living in Chicago and are business guys." With such touchstones for success, Rob told me, he had "better do something good" or he "will be like the one that didn't." Even fraternity brothers from less affluent families feel pressure to make it. Seth, a confessed country boy from Kentucky, discussed with me his family's expectations for his future. "I am the first, really, to go to college. They are always bragging about me at home, my grandpa a lot. I can tell they really want me to do good for them."

As telling as these men's stories are, the fact that few of the women told such stories is equally telling. While most of the women reported pressure to do well in school, very few reported similar pressure to excel in the workforce. Conversely, while few of the men reported (external or internal) pressure to excel in class, most reported pressure to excel in the workforce, indeed, agonizing over not meeting professional expectations after graduation. It appears, therefore, that little has changed for these young people since they entered elementary school. Schoolgirls and sorority women are still expected to study hard and be conscientious in class, schoolboys and fraternity men to be active, social, energetic, and spirited, not contemplative. These expectations are then inverted after college: a dutiful woman should be too concerned about her family to prioritize her career, and a good man should be too focused on his career to privilege his family.

The obvious tragedy here is the elimination of choices from these young student's lives. Just think about how many wonderful female minds have been stifled, prevented from making a legitimate professional and civic contribution to our society, or how many sons and daughters have been denied the love and attention of a father working sixty-hour weeks.

The Ideal Wife and the Fragile Male Ego

Given the amount of time and energy fraternity men devote to partying and chasing sorority women, it is hard to imagine that they

have the wherewithal to contemplate long-term monogamous relationships. But, by their own admission, the vast majority believe
that, in ten years, they will marry and start a family. Among these
optimistic romantics, however, the conception of the ideal wife and
mother varies significantly.

There are, of course, those men who want a very traditional dutiful wife and stay-at-home mother. Surprisingly, however, these
brothers constituted only a small minority of the fraternal ranks.
Some, like the second-year John, seemed to come from an earlier
era when labor domains were simply (and oppressively) delineated.
"Women should not work," he told me. "They are meant to take
care and raise children. That's very important, and people have forgotten, you know." When asked "what men were *meant* to do,"
John replied, consistently with his traditional views: "Men are to
work and provide for our families . . . be dads and good husbands."
Another anachronistic brother, Kenneth from the Delta house, adopted a similar perspective but was clearer on the origins of his gender philosophy: "God tells us what the husband and wife are to do. I
believe it. My wife will, my mom did it, take care of the house, shopping, cooking, and the kids, raising them." Kenneth was concerned,
however, that I understood that he was not sexist. He stressed that
"raising kids" was as important as working outside the home. "A
man," he concluded, "needs to honor and respect his wife too."

While some, like Kenneth, saw their mothers as models of feminine behavior, others, like Raymond, one of the few African Americans in GU's white Greek system, remembered their mothers' hard
work outside the house and vowed to provide a "better life" for
their wives. "My mom worked her ass off," Ray told me, "and it
was hard for all of us, especially her." Consequently, Ray was going
to make sure that his wife "will not have to do all that. I need to do
that as a man, you know what I'm saying?"

The large majority of these young fraternity men, however, adopted a more modern—but not completely enlightened—perspective on women working outside the home. More than three-quarters

claimed that they had no problem with their wives being employed. However, two qualifications surfaced repeatedly, belying claims of belief in workforce equality.

The first qualification was that a wife should stop working, or, at the very least, dramatically reduce her hours outside the home, once she has children. As Luke matter-of-factly explained, "A woman has got to stop when she has babies. I mean, who else is gonna take care of them, a nanny or something?" Nathan, a third-year Phi brother, talked with me about his and his steady girlfriend Nancy's plans after graduation: "Nancy and I both want to work right out, but she will take a few years off once we have a family." For Tony, a "few years off" is not long enough: "A mother should stop working until the kids are finished with high school, I think. She can always go back to work again, if she even wants to, once the kids are away, at college or something." For these brothers, work is something a woman does while she is not mothering. Once she begins procreating, her emphasis must shift from the public to the private. For, in the minds of Luke, Nathan, and Tony, caregiving is the natural and God-given sphere for women.

The second qualification was that a wife's employment is acceptable only as long as she has a job that is not as good as her husband's. For some, like Steven, it was an issue of income: "I could not take it if my wife earned more money that I did." Brian thought he "would feel like a little bitch" if his wife outearned him. For Kevin, it was the "loss of control in the house": "I mean, how can you be the man if she is the man, you know?" Big Mike had "never even let a girl pay for a drink or dinner, nothing." "No, no," he concluded, "no way, my ego could not take that."

But being outearned was not the men's greatest fear. More were concerned about being outprestiged. The brothers of the Gamma house debated which of the two was the greater evil:

AD: What would your reaction be if your wife had a better job than you did?

Mark: I would have a problem if she made more money than I did.

Jason: I would. It's a power thing. It would just be weird hearing my mom tell my dad, "Well, I pay the house bill around here." I know I would want my wife, like, I know it would never happen, but to hear her say, "Well, I make more money than you do, so. . ."

Ken: I think that it wouldn't bother me; the social prestige would. That kind of cuts into your self-conscious and assertiveness as a man. As far as who you marry, I don't think making more money would cause problems. I mean, if she was cleaning houses—she wouldn't really do that, you know, but something like that—and I was a lawyer making a little less, I would still be the man.

Mark: If you're going to all her dinner parties and she is introducing you like she is in charge.

Ken: If she is introducing you to doctors and surgeons driving Beamers [BMWs] and Land Rovers. They would look at you like [*he makes a face as if smelling something rotten*].

Richard: Like if she was the first president, you'd be the first man. How would that feel? Just take my dick.

The guys at the Sigma house also had a problem with marrying a more socially prominent wife. Josh, for example, wouldn't mind "hooking up with a hot-ass sugar momma," but he would have problems with a wife who had more cultural clout. "What would suck," he imagined, "is when you are playing cards with the boys or something like that and they'd probably make fun of me the whole fucking time." But he would not be the only one to suffer from this matriarchal arrangement. After nights out with the boys, Josh speculated, he "would come home pissed off at her, pissed for that." He wondered how such a relationship could ever work. "You'd be always fighting about that shit."

Stan, a third-year Rho brother, was so concerned about not wearing the proverbial pants in the family that, at twenty years of age, he was already strategically planning for his empowered life: "I think I can handle better her making more money than me. But, no, if she was socially better, you know higher on that ladder, then, yeah. I wouldn't want her all in my face the whole time, and people would laugh at you all the time. I think that's one reason why I am going to school to get a CPA and go to law school, not that that's the only reason, but I have to be the head of the household."

For most of these men, succeeding professionally was intrinsically tied to meeting social expectations, maintaining relational power, and avoiding scorn. The possible financial and material advantages of a dual-income family were of little or no concern. Evidently, any benefit that would come from marrying a successful wife would be eclipsed by the loss of their masculinity. In fact, these men would rather live a less affluent and comfortable life than relinquish any financial or social control to a woman, supply their friends any fodder for emasculating humor, or be viewed by society as a professional loser.

This fear of social humiliation does not plague GU's Greek men alone. Men throughout America fear "being laughed at" as much as women fear being "raped and murdered" (Noble, 1992, pp. 105–106). According to Gaylin (1992), men are also three times more likely to commit suicide because of the "perceived social humiliation" associated with professional failure. "Men become depressed because of loss of status and power in the world of men," Gaylin writes. It is not the loss of money or material, however, that "produces the despair that leads to self-destruction." It is the "shame" and "humiliation" of professional failure. "A man," Gaylin concludes, "despairs when he ceases being a man among men" (p. 32).

Conclusion

Our culture's rigid gender roles are the source of myriad social ills. They have been used to justify discriminatory hiring and promotion practices. They have taken generations of fathers away from their wives and children and consigned generations of women to a life of domestic labor. And they have prevented both men and women from developing intimate, meaningful, and equal relationships, leaving the genders isolated and estranged.

But, for the young men and women in this study, who have not yet embarked on their postcollege lives, they primarily produced confusion, guilt, and discord. Regardless of whether they are male or female, traditional or progressive, rich or poor, all described the anxiety produced by being caught between social expectations and personal desires, the customary and the contemporary, the public and the private. Women who wanted to be stay-at-home mothers felt guilty for not wanting to work outside the home. Women who wanted to work outside the home felt guilty for wanting to leave their families. The men were no better off. After a two-decade-long free ride when it came to matters academic, they found themselves expected to be a professional and social success—and ill prepared to meet the challenge.

What is, perhaps, most disturbing about these findings is not how concerned men are about their professional futures but how unconcerned they are about their relational futures. A case in point: of the thousands of male students whom I have encountered over the years, only a very few have ever expressed significant concern about how they were going to balance their work lives and their family lives. Men only very rarely select their majors with the emotional well-being of their future families in mind. And none—Greek or independent—have ever expressed an obligation to stay at home with the children or to sacrifice their careers to the wives'. The emotional welfare of the family and the stability of the marriage was, for them, the wife's responsibility. They are blindly enacting the gender roles that their fathers and grandfathers before them blindly enacted.

7. Cleaning Up after the Party

The brothers and sisters at GU are not radically different from the thousands of other young adults I have come to know over the last twenty-one years as a teacher and an adviser. But this conclusion should come as no surprise to anyone. The young men and women examined in this study were not raised in isolation; for the first eighteen years of their lives, they were shaped by the same social forces that shape most young people in this country

This is not to imply, however, that there is nothing unique about the Greek experience. The students that come through the system, unlike the non-Greek population on campus, voluntarily live isolated lives, removed from the larger student body and the university culture generally. Once they enter their respective houses, doors are shut, secrets are kept, outsiders are excluded, and years of tradition and protocol are rigidly reproduced. Greek organizations pride themselves, in fact, on connecting the experiences of the active sisters and brothers to that of their eighteenth- and nineteenth-century foremothers and forefathers. Maintaining the status quo is a virtue.

Greek organizations also set themselves apart from the larger university culture through their unique rushing and pledging practices. As we have seen, only the most hypermasculine/feminine of the incoming freshman men and women will be rushed and offered bids. This means that the men who are the most promiscuous, violent, aggressive, competitive, cut, and social will be the most sought after among the elite fraternities and that the women who are the most supportive, interdependent, sexually chaste, pretty, and thin will be the most sought after among the elite sororities. It goes without saying, of course, that all potential initiates will be white, heterosexual, Christian, and, at the very least, middle class.

Once bids go out and are accepted, another form of indoctrination into gender roles takes place. Through rules, rituals, and daily practices, neophytes learn what is expected of them and what will not be tolerated. The men learn, for instance, that no fags are allowed, that fighting for your frat is required, that drinking and womanizing are rewarded with increased popularity, and that blind loyalty to your brothers is demanded. The women learn that sleeping around is unacceptable, that being overweight is unbecoming, and that loud, assertive, or bitchy conduct is anathema, tarnishing as it does the sorority image.

Why, it may be asked, would any students willingly subject themselves to such dogmatic and tyrannical treatment? The answer is threefold. First, and most obviously, they want to be a part of Greek social life. On any given night, fraternity brothers and sorority sisters are drinking, dancing, and hooking up with each other while much of the rest of the non-Greek campus sleeps, studies, watches TV, or drinks in smaller, same-sex groups. As every one of my interviewees unapologetically asserted, Greek life is fun. Second, by pledging (especially elite organizations), first-year students get instant access to the older, more established, more popular students—the cool kids on campus. Finally, they become part of a pack to run with, acquire a sense of communal purpose and collective belonging, a sergeant family. They find a group of friends who swear loyalty to them, who fight for them, who talk with, listen to, and empathize with them. And, ultimately, it is this very special human connection, not the keg parties or the cool kids, that keeps the brothers and sisters together and the alumni coming back for more.

Is the exchange of autonomy for an active social life, popularity, and an emotional connection worth it? For the overwhelming majority of alumni I have talked with, the answer was an unqualified yes. The advantages of going Greek overwhelmingly outweighed the disadvantages. The question left unanswered, however, is whether this self-selected group of people is introspective enough to critically evaluate the hidden ideological costs of membership in such conservative organizations.

Summary

Each chapter of this book was intended to illuminate a different aspect of the intersection of gender and Greek life on the GU campus. I discussed how fraternity brothers and sorority sisters conceive of such interrelated issues as sexuality, education, their bodies, same-sex and opposite-sex relationships, and the tension between competition and cooperation. I also drew some larger conclusions that served as a common thread connecting these chapters. In no specific order, the five most important of these are the following:

- Greek organizations on GU's campus are not monolithic or homogenized. Some groups allow significantly more deviance from traditional conceptions of gender than others. As a rule, however, the more elite, selective, and coveted an organization is, the more intolerant it is toward difference, and the less freedom it affords its members in adopting nontraditional gender scripts. The price that students pay for being part of the Greek system, therefore, is a greater loss of autonomy.
- Elite Greek organizations are locales where traditional ideas of masculinity and femininity are not just reinforced but are strengthened. In many cases, gender becomes hyperaccentuated because these groups demand adherence to an even more limiting conception of acceptable behavior than does white middle-class society in general.
- When the men and women in this study were asked to describe how they conceived of masculinity and femininity in their own lives, most, regardless of organizational affiliation, supplied very predictable and orderly answers. In practice, however, these same men and women were constantly pushing the limits and challenging the assumptions of their own ideas of appropriate behavior. Lived gender was far messier and far more malleable than they expected it to be, whether it was their lives or the lives of others that were in question.

- Even with this blurring, however, the genders were still defined relationally. To understand fraternal masculinity, therefore, we must understand sororal femininity, and vice versa. Each influences, and is influence by, the other.

- The men and women in this study should not be viewed as malicious villians conspiring to oppress nonconformists, as Greeks are often portrayed in popular culture. This characterization is both too simplistic and too unempathetic. Instead, as I have suggested, a more accurate and productive conception is that they are young adults who are trying to find meaning, acceptance, love, and direction in their lives and, as a result, have become complicit in the system's reproduction. The lack of transformative action on their part may be disappointing, but remember that all these young people were indoctrinated as children by a patriarchal system that promised acceptance and popularity in return for adherence to traditional gender performances. Now in college, they have joined organizations that demand even greater obedience and conformity and promise in return even greater acceptance and popularity—a seductive proposition for even the most enlightened young adult. The result of this Faustian bargain is the tragic loss of their enlightenment in college and the attenuation of their life choices after graduation.

Using these five overarching concepts as a foundation, I will in what follows evaluate the merits of Greek life at GU and offer a series of suggestions for stakeholders aimed at moving fraternities and sororities closer to the idealized goals of both higher education and Greek life as envisioned by their founding mothers and fathers.

The Evaluation

I myself was drawn to higher education first as a student and now as a professor because of its liberating and life-altering potential. It is one of the few places in America where individuals are encouraged to test the boundaries of their comfort zones and challenge their most deeply rooted assumptions. When managed correctly, higher education should transform, complicate, and expand lives.

College should also be a place where young adults explore a wide range of social interests and cultural experiences not previously available to them. As students often testify, making and breaking close relationships, attending cultural events, managing their own finances, and meeting people from around the world have been as important to their education as the lessons learned in classrooms.

Many of the students in this study, however, viewed becoming a Greek as the most important and life-changing decision of their college careers. The affection felt for their brothers and sisters, the good times spent at parties and tailgates, and the unique experience of living with so many like-minded friends in such intimate settings are often cited as being far more influential and memorable than classes or professors.

Consequently, stakeholders in these students' lives must ask whether the Greek experience is a worthy augmentation of the college experience or whether it works against the goals of higher education. And I am saddened to conclude that, for many men and women at GU, it has further restricted their already narrow comfort zones and reinforced many of the most traditional and dangerous ideas of their childhood. Of all the harmful lessons learned, however, none affects Greek students' lives more than the limiting conceptions of gender that the system reinforces. More than any other single factor, these conceptions impede students' intellectual and emotional growth and limit the range of possibilities open to them in their postcollege lives.

It should be noted, however, that I am *not* advocating the abolishment of the institution. The Greek experience has meant too much to me, and to thousands of others whom I have known, to turn my back on it now. It introduced me to many of the most important people in my life, taught me how to be a loyal and selfless friend, and gave me the freedom, confidence, and safety to take big risks and make big mistakes. What I am advocating instead is the implementation of measures that will move the Greek system closer to the higher ideals envisioned by its founding fathers and mothers. Long before toga and tailgate parties ever became staples of Greek life, these visionary men and women wanted to form societies that would encourage their members to debate the merits of ideas, improve the human condition through philanthropic work, and enjoy good food, drink, and conversation with kindred minds and souls.

Of course we cannot turn the clock back to the nineteenth century. But it is, I believe, a reasonable goal to aim at rewriting the gender scripts of the Greek system in such a way that they allow for greater possibilities. With such a change, the Greek experience would no longer stifle students' potential but expand the opportunities available to them. If managed well, in fact, fraternities and sororities have the potential to create an even safer and more supportive climate for change than does society in general. Within the already protective atmosphere of their houses, brothers and sisters could safely challenge the status quo without fear of ridicule or reprisal. While *The Dead Poets Society* is, admittedly, a bit corny, I am drawn to the film as a model of what an inspiring teacher and a group of students hungry for both friendship and enlightenment can create. Along with smoking cigarettes and chasing girls, the film's young protagonists also found in their secret order a safe and supportive atmosphere that allowed them to dream, debate, and think creatively. Balancing the social with the intellectual in their fraternal experience, they actually expanded their notion of what a man can do and be.

Left to their own devices, however, today's Greeks are highly unlikely to achieve such personal or organizational transformations. It is more likely that they will simply continue to reproduce traditional gender performances. If significant and lasting change is to take place, there must be a concerted effort on the part of everyone involved in the lives of these young people. Professors, alumni, students, parents, and administrators will all need to work together toward expanding gender conceptions. This, I argue, is not only the solution to making the Greek experience worthy of being part of the university experience but also the key to attenuating the campus problems of date rape, eating disorders, violence, and sexism. Other approaches merely treat the symptoms, not the disease.

Recommendations to Stakeholders

University Professors

Like Robin Williams's character in *Dead Poets Society*, teachers have the potential to influence the lives of even the most traditional and privileged (or underprivileged) students. This is one of the main reasons, in fact, that most of my colleagues have dedicated their lives to education. Few of them, however, have the time or the patience to deal with Greeks, an attitude found on campuses nationwide. Greeks are generally viewed as the scourge of campuses, responsible for date rape, binge drinking, missed classes, cheating, hazing, elitism, sexism, and racism, to name just a few of the problems pinned on them.

While such a view is often warranted, the reality is that fraternities and sororities are here to stay, and their influence is powerful and pervasive. Not only do they produce a staggering number of American leaders, as we saw in the introduction, but Greeks are also among the most generous alumni when it comes to supporting their alma mater financially. With the increasing pressure placed on institutions of higher education to generate external sources of funding, the importance of this latter point should not be underestimated. As one GU administrator recently told me, it would be professional suicide for university administrators to alienate or anger Greek organizations: "They're very rich, and most of them run everything. . . . Just ask our governor or our president."

Faculty members must, therefore, stop futilely wishing for the abolishment of the Greek system and get involved with its renovation. Toward this end, they must first realize their own persuasive power. While peer groups are certainly important in the lives of Greek students, professors are potentially more influential. I am constantly amazed, for instance, by how enthusiastic and receptive students are when professors visit them at their houses, talk with them on campus, or attend their functions.

With that said, I also realize that not all professors are created equal in the eyes of all students. Certain personality types (e.g., professors who are extroverted and humorous) will find the going easier, as will individuals with similar backgrounds. With time, dedication, and a show of commitment, however, most interpersonally competent professors will be welcomed warmly at most Greek organizations.

For significant change to take place, however, getting involved must entail more than just selecting an organization and showing up once a month for a formal meeting. Professors will need to get to know the brothers and sisters in more intimate and natural settings. Here are few strategies that have worked well for me in getting to know my Greek students and giving them an opportunity to get to know me:

- Stop by their house and eat breakfast, lunch, or dinner with them.
- Spend an evening watching television with them (*Monday Night Football, Sex in the City, Friends,* etc.).
- Help around the house (with yard work, painting, etc.).
- Invite them to your house for a cookout.
- Work on charity events with them.
- Introduce them to your family.
- Meet their families.
- Attend homecoming events, and meet their alumni.
- Sit with them at university sporting events.
- Go to religious services with them.
- Have a beer with the members, and serve as a model for responsible and moderate drinking (something they rarely see).

- Support them at their intramural sports or performance/talent competitions.
- Attend Greek conferences and/or workshops with them. Most national organizations will gladly sponsor your trip.

Once professors have gained the trust, respect, and friendship of the membership, they will be in a position to suggest significant changes. The key, of course, is knowing when to push and when to back away, which battles are worth fighting and which ones are not. Change cannot be crammed down anyone's throat; it must be accepted willingly, and it must be a matter of consensus. The best that any adviser can do is to introduce topics, facilitate debate, and help implement agreed-on changes. If pushed too fast or bullied too much, the organization will close ranks and freeze out the offending outsider. Young people want guidance, not a nagging surrogate mother or father. And they want to be treated like adults. I have found it effective to think (and refer) to myself as their much older "big brother." The metaphor keeps me within the family structure of the organization, but it also creates a clear social and professional demarcation between me and the brothers and sisters.

But change within such a traditional institution does not come overnight, and it cannot be achieved without effort. Professors will need to make a long-term commitment to their organizations. This is especially important given the ephemeral nature of campus life. Changes implemented one year can be easily forgotten the next as seniors graduate and neophytes take their place. At best, the institutional memory of any Greek organization—without consistent and involved advising—is three years. The good news is that involvement becomes more enjoyable and easier with each invested semester. The hardest period is usually the first year.[1]

Finally, professors who for whatever reason are unable to involve themselves directly with Greek organizations can still participate in the process of change by adjusting the content of their courses to focus on problem areas. While certain courses are more conducive than others to discussion of gender, race, and class, most informed teachers, regardless of discipline, should be able to find ways to address these issues in the classroom. After all, power and privilege penetrate all aspects of our lives (e.g., business, education, government, science, religion, family). We professors just need to know where to look for them in our chosen fields and how to communicate their deleterious effects to our students, many of whom will be Greek.

Greek Alumni

In the effort to reshape Greek life, alumni are the great untapped resource. No other stakeholders care as much, are more invested, or know the inner workings of the institution better. Unfortunately, they are also difficult to find, except on homecoming weekend, and, even then, they spend most of their time with *their* contemporaries, not the younger, active chapter members.

When I ask alumni why they have stayed away for so long and whether they are interested in getting involved again, the typical response is that they are too busy, that they have outgrown Greek life, or that, on the rare occasions when they have visited their old house, they have felt unwanted and uncomfortable. And I have to admit that, before committing to serving as an alumni volunteer, I felt the same way. All I can say in response is that the reward is well worth the effort, however difficult it may be at first.

While alumni's first few visits to their old houses may be awkward and conversation strained, within a relatively short period of time most will be welcomed back warmly. Undergraduates generally enjoy meeting their older brothers and sisters who are professionally successful and domestically happy. Surely most everyone remembers the anxiety engendered by the thought of life after college (see chapter 6). When mature and thoughtful alumni become a presence at a house, they serve as living models of what can be achieved when the proverbial party is over.

Along with serving as role models, however, I also encourage alumni to let their little brothers and sisters learn from their mistakes. Let them know what attitudes and behaviors you learned as a Greek are unacceptable in the real world. Tell them what you would do differently if you could do it again. For example:

- Would you party less and study more?
- Would you surround yourself with more culturally diverse friends?
- Do you wish you had studied abroad and spent less time in basements, bars, and bedrooms?
- Do you regret not taking a more diverse range of courses, including courses that were not seen as gender appropriate at the time (e.g., interior design, mechanical engineering, early childhood education, finance, sculpting)?
- Would you have treated outsiders better?
- Would you have held insiders more accountable for their actions?
- Would you have been more proactively involved in the lives of emotionally troubled brothers and sisters?
- Do you wish you intervened more often when confronted with excessive drinking, fighting, and unsafe sexual behavior?
- Did you ignore the early warning signs of alcoholism, eating disorders, or drug addiction?
- Do you wish there had been more discussion of intellectual, moral, and political issues in your house and fewer sexist, racist, and homophobic jokes?
- Do you wish your chapter had engaged in more sincere and more legitimate philanthropic work to improve the living conditions in your community?

While most alumni wanting to reconnect have good intentions, there are a few common mistakes made in the process that need to be avoided. The most common is usually committed by male alumni, especially the recent graduates, who come back to their houses looking to relive their undergraduate days. Not only will such individuals be of little help in effecting positive change; they will also be seen as pathetic losers by their little brothers and sisters. Yes, undergraduates do enjoy their social life, but most also understand that, when their school days are over, it is time to grow up, get a job, and act responsibly. A thirty-five-year-old who is still pounding back the beers and chasing coeds with his little brothers is not cool; he is an embarrassment.

A second common mistake is sporadic attendance or extended absence. Given the professional and domestic demands on the average alumnus, it is easy to see how checking in, hanging out, and making meetings are often pushed aside, especially if getting to campus involves a substantial commute. And, as I have experienced myself during a sabbatical year, the longer you stay away, the easier it is to stay away. You feel less connected to the brothers and sisters, and they feel less connected to you. The best strategy, therefore, is not to sever your ties once you have developed a rapport. Even five-minute visits once a week can be sufficient to maintain ties during those inevitable hectic periods.

Finally, like most people, alumni volunteers often make popularity their first concern. The right thing to do is often the least popular thing to do. And I must confess to having backed down, compromised, and looked the other way sometimes when I should have stood my ground and fought the good fight. Keep reminding yourself, as I often have to, that you are not these students' peer but their mentor. They need you to broach the uncomfortable topics, advocate the unpopular ideas, and champion the right course of action. Your interpersonal astuteness and character will get you through the rough patches. Remember, it is precisely the rough patches that offer the best opportunities for significant change.

Concerned Greek Students

The final group of stakeholders that has the ability to facilitate change from *within* the institution consists of the concerned and enlightened members of the Greek system. One of the affirming aspects of this project was finding so many students who sensed that the system was somehow broken. These are the students who will need to continue to voice discontent with the traditional ways. They will need to find like-minded sisters and brothers and work together to challenge the status quo. They will need to engage their membership in thoughtful conversation, both formally and informally. Change cannot happen without them.

For those students who want to make a difference, here are some specific suggestions to begin the long process of reformation:

- Make your house an unsafe environment for racism, sexism, and homophobia. When you hear a hateful or hurtful joke, let your brothers and sisters know that such remarks are beneath them, antithetical to their organization's creed, and personally distasteful to you. You will be amazed how this small act will affect people's behavior.
- Speak up when something is wrong, even if you think you are outnumbered or will be outvoted. You may be surprised by how many people will follow your lead. Research in social psychology has demonstrated that, often, one brave voice is enough to smash the illusion of unanimity and open the door to debate.[2] Even if no one follows your lead, you will at least have followed your conscience.
- Be a mentor and model. Every year, by the very nature of the institution, you have the opportunity to shape the thoughts and behaviors of new pledge classes. While it may take a few years to see your investment pay off, the pledges you mentor today will be your organization's leaders tomorrow.
- Work to rush and pledge diversity. This is perhaps the single most effective way to expand gender scripts. When given the opportunity to affect your organization's makeup, push boundaries, don't seek out just one "type," look past physical appearance for character, and advocate for those who are overlooked

for being "just a little too"—whether it's fat, poor, ethnic, effeminate, butch, unattractive, uncool, or unique. While change won't happen overnight, diversity will breed diversity.

- Encourage the integration of your organization into mainstream campus life. On many campuses, Greeks have scant contact with non-Greek students, organizations, and events. An insulated and isolated Greek culture cuts its members off from diversity of thought and action.

Parents

Perhaps the most important stakeholders not directly involved with university life are the parents of students. Although their sons and daughters are officially adults, parents still have a great deal of sway over the decisions their children make. Consequently, parents need to stay involved in their children's search for the right Greek organization. But how can parents tell the right Greek organizations from the wrong ones? Simply asking their children's opinion will not always be the best approach. The qualities that impress first-year college students will not necessarily be the qualities that will ensure that they mature into critically thinking adults. Here are a few strategies that can more adequately equip parents to engage their sons and daughters in thoughtful decisionmaking.

- Obtaining simple demographic data is a good start. Most university officials will gladly supply you with such information (and, regardless, they are under a legal obligation to do so). Another way to get a sense of the organization's makeup is to look at the chapter's annual composite picture proudly hanging in the front entryway—and these days posted on its Web page as well. Do members look like clones of each other? Do you see any minorities? Do the names supply any clues as to ethnic or cultural diversity? Do you see diversity in body shape and size? Are the women too thin? Do all the men look like bodybuilders?

- Visit the house, and not just during arranged parents' weekends. Greek organizations have learned to clean up, dry out, and hide incriminating evidence before such well-publicized events. Meet your son or daughter's potential brothers and sisters. Good organizations will welcome you and will appreciate your involvement.
- Be an investigative parent. Look around; study the culture of the group. One very astute parent, for example, told me that she was "turned off" by a fraternity her son was interested in because she observed too many neon beer signs, decorative liquor bottles, and homemade bars in individual rooms. "This just wasn't a place that I felt comfortable with." Other parents have told me they rejected organizations because of their lack of cleanliness. Any group, they asserted, that trashes its own house or lives like pigs will probably treat its pledges with the same disregard. One of the most interesting observations came from a parent who noticed that none of the women at the sorority her daughter was rushing ate dessert. "They were all really skinny and drank lots of water."
- Ask informed university administrators and professors for their insight. The key, of course, is to ask, not which houses are the most popular, but which are the most diverse and accepting of individuality, which do the most philanthropic work in the community, which have the highest GPAs, which produce the most campus leaders, which have been on social or academic probation in recent years, which have reputations as hazers, which have reputations as partiers.
- Trust your parental intuition. It has probably served you well up to this point. Don't abandon it now just because your children are beginning their adult lives away from home.

University Administrators

At the risk of offending university administrators around the country, my advice to them would be, Start doing your job! I believe that most of you who are involved with student life are aware of what is happening on Greek row. The general strategy used in managing these organizations is often the all too familiar "don't ask, don't tell" approach. As long as the Greeks do not draw attention to their activities, administrators look the other way. When a sorority or fraternity attracts parental, legal, or media attention, however, these same complacent administrators will publicly demonstrate their "tough-on-Greeks" persona to appease and impress the critics. But such posturing usually comes only after the rare, and well-publicized, rape or death on campus.

If significant change is going to take place within Greek organizations, a far more proactive approach must be adopted by administrators. These are the only stakeholders, after all, who have the power to demand change and suspend or expel members and organizations for noncompliance. Regardless of how politically or financially imprudent it may be, the hard choices must be made and the Greek student body held accountable to the higher ideas of university life. For what it is worth, here are some of my thoughts:

- Your once-a-semester mass presentation or workshop on the evils of drinking or the ills of drug use is not enough. It is often simply a public relation ploy or a safeguard against litigation, and it is viewed by Greeks as insincere and annoying.
- Get out from behind your desks, and get to know the students in your charge. Appoint specific administrators to be responsible for maintaining close and constant ties with the Greek community. On most campuses, deans and directors of student life rarely make their presence felt. And, when they do, their visits are often well publicized in advance. Just like faculty and alumni, administrators must "be there"—regardless of whether it is a Friday night or a Saturday morning—listening to, learning from, influencing, and shaping the lives of students. While establishing such lines of communication may mean hir-

ing new liaisons (with unique job descriptions), the investment will surely pay dividends.

- Evaluate and assess all Greek organizations annually. Remaining active on campus should not be a right; it should be a privilege and, as such, earned. As things are now, most organizations remain active as long as they have done nothing terribly wrong, regardless of whether they have done anything exceptionally right. This precedent needs to be changed. If an organization is not living up to the higher ideals of university life, its charter should be revoked. Set the bar higher, and you will be amazed by how high students will ascend.

The Future without Stakeholder Investment

I wish I had the magic bullet that would solve the Greek problem, painlessly and effortlessly. But I don't. Unfortunately, when it comes to transforming something as stubborn as gender construction, no such easy remedy exists. Notions of masculinity and femininity have been evolving slowly over thousands of years—shaped (or misshaped) by power, environment, biology, superstition, law, war, imperialism, disease, religion, and MTV—and nothing short of a cataclysm is going to alter them dramatically.

Consequently, my suggestions for change focus on grassroots activism: concerned stakeholders, working in tandem, beginning to affect small, localized sites where harmful gender performances have been normalized. To borrow from the environmentalists, our only hope is to "think globally, act locally—one person at a time." While we may not have the power to revolutionize ideas of equality and justice, we can begin to change the people who may eventually have that power.

It would be misleading of me to imply that involvement in the Greek system is always going to be easy, fun, and rewarding. It won't be. I am confident, however, that, with time and effort, dedicated and concerned stakeholders can make a difference. And a difference made in the Greek system is an important difference indeed. More enlightened brothers and sisters means more enlightened graduates making their way from Greek row to Fortune 500 companies, the Supreme Court, Congress, and the White House. Without stakeholder involvement, however, change will not come. Traditional notions of gender will continue to reproduce themselves, and our students and our society will continue to be cheated by such limited and limiting rules of acceptable behavior and thought.

Acknowledgments

First and foremost I am indebted to the hundreds of Greek students who invited me into their lives and shared their stories with me. They trusted me to write a fair and accurate book about their lives that would help move the Greek system toward the idealized goals of its creeds. I hope that I did not disappoint them.

If it is true that behind every book there is a patient and selfless friend, then mine is Audrey Curtis Hane (Newman University, Kansas). Whether brainstorming ideas, unpacking gender theory, or reading the endless drafts, Audrey was always encouraging, insightful, and supportive.

Thank you to my three very generous readers: my mentor Eva McMahan (James Madison University), Scott Kiesling (University of Pittsburgh), and Cindy Griffin (Colorado State University). Their insights, suggestions, and support helped make this work significantly more interesting and readable.

I also need to thank Erin Foley-Reynolds and Amy Akers, two of the funniest and brightest graduate students in America. Their help and encouragement during the conceptualization and data-gathering segments of this project were immeasurable.

For their editorial guidance at every stage of the process, I would like to thank Anne Dean Watkins, David Cobb, Joe Brown, and most especially, Stephen Wrinn at the University Press of Kentucky.

Finally, thank you to my wife, Lori, and my children, Abigail and James, for unselfishly letting me research and write this book. They were always supportive and patient, no matter how "crazy" I got.

Notes

Introduction

1. While most Greek organizations use Greek letters for identification, there are three notable exceptions found in the ranks of white fraternities: Acacia, Farm-House, and Triangle.

2. While professional fraternities/sororities and honor societies use Greek letters as designators, they have little else in common with their distant social cousin. Their members don't pledge or haze, live in communal housing, refer to or conceive of each other as brothers or sisters, or socialize with each other outside the rare chapter meeting or philanthropic event.

3. It should be noted that, whereas individuals can, given eligibility, belong to as many professional fraternities/sororities and honor societies as they choose, membership in more than one social institution is prohibited. Membership in a social institution does not, however, make one ineligible for membership in professional fraternities/sororities or honor societies.

4. Shortly after its inception, Phi Beta Kappa became an honor society. The group is still in existence, with over fifteen thousand new members initiated every year in 270 chapters across the United States.

5. Today, fraternities are governed by the North-American Interfraternity Conference (NIC). As of April 2007, the NIC represented sixty-eight national and international men's fraternities: Acacia, Alpha Chi Rho, Alpha Delta Gamma, Alpha Delta Phi, Alpha Epsilon Pi, Alpha Gamma Rho, Alpha Gamma Sigma, Alpha Kappa Lambda, Alpha Phi Alpha, Alpha Phi Delta, Alpha Sigma Phi, Alpha Tau Omega, Beta Chi Theta, Beta Sigma Psi, Beta Theta Pi, Chi Phi, Chi Psi, Delta Chi, Delta Kappa Epsilon, Delta Phi, Delta Psi, Delta Sigma Phi, Delta Tau Delta, Delta Upsilon, FarmHouse, Iota Phi Theta, Kappa Alpha Order, Kappa Alpha Psi, Kappa Alpha Society, Kappa Delta Phi, Kappa Delta Rho, Lambda Chi Alpha, Lambda Phi Epsilon, Lambda Sigma Upsilon, Lamda Theta Phi, Phi Gamma Delta, Phi Iota Alpha, Phi Kappa Psi, Phi Kappa Sigma, Phi Kappa Tau, Phi Kappa Theta, Phi Lambda Chi, Phi Mu Delta, Phi Sigma Kappa, Phi Sigma Phi, Pi Kappa Alpha, Pi Kappa Phi, Pi Lambda Phi, Psi Upsilon, Sigma Alpha Epsilon, Sigma Alpha Mu, Sigma Chi, Sigma Lambda Beta, Sigma Nu, Sigma Phi Delta, Sigma Phi Epsilon, Sigma Phi Society, Sigma Pi, Sigma Tau Gamma, Tau Delta Phi, Tau Epsilon Phi, Tau Kappa Epsilon, Theta Chi, Theta Delta Chi, Theta Xi, Triangle, Zeta Beta Tau, and Zeta Psi.

6. Today, sororities are governed by the National Panhellenic Conference

(NPC). The NPC represents twenty-six national and international women's sororities: Alpha Chi Omega, Alpha Sigma Tau, Delta Zeta, Pi Beta Phi, Alpha Delta Pi, Alpha Xi Delta, Gamma Phi Beta, Sigma Delta Tau, Alpha Epsilon Phi, Chi Omega, Kappa Alpha Theta, Sigma Kappa, Alpha Gamma Delta, Delta Delta Delta, Kappa Delta, Sigma Sigma Sigma, Alpha Omicron Pi, Delta Gamma, Kappa Kappa Gamma, Theta Phi Alpha, Alpha Phi, Delta Phi Epsilon, Phi Mu, Zeta Tau Alpha, Alpha Sigma Alpha, and Phi Sigma Sigma.

7. Today, black fraternities and sororities are governed by the National Pan-Hellenic Council (NPHC). The NPHC represents nine historically black Greek-letter organizations: Alpha Kappa Alpha Sorority, Alpha Phi Alpha Fraternity, Delta Sigma Theta Sorority, Zeta Phi Beta Sorority, Iota Phi Theta Fraternity, Kappa Alpha Psi Fraternity, Sigma Gamma Rho Sorority, Phi Beta Sigma Fraternity, and Omega Phi Psi Fraternity.

8. For a more detailed history of hazing in America's social Greek system, see Nuwer (1999).

9. This translates to approximately 750,000 active members in 12,000 chapters on 800 campuses in the United States.

10. Before beginning this project investigating the lives of GU's Greeks, I first obtained permission from the university's Institutional Review Board (IRB). The IRB, which reviews research studies involving human subjects, is federally mandated to ensure that proper safeguards are in place to protect human subjects enrolled in research studies.

I also had each interviewee involved with this project sign an informed-consent form. This form details the goals of my project, describes the rights that subjects have in the research process, and gives me legal permission to use the data obtained in my research.

11. These experiences in such varied and diverse contexts allow me to identify recurring aspects of gender that remain constant, trace developmental factors of gender that have changed, and isolate aspects of femininity and masculinity that appear to be contextually specific to a given campus or geographic location.

12. The chapter director holds an advisory position sponsored by the national fraternity; the faculty adviser holds an advisory position sponsored by the university.

13. In return for their help, all point people received one academic credit, an insider's look at how academic research is conducted, an invitation to participate in the study throughout its duration (none chose to do so), and greater insight into how gender is constructed in their organization.

14. On average, these nineteen videotaped interviews lasted one hour, forty minutes each. The sorority interviews typically lasted fifteen minutes longer than the fraternity interviews.

15. That is, aspirer organizations were more likely to have a token Asian American, Latino, or African American in their ranks than were elite organizations.

16. While most members of strugglers claimed to have found happiness and fellowship in their smaller groups, all those whom I interviewed were painfully aware of the negative way in which they were perceived—when perceived at all—by the rest of the GU Greek community.

I. Understanding Gender

1. As with most *public* universities, GU attracts a wide range of students from diverse socioeconomic backgrounds. Its Greek system, however, is not so welcoming; it disproportionately attracts, and courts, middle- and upper-class undergraduates. This economic divide can be understood by considering a number of interrelated factors.

First, students are more likely to know about the Greek system and be encouraged to rush (a process that, at GU, begins a week before the first day of classes) and pledge if friends and family members have previously attended college and gone Greek. This type of privileged information and guidance is often unavailable to GU's lower-middle-class students, who tend to hail from small farm towns and inner cities and be the first in their families to attend college.

Second, going Greek is not cheap. The average cost per *semester* of joining a sorority at GU, e.g., ranges from $2,050 to $3,000 for room and board in a communal Greek house and chapter dues. Many Greek organizations also require a onetime initiation fee that ranges from $700 to $1,100. And beyond these "official" expenses are the social expenses, e.g., out-of-state, overnight formals and semiformals, Greek paraphernalia, appropriate clothing, and, of course, the alcohol that is de rigueur at every party. The average GU Greek can, over the course of a five-year college career, expect to spend $30,000–$35,000 on the Greek experience.

Finally, elite organizations seek out elite (like-minded, privileged) pledges, and vice versa. For a more detailed description of how this selection process works, see the section "The Interplay between Groups, Recruits, and Culture."

It should be noted that less privileged students are more likely to be rushed and bid by the less selective and prestigious aspirer and struggler organizations.

2. It should be noted that GU's strugglers do not have houses and, thus, have a far more difficult time recruiting new members. While the elites and the aspirers open up their centrally located houses to attract and impress visitors, the strugglers have to find available space on campus to publicize the benefits of membership in their group.

3. While most traditional gender themes have remained ideologically stable for generations, I did discover some exceptions to this rule. Specifically, some gender themes have recently morphed into amplified versions of themselves. An analysis of the men in the study, e.g., revealed that a new *hypermasculinity*—in terms of violence, aggression, and physical strength—has emerged. Young men in alarming numbers are joining gyms, lifting weights, and taking muscle-enhancing supplements. At the same time, a new *hyperfemininity* has also emerged. The object, however, is about becoming, not more imposing, but less. Approximately 80 percent of all the women I have worked with have admitted to having problems with enjoying food, or, to put it another way, are obsessively dieting, counting calories, carbs, and fat, exercising, or abstaining from food completely. On college campuses around America, the men are getting bigger, and the women are getting smaller.

I also found that the concept of *frontiersmanship*, once a standard component of the American notion of masculinity, no longer figures in the lives of young college men. Frederick Jackson Turner's so-called frontier thesis asserts that deep in the heart of every American man is the drive to conquer, control, and connect with the great outdoors. So central has this idea been to the national conversation, in fact, that Cawelti (1976), Kimmel (1987), Maynard (1974), and Rushing (1983) have all argued that the "daring and romantic cowboy" (Trujillo, 1991, p. 183) has become an archetype in America's collective masculine unconscious. But things appear to have changed, at least for an elite segment of American men. Perhaps this ideological development can be blamed on the computer age (our new uncharted frontier), conspicuous mass consumption (our new obsession), or the industrialization of America's last Western frontiers, but, whatever the reason, the drive to conquer, control, and connect with nature is largely extinct in the next generation of American's leaders.

4. The differences in verbal expressiveness between the men and the women in this study were both striking and disturbing. The women employed a vocabulary that was more precise and complex, incorporated more intimate details when describing their experiences, constructed longer narratives in discussions, relied far less on vulgar expressions and profanities, and demonstrated fluency and ease while discussing relationships, emotions, and vulnerabilities. Conversely, most of the men struggled to articulate ideas clearly, especially when the topic was intimacy. They spoke in shorter spurts, cursed more, struggled for appropriate words, and demonstrated unease with questions probing relationships and emotions.

2. Studs and Virgins

1. The National Panhellenic Conference, founded in 1902, is an umbrella organization for twenty-six international sororities. Member groups are found on over

620 college and university campuses in the United States and Canada and in over 4,800 alumnae associations, representing over 3.5 million sorority women worldwide. See NPC (2003).

2. The Kinsey Reports (1948, 1953) found that oral sex was pretty much the province of married couples. Even then, Kinsey found that only 50 percent of married women had participated in oral sex, suggesting that it was not a widely accepted form of sexual expression (as reported by Elliott & Brantley, 1997, 113).

3. For more detail, see Birnbaum (2000), Jarrell (2000), Schuster, Bell, and Kanouse (1996), "*Seventeen* News" (2000), and Stepp (1999a, 1999b).

4. For national figures on this trend, see Elliott & Brantley (1997).

5. It is interesting to note that no one, male or female, ever made any reference, either in formal interviews or in informal conversations, to sexually transmitted diseases (STDs). With 3 million new cases of chlamydia, 650,000 new cases of gonorrhea, 70,000 new cases of syphilis, 1 million new cases of herpes, 5.5 million new cases of human papillomavirus, and 5 million new cases of trichomoniasis being diagnosed each year and AIDS the leading killer of Americans between the ages of twenty-five and forty-four, inevitability dictates that many of these sexually active young adults are infecting each other. Nonetheless, STDs remain *the* great taboo topic in the Greek system (see CDC 2004).

3. The Tough Guy and His Date (Rape)

1. On the GU campus, most fraternities rush during both the fall and the spring semesters. It is the fall rush, however, attracting as it does the largest pledge classes, and thus serving as a sign of the organization's health, that takes priority.

2. Most campuses in America have implemented a dry-rush policy. Alcohol of any kind is officially banned from any fraternity function during the week. As a result, most organizations have been forced to go underground and sponsor late-night, secret "wet rushes" or "dirty parties."

3. Interestingly, the most horrifying stories that I have heard over the last twenty-five years have never been experienced by the teller. These narratives, mythic in quality, have all been passed down as part of Greek lore, becoming the urban legends of the Greek community. Among them are the following:

- "One of the worst things I have ever heard was from one of my buddies who pledged in another state. They would make the room in the basement, like, freezing, and they had glue all across the rails on the top, and then they would take bottles and break them over the rail so the glue would make the glass stick to the rails, and then they would make them, like, hang for five minutes and then drop down. He's still got some scars from where he did it. This guy was very headstrong and was like, 'If I am going to do it, then I am going to do it.'"

- "There was that chapter that had the kid chained in the doghouse? They stripped him bare and tied him to the doghouse for a week. He finally escaped, and I think he's still fucked up."
- "I heard about these houses that make the brothers do circle jerks. They all have to beat off together."
- Oh yeah, I know for a fact that some of these guys had to fuck goats and stuff. Horses I think too."

4. When factors such as excessive alcohol consumption, the isolation and segregation of fraternity houses, and the traditional ideas of aggressive masculinity and passive femininity promoted by most fraternities and sororities are added to the equation, the risk of sexual assault and date rape increases exponentially (Boswell & Spade, 1996; Martin & Hummer, 1989; O'Sullivan, 1991; Sanday, 1990).

5. For further discussion, see chapter 6.

6. Unlike GU's fraternities, which rush twice a year, GU's sororities rush only once, at the beginning of the fall semester.

7. Usually only elite and aspirer sororities compete in Greek Sing. As one sister from the Rho sorority, a struggler, told me: "We would not stand a chance. We just don't have enough members to do it like the others." She adds, with a self-deprecating laugh: "We also don't get a whole lot of the cheerleader types pledging us."

4. Her Laxatives, His Steroids

1. I started taking this informal poll in my mass-lecture theory class in 1997. Normally, it follows a discussion of sex in American advertising. Of the roughly twelve hundred students that this class attracts annually, at least half are women.

2. These references and more can be found at http://www.about-face.org, an excellent example of how the Web can be responsibly used to empower and educate, its purpose being to promote "positive self-esteem in girls and women of all ages, sizes, races and backgrounds."

3. I am often asked what has changed the most since the days when I was an active Greek. My response is always threefold. First, many more students are working part-time jobs while attending college. Second, oral sex has replaced vaginal sex as the most popular form of heterosexual intercourse. Finally, and most strikingly, whereas

all that used to be expected of fraternity men was that they be lean, reasonably well groomed, and preppy, today the emphasis is on clean, chiseled, muscular bodies.

4. Creatine is used in muscle cells to store energy for sprinting and explosive exercise. Athletes can increase the amount of creatine in their muscle tissue by taking creatine supplements. Although some studies report no ergogenic effect of creatine supplementation (e.g., twenty grams a day for five to seven days), most indicate that it increases sprint performance by 1–5 percent and work performed in repeated sprints by up to 15 percent. The effect evidently varies with the extent of uptake of creatine into muscle tissue. Creatine supplementation for a month or two during training has been reported to promote further gains in sprint performance (5–8 percent) as well as gains in strength (5–15 percent) and lean body mass (1–3 percent). The only known side effect is increased body weight (see Kreider, 1998). More research is needed on individual differences in response to creatine, the periodic or cyclical use of it, other possible side effects, and long-term effects on endurance.

5. Deca Durabolin is the Organon brand name for nandrolone decanoate. Worldwide, Deca is one of the most popular injectable steroids. Its popularity is likely due to the fact that it exhibits significant anabolic effects with minimal androgenic side effects. Considered by many the best overall steroid for a man to use (side effects vs. results) Deca is most commonly injected once per week at a dosage of two to four hundred milligrams. At this amount, estrogen conversion is slight, so gynecomastia is usually not a problem. Also uncommon are problems with liver enzymes, blood pressure, or cholesterol level. At higher dosages, side effects may occur more frequently, but this is still a very well tolerated drug. It should also be noted that, in HIV studies, Deca has been shown not only to be effective at safely bringing up the lean body weight of patients but also to be beneficial to the immune system.

For the purposes of bodybuilding, Deca can effectively be incorporated in both mass and cutting cycles. One major drawback to Deca is that it can be detected in a drug screen for as long as a year after use. Unfortunately for many competitive athletes, this renders Deca and other nandrolone products off-limits. Deca is also comparatively expensive. Purchased on the black market, two hundred milligrams will cose upwards of twenty dollars. Commonly available in the United States is the Mexican veterinary version Norandren 50 from Brovel. This is a fifty-milliliter vial of what is supposed to be fifty milligram per millileter nandrolone decanoate. Brovel, however, has a reputation for underdosing its products, so this may be closer to thirty-five milligrams per milliliter. Extraboline and Deca-Durabolin from Greece are also commonly found (Extraboline usually being slightly cheaper), as is Retabolil from Bulgaria ("Russian Deca"). Retabolil ampoules come one to a box and in twenty-five- and fifty-milligram strength, the latter being almost exclusively brought to the United States. The ampoules have no band around the neck and no scoring. The larger box comes with a file, which is required to open the ampoules. Riabolil ampoules have been made with two labeling styles, one being a very-easy-to-rub-off red-and-yellow silk-screened directly on the glass, the other a simple paper label with gray text. Deca is also widely counterfeited, so caution should be taken when purchasing this on the black market. Information obtained from http://www.anabolicsteroidsuccess.com/products/deca_durabolin_norma.html.

5. Bros before Hos

1. This story was related to me by Lisa after the ceremony. The candlelight is a restricted ritual, with only sisters allowed in attendance.

2. GU has never allowed an official little sister program.

3. Another effect of the metaphor of fraternity brothers as family members, it seems to me, is the frequency with which fraternity brothers touch each other and the form of physical contact in which they engage. Like biological brothers, they hug, wrestle with, greet (they shake hands with each other as often as fifteen or twenty times a day), grab, embrace, affectionately punch, and humorously slap each other far more often than is usual among heterosexual American men—a demographic group that touches less than any other segment of our culture (Deaux, 1976; Leathers, 1986).

4. This information was compiled in the report *A Call to Action: Changing the Culture of Drinking at U.S. Colleges* (Task Force of the National Advisory Council on Alcohol Abuse and Alcoholism, 2002). The report was developed by a special task force composed of college presidents, alcohol researchers, and students that conducted an extensive analysis of the research literature in order to provide the most current scientifically based information on college drinking.

5. For a more detailed analysis of fraternity drinking songs, see Workman (2001).

6. Throughout the years, these songs have been appropriated, adapted, and sung by almost every fraternity in the nation.

7. This list was reproduced from the Web page of the Lousiana State University Greek Affairs Office: http://appl003.lsu.edu/slas/GreekAffairs2.nsf/$Content/IFC+Hazing+Policy?OpenDocument.

8. There are, of course, exceptions to this rule. For instance, the most tightly bonded organization that I have ever encountered was a small, local sorority on the campus of Brandywine College in Wilmington, Delaware. The Zeta women, as they referred to themselves, were deeply committed and connected to each other in ways that most fraternities could only envy. Interestingly, the Zetas were not the biggest or the most popular sorority on campus. They did, however, haze hard,

remain small, define themselves (both privately and publicly) as the sorority with real sisterhood, and create a culture of intolerance for catty dissent and cliques. These four ingredients produced a sisterhood that was fiercely loyal, dedicated, and committed to each other's welfare. While GU's sororities may be bigger, richer, more attractive, more influential, and older, they have been unable to generate such collective loyalty and devotion.

9. What is perhaps most interesting about these women's attitude toward the endemic cattiness is that they all recognize it as a problem but do nothing to combat it—despite being remarkably proactive when it comes to addressing and solving other problems. For example, there have been many incidents of sexual promiscuity, excessive drinking, tardiness at meetings, dropping GPAs, and apathy that have been directly addressed and resolved by sororities. Why, I am left to wonder, don't these women take a similar approach to what many see as the real cancer to sisterhood? Have they been programmed by the patriarchy to believe that women are inherently bitchy and gossipy? Have they accepted the myth that such dysfunctional communication is the natural, God-given state of affairs for women in large groups? I am left with more questions than answers.

6. Soccer Moms and Corporate Dads

1. As of the spring 2005 semester, my department had 398 majors, 59 percent women, 41 percent men. The department's selective admissions policy requires that students earn a 2.6 overall GPA during their first sixty credit hours and a 3.0 GPA in five courses preliminary to the major before being admitted into our college.

2. This state of affairs is not unique to white America. Harris (1992) found a similar pressure on black men to underperform in the classroom. In their quest not to be seen as feminine, Harris argues, African American boys will sometimes neglect schoolwork, misbehave, and challenge authority.

7. Cleaning Up after the Party

1. I want to make it very clear that I am not claiming to be an exemplary faculty adviser. I do not devote enough time to the mundane workings of the organizations for which I am responsible, and I am probably too cautious about intervening in their decisionmaking process.

2. Readers interested in empirical demonstrations of this phenomenon should consult Asch (1955) and Insko, Smith, Alicke, Wade, and Taylor (1985).

References

Andersen, A. E., & DiDomenico, L. (1992). Diet vs. shape content of popular male and female magazines: A dose-response relationship to the incidence of eating disorders. *International Journal of Eating Disorders, 11*(3), 283–287.

Anzuldúa, G. E. (1999). *Borderlands/La frontera: The new mestiza* (2nd ed.). San Francisco: Spinsters/Aunt Lute. (Original work published 1987)

Are you a metrosexual? (2003, September 23). ESPN Sports Nation. Retrieved March 10, 2004, from http://proxy.espn.go.com/chat/sportsnation/quiz?event_id=418.

Aries, E. J., & Johnson, F. L. (1983). Close friendship in adulthood: Conversational content between same-sex friends. *Sex Roles, 9,* 1183–1197.

Asch, S. D. (1955, November). Opinions and social pressure. *Scientific American, 19,* 31–35.

Bachman, R., & Saltzman, L. E. (1995). *Violence against women: Estimates from the redesigned survey* (NCJ 154348). Washington, DC: U.S. Department of Justice, Bureau of Justice Statistics.

Balswick, J. O., & Peek, C. W. (1976). The inexpressive male: A tragedy of American society. In D. Brannon & R. Brannon (Eds.), *The forty-nine percent majority: The male sex-role* (pp. 55–57). Reading, MA: Addison-Wesley.

Bartlett, K. T., & Kennedy, R. (Eds.). (1991). *Feminist legal theory: Readings in law and gender.* Boulder, CO: Westview.

Becker, C. S. (1987). Friendship between women: A phenomenological study of best friends. *Journal of Phenomenological Psychology, 18,* 59–72.

Beemyn, B., & Eliason, M. (Eds.). (1996). *Queer studies: A lesbian, gay, bisexual, and transgender anthology.* New York: New York University Press.

Bem, S. L. (1993). *The lenses of gender: Transforming the debate on sexual inequality.* New Haven, CT: Yale University Press.

Birnbaum, C. (2000, October/November). The love and sex survey, 2000. *Twist,* 54–56.

Blackwell, R. E. (1957). *Improvement of fraternity scholarship.* Oxford, OH.

Boeringer, S. B., Sherhan, C. L., & Akers, R. (1991). Social contexts and social learning in sexual coercion and aggression: Assessing the contribution of fraternity membership. *Family Relations, 40,* 58–64.

Bordo, S. (1999). *The male body: A new look at men in public and in private.* New York: Farrar Straus Giroux.

Boswell, A. A., & Spade, J. Z. (1996). Fraternities and collegiate rape culture: Why are some fraternities more dangerous places for women? *Gender and Society, 10,* 133–147.

247

Brehm, S. S. (1992). *Intimate relationships* (2nd ed.). New York: McGraw-Hill. (Original work published 1988)

Brewer, M. (1979). In-group bias in the minimal intergroup situation: A cognitive-motivational analysis. *Psychological Bulletin, 86,* 307–324.

Brod, H. (1994). Some thoughts on some histories of some masculinities: Jews and other others. In H. Brod & M. Kaufman (Eds.), *Theorizing masculinities* (pp. 82–96). Thousand Oaks, CA: Sage.

Brod, H., & Kaufman, M. (Eds.). (1994). *Theorizing masculinities.* Thousand Oaks, CA: Sage.

Bryan, W. A. (1987). Contemporary fraternity and sorority issues. In R. B. Winston, W. R. Nettles III, & J. H. Opper (Eds.), *Fraternities and sororities on the contemporary college campus* (pp. 37–56). San Francisco: Jossey-Bass.

Butler, J. (1990). *Gender trouble: Feminism and the subversion of identity.* New York: Routledge.

Butler, J. (1993). *Bodies that matter: On the discursive limits of "sex."* New York: Routledge.

Byrne, D. (1971). *The attraction paradigm.* New York: Academic.

Caldwell, M. A., & Peplau, L. A. (1982). Sex differences in same-sex friendships. *Sex Roles, 8,* 721–732.

Campbell, A. (2002). *A mind of her own: The evolutionary psychology of women.* Oxford: Oxford University Press.

Cancian, F. M. (1987). *Love in America: Gender and self-development.* Cambridge: Cambridge University Press.

Cancian, F. M. (1989). Love and the rise of capitalism. In B. J. Risman & P. Schwartz (Eds.), *Gender in intimate relationships: A microstructural approach* (pp. 12–25). Belmont, CA: Wadsworth.

Cashin, J. R., Presley, C. A., & Meilman, P. W. (1998). Alcohol use in the Greek system: Follow the leader? *Journal of Studies on Alcohol, 59*(1), 63–79.

Cawelti, J. G. (1976). *Adventure, mystery, and romance: Formula stories as art and popular culture.* Chicago: University of Chicago Press.

Center for the Study of the College Fraternity. (n.d.). Frequently asked questions: Where can I find the source of those great-sounding stats that are always used to promote Greek Life? Retrieved March 2, 2007, from http://www.indiana.edu/~sao/cscfsite.

Centers for Disease Control and Prevention (CDC). (2004). *Trends in reportable sexually transmitted diseases in the United States, 2004: National surveillance data for chlamydia, gonorrhea, and syphilis.* Retrieved April 15, 2007, from http://www.cdc.gov/std/stats04/trends2004.htm.

Centers for Disease Control and Prevention (CDC). (2003, October 10). Cigarette smoking among adults—United States, 2001. *Morbidity and Mortality*

Weekly Report, 52(40), 953–956. Retrieved October 2004 from www.cdc. gov/mmwr//preview/mmwrhtml/mm5240a1.htm.

Cialdini, R. B. (2001). *Influence: Science and practice* (4th ed.). Boston: Allyn & Bacon. (Original work published 1985)

Connell, R. W. (1983). *Which way is up? Essays on sex, class, and culture.* Sydney: Allen & Unwin.

Connell, R. W. (1987). *Gender and power.* Stanford, CA: Stanford University Press.

Connell, R. W. (1990). An iron man: The body and some contradictions of hegemonic masculinity. In M. A. Messner & D. F. Sabo (Eds.), *Sport, men, and gender order: Critical feminist perspectives* (pp. 83–95). Champaign, IL: Human Kinetics.

Connell, R. W. (1995). *Masculinities.* Berkeley and Los Angeles: University of California Press.

Connell, R. W. (2002). *Gender.* Cambridge: Polity.

Copenhaver, S., & Grauerholz, E. (1991). Sexual victimization among sorority women: Exploring the link between sexual violence and institutional practices. *Sex Roles, 24,* 31–41.

Davidson, K. J., & Moore, N. B. (1994). Masturbation and premarital sexual intercourse among college women: Making choices for sexual fulfillment. *Journal of Sex and Marital Therapy, 20,* 178–199.

Deaux, K. (1976). *The behavior of men and women.* Monterey, CA: Brooks/Cole.

Delamont, S. (2001). *Changing women, unchanged men? Sociological perspectives on gender in a post-industrial society.* Philadelphia: Open University Press.

Dillon, S. (2007a, February 25). Evictions at sorority raise issue of bias. *New York Times.* Available at http://www.nytimes.com.

Dillon, S. (2007b, March 13). After evicting members, sorority is itself evicted. *New York Times.* Available at http://www.nytimes.com.

Doyle, J. A. (1995). *The male experience* (3rd ed.). Dubuque, IA: William C. Brown. (Original work published 1983)

Eagly, A. H. (1978). Sex differences in influenceability. *Psychological Bulletin, 85,* 86–116.

Eckert, P., & McConnell-Ginet, S. (2003). *Language and gender.* Cambridge: Cambridge University Press.

Eder, D. (2001). *School talk: Gender and adolescent culture.* New Brunswick, NJ: Rutgers University Press.

Eichenbaum, L., & Orbach, S. (1987). *Between women: Love, envy, and competition in women's friendships.* New York: Viking.

Elliott, L., & Brantley, C. (1997). *Sex on campus: The naked truth about the real sex lives of college students.* New York: Random House.

Engs, R. C., Diebold, B. A., & Hansen, D. J. (1996). The drinking patterns and problems of a national sample of college students, 1994. *Journal of Alcohol and Drug Education, 41,* 13–33.

Epstein, C. F. (1971). *Women's place: Options and limits in professional careers.* Berkeley: University of California Press.

Espiritu, Y. L. (1997). *Asian American women and men: Labor, laws, and love.* Thousand Oaks, CA: Sage.

Faludi, S. (1992). *Backlash: The undeclared war against American women.* New York: Anchor.

Faludi, S. (1999). *Stiffed: The betrayal of the American man.* New York: Morrow.

Ferguson, C. W. (1937). *Fifty million brothers.* New York: Farrar & Rinehart.

Flagg, B. J. (1997). Transparently white subjective decisionmaking: Fashioning a legal remedy. In R. Delgado & J. Stefancic (Eds.), *Critical white studies: Looking behind the mirror* (pp. 85–88). Philadelphia: Temple University Press.

Foucault, M. (1994). *The order of things: An archaeology of the human sciences.* New York: Vintage.

Friedan, B. (1963). *The feminine mystique.* New York: Norton.

Gadamer, H.-G. (1975). *Truth and method* (J. Weinsheimer & D. G. Marshall, Trans.). New York: Crossroad. (Original work published 1960)

Gates, G. J., & Sonenstein, F. L. (2000). Heterosexual genital sexual activity among adolescent males: 1988 and 1995. *Family Planning Perspectives, 32,* 295–304.

Gauntlett, D. (2002). *Media, gender, and identity: An introduction.* New York: Routledge.

Gaylin, W. (1992). *The male ego.* New York: Viking/Penguin.

Gazmararian, J. A., Petersen, R., Spitz, A. M., Goodwin, M. M., Saltzman, L. E., & Marks, J. S. (2000). Violence and reproductive health: Current knowledge and future research directions. *Maternal and Child Health Journal, 4*(2), 79–84.

Gerson, K. (2004). Moral dilemmas, moral strategies, and the transformation of gender: Lessons from two generations of work and family change. In J. Spade & C. Valentine (Eds.), *The kaleidoscope of gender: Prisms, patterns, and possibilities* (pp. 413–424). Belmont, CA: Wadsworth.

Gilmore, D. D. (1990). *Manhood in the making: Cultural concepts of masculinity.* New Haven, CT: Yale University Press.

Goode, E. (2001, August 1). 20% of girls report abuse by a date. *Raleigh News and Observer,* 10A.

Greenfeld, L. A., Rand, M. R., Craven, D., Klaus, P. A., Perkins, C. A., Ringel, C.,

Warchol, G., Maston, C., & Fox, J. A. (1998, March). *Violence by intimates: Analysis of data on crimes by current or former spouses, boyfriends, and girlfriends* (NCJ-167237). Washington, DC: U.S. Department of Justice, Bureau of Justice Statistics.

Gustafson-Larson, A. M., & Terry, R. D. (1992). Weight-related behaviors and concerns of fourth-grade children. *Journal of the American Dietetic Association, 92*(7), 818–822.

Gwartney-Gibbs, P., & Stockard, J. (1989). Courtship aggression and mixed-sex peer groups. In M. A. Pirog-Good & J. E. Steds (Eds.), *Violence in dating relationships: Emerging social issues* (pp. 185–204). New York: Praeger.

Hackbarth, A. (2003, November 17). Vanity, thy name is metrosexual. *Washington Post*.

Hacker, A. (2003). *Mismatch: The growing gulf between women and men*. New York: Scribner.

Halberstam, D. (1994). *The fifties*. New York: Ballantine.

Harris, S. (1992). Black male masculinity and same sex friendships. *Western Journal of Black Studies, 16,* 74–81.

Herek, G. (1987). On heterosexual masculinity: Some psychical consequences of the social construction of gender on sexuality. In M. Kimmel (Ed.), *Changing men: New directions in research on men and masculinity* (pp. 68–82). Newbury Park, CA: Sage.

Hewitt, J. P. (1991). *Self and society: A symbolic interactionist social psychology*. Boston: Allyn & Bacon.

Hingson, R. W., Heeren, T., Zakocs, R. C., Kopstein, A., & Wechsler, H. (2002). Magnitude of alcohol-related mortality and morbidity among U.S. college students ages 18–24. *Journal of Studies on Alcohol, 63*(2), 136–144.

Hochschild, A., with Machung, A. (2003). *The second shift: Working parents and the revolution at home* (rev. ed.). New York: Viking/Penguin.

Holmstrom, L. L. (1972). *The two-career family*. Cambridge, MA: Schenkman.

Hondagneu-Sotelo, P., & Messner, M. A. (1994). Gender displays and men's power: The "new man" and the Mexican immigrant man. In H. Brod & M. Kaufman (Eds.), *Theorizing masculinities* (pp. 200–218). Thousand Oaks, CA: Sage.

hooks, b. (2000). *Feminist theory: From margin to center*. Boston: South End.

Horan, P. F., Phillips, J., & Hagan, N. E. (1998). The meaning of abstinence for college students. *Journal of HIV/AIDS Prevention and Education for Adolescents and Children, 2,* 51–66.

House, A., Dallinger, J., & Kilgallen, D. (1998). Androgyny and rhetorical sensitivity: The connection of gender and communicator style. *Communication Reports, 11,* 11–20.

Insko, C. A., Smith, R. H., Alicke, M. D., Wade, J., & Taylor, S. (1985). Conformity and group size: The concern with being right and the concern with being liked. *Personality and Social Psychology Bulletin, 11*, 41–50.

Jarrell, A. (2000, April 2). The face of teenage sex grows younger. *New York Times.*

Joseph, G. I., & Lewis, J. (1981). *Common differences: Conflicts in black and white feminist perspectives.* Garden City, NY: Doubleday/Anchor.

Kalof, L., & Cargill, T. (1991). Fraternity and sorority membership and gender dominance attitudes. *Sex Roles, 25*, 417–423.

Kanter, R. M. (1977). *Men and women of the corporation.* New York: Basic.

Kiesling, S. F. (2001). Playing the straight man: Displaying and maintaining male heterosexuality in discourse. In K. Campbell-Kibler, R. Podesva, S. Roberts, & A. Wong (Eds.), *Language and sexuality: Contesting meaning in theory and practice* (pp. 249–266). Stanford, CA: CSLI.

Kilbourne, J. (1999). *Can't buy my love: How advertising changes the way we think and feel.* New York: Touchstone.

Kimmel, M. S. (1987). The cult of masculinity: American social character and the legacy of the cowboy. In M. Kaufman (Ed.), *Beyond patriarchy: Essays by men on pleasure, power, and change* (pp. 235–249). Toronto: Oxford University Press.

Kimmel, M. S. (2003). Masculinity as homophobia: Fear, shame, and silence in the construction of gender identity. In T. E. Ore (Ed.), *The social construction of difference and inequality* (pp. 119–135). Boston: McGraw-Hill.

Kindlon, D., & Thompson, M. (2000). *Raising Cain: Protecting the emotional life of boys.* New York: Ballantine.

Knight, J. R., Wechsler, H., Kuo, M., Seibring, M., Weitzman, E. R., & Schuckit, M. (2002). Alcohol abuse and dependence among U.S. college students. *Journal of Studies on Alcohol, 63*(3), 263–270.

Komisar, L. (1980). Violence and masculine mystique. In D. D. Sabo & R. Runfola (Eds.), *Jock: Sports and male identity* (pp. 131–157). Englewood Cliffs, NJ: Prentice-Hall.

Koss, M. P., Gidycz, C. A., & Wisniewski, N. (1987). The scope of rape: Incidence and prevalence of sexual aggression and victimization in a national sample of higher education students. *Journal of Consulting and Clinical Psychology, 55*, 162–170.

Kposowa, A. J. (2000). Marital status and suicide in the National Longitudinal Mortality Study. *Journal of Epidemiology and Community Health, 54*, 254–261.

Kreider, R. B. (1998, September). Creatine, the next ergogenic supplement? *Mesomorphosis, 1*(4). Retrieved February 2007 from http://www.mesomorphosis.com/exclusive/kreider/creatine.htm.

Lakoff, G., & Johnson, M. (2003). *Metaphors we live by* (updated ed., with a new afterword by the authors). Chicago: University of Chicago Press. (Original work published 1980)

Leathers, D. G. (1986). *Successful nonverbal communication: Principles and applications.* New York: Macmillan.

Lees, S. (1986). *Losing out: Sexuality and adolescent girls.* London: Hutchinson.

Lehne, G. (1989). Homophobia among men: Supporting and defining the male role. In M. Kimmel & M. Messner (Eds.), *Men's lives* (pp. 416–429). New York: Macmillan.

Lorde, A. (1984). *Sister outside.* Freedom, GA: Crossing.

Mac an Ghaill, M. (1994). The making of black English masculinities. In H. Brod & M. Kaufman (Eds.), *Theorizing masculinities* (pp. 183–199). Thousand Oaks, CA: Sage.

Maltz, D. N., & Borker, R. (1982). A cultural approach to male-female miscommunication. In J. J. Gumpertz (Ed.), *Language and social identity* (pp. 196–216). Cambridge: Cambridge University Press.

Martin, P. Y., & Hummer, R. A. (1989). Fraternities and rape on campus. *Gender and Society, 3,* 457–473.

Maynard, R. M. (1974). *The American West on film: Myth and reality.* Rochelle Park, NJ: Hayden.

McIntosh, P. (1997). White privilege and male privilege: A personal account of coming to see correspondence through work in women's studies. In R. Delgado & J. Stefancic (Eds.), *Critical white studies: Looking behind the mirror* (pp. 291–299). Philadelphia: Temple University Press.

McNutt, S. W., Yuanreng, H., Schreiber, G. B., Crawford, P. B., Obarzanek, E., & Mellin, L. (1997). A longitudinal study of the dietary practices of black and white girls 9 and 10 years old at enrollment: The NHLBI growth and health study. *Journal of Adolescent Health, 20*(1), 27–37.

Messner, M. A. (1988). Sports and male domination: The female athlete as contested ideological terrain. *Sociology of Sport Journal, 5,* 197–211.

Miedzian, M. (1991). *Boys will be boys: Breaking the link between masculinity and violence.* New York: Anchor.

Miller, C. L. (1987). Qualitative differences among gender-stereotyped toys: Implications for cognition and social development. *Sex Roles, 16,* 473–487.

Mohler-Kuo, M., Dowdall, G. W., Koss, M. P., & Wechsler, H. (2004). Correlates of rape while intoxicated in a national sample of college women. *Journal of Studies on Alcohol, 65,* 37–45.

Moos, R. (1979). *Evaluating educational environments.* San Francisco: Jossey-Bass.

Morrison, T. (1993). *Playing in the dark: Whiteness and the literary imagination.* New York: Vintage.

Nardi, P. (1992). Seamless "souls": An introduction to men's friendships. In P. Nardi (Ed.), *Men's friendships* (pp. 1–14). Newbury Park, CA: Sage.

National Center for Victims of Crime. (2004, January). *Stalking.* Problem-Oriented Guides for Police, Problem-Specific Guides Series, Guide No. 22. Washington, DC: U.S. Department of Justice, Office of Community Oriented Policing Services. Available at http://www.cops.usdoj.gov/mime/open. pdf?Item=1042.

National Panhellenic Conference (NPC). (2003). *Annual report.* Indianapolis: NPC. Available online at http://www.npcwomen.org/newsevents/pdf/03/ 2003AnnualReport.pdf.

Nelson, M. B. (1994). *The stronger woman get, the more men love football: Sexism and the American culture of sports.* New York: Harcourt Brace.

Noble, V. (1992). A helping hand from the guys. In K. L. Hagan (Ed.), *Women respond to the men's movement* (pp. 105–106). San Francisco: HarperCollins.

North-American Interfraternity Conference (NIC). (n.d.). Who we are and what we do. Retrieved March 3, 2007, from http://nicindy.org/about_us/who_we_are/.

Nuwer, H. (1990). *Broken pledges: The deadly rite of hazing.* Atlanta: Longstreet.

Nuwer, H. (1999). *Wrongs of passage: Fraternities and sororities, hazing, and binge drinking.* Bloomington: Indiana University Press.

O'Sullivan, C. S. (1991). Acquaintance gang rape on campus. In A. Parrot & L. Bechhofer (Eds.), *Acquaintance rape: The hidden crime* (pp. 140–156). New York: Wiley.

Overcoming obesity in America. (2004, June 7). *Time.*

Paglia, C. (1992). *Sex, art, and American culture: Essays.* New York: Vintage.

Paglia, C. (1994). *Vamps and tramps: New Essays.* New York: Vintage.

Pike, K. M., & Rodin, J. (1991). Mothers, daughters, and disordered eating. *Journal of Abnormal Psychology, 100*(2), 198–204.

Pipher, M. (1994). *Reviving Ophelia: Saving the selves of adolescent girls.* New York: Ballantine.

Presley, C. A., Meilman, P. W., & Cashin, J. R. (1996). *Alcohol and drugs on American college campuses: Use, consequences, and perceptions of the campus environment: Vol. 4. 1992–1994.* Carbondale: Core Institute, Southern Illinois University.

Remez, L. (2000). Oral sex among adolescents: Is it sex or is it abstinence? *Family Planning Perspectives, 32,* 6.

Richins, M. L. (1991). Social comparison and the idealized images of advertising. *Journal of Consumer Research, 18,* 71–83.

Riessman, C. K. (1990). *Divorce talk: Women and men make sense of personal relationships.* New Brunswick, NJ: Rutgers University Press.

Rise of the metrosexual. (2003, March 11). *The Age.* Retrieved March 10, 2004, from http://www.theage.com.au/articles/2003/03/10/1047144914842.html.

Roiphe, K. (1993). *The morning after: Sex, fear, and feminism on campus.* Boston: Little, Brown.

Ross, L. C. (2000). *The divine nine: The history of African American fraternities and sororities.* New York: Kensington.

Ross, T. (1997). The rhetorical tapestry of race. In R. Delgado & J. Stefancic (Eds.), *Critical white studies: Looking behind the mirror* (pp. 89–97). Philadelphia: Temple University Press.

Rubin, L. (1985). *Just friends: The role of friendship and women together.* New York: Harper & Row.

Rushing, J. H. (1983). The rhetoric of the American Western myth. *Communication Monographs, 50,* 14–32.

Ryan, M. (1979). *Womanhood in America: From colonial times to the present* (2nd ed.). New York: Harper & Row. (Original work published 1975)

Salih, S. (2002). *Judith Butler.* New York: Routledge.

Sanday, P. R. (1990). *Fraternity gang rape: Sex, brotherhood, and privilege on campus.* New York: New York University Press.

Schaef, A. W. (1981). *Women's reality.* St. Paul, MN: Winston.

Scherrer, J. (2004, February 3). Two words for the metrosexual. Clark Schpiell Productions. Retrieved March 10, 2004, from http://www.clarkschpiell.com/home/metrosexual.shtml.

Schuster, M. A., Bell, R. M., & Kanouse, D. E. (1996). The sexual practices of adolescent virgins: Genital sexual activities of high school students who have never had vaginal intercourse. *American Journal of Public Health, 86*(11), 1570–1576.

Seventeen news: National survey conducted by *Seventeen* finds that more than half of teens ages 15–19 have engaged in oral sex (News Release). (2000, February 28). *Seventeen.*

Silverman, J. G., Raj, A., Mucci, L. A., & Hathaway, J. E. (2001). Dating violence against adolescent girls and associated substance use, unhealthy weight control, sexual risk behavior, pregnancy, and suicidality. *Journal of the American Medical Association, 286,* 895–905.

Silverstein, B., Peterson, B., & Perdue, L. (1986). Some correlates of the thin standard of bodily attractiveness for women. *International Journal of Eating Disorders, 5*(5), 145–155.

Simpson, M. (1994, November 15). Here come the mirror men. *Independent.*

Smolak, L. (1996). *Statistics: Eating disorders and their precursors*. Seattle: National Eating Disorders Association. Also available at http://www.nationaleatingdisorders.org/p.asp?WebPage_ID=286&Profile_ID=41138.

Stein, P. (1986). Men and their friendships. In R. Lewis & R. Salt (Eds.), *Men in families* (pp. 261–270). Beverly Hills, CA: Sage.

Stepp, L. S. (1999a, July 8). Parents are alarmed by an unsettling new fad in middle schools: Oral sex. *Washington Post*.

Stepp, L. S. (1999b, July 8). Talking to kids about sexual limits. *Washington Post*.

Stewart, L. P., Cooper, P. J., Stewart, A. D., & Friedley, S. A. (1998). *Communication and gender* (3rd ed.). Boston: Allyn & Bacon. (Original work published 1986)

Stice, E., Schupak-Neuberg, E., Shaw, H. E., & Stein, R. I. (1994). Relation of media exposure to eating disorder symptomatology: An examination of mediating mechanisms. *Journal of Abnormal Psychology, 103*(4), 836–840.

Stice, E., & Shaw, H. E. (1994). Adverse effects of the media portrayed thin-ideal on women and linkages to bulimic symptomatology. *Journal of Social and Clinical Psychology, 13*(3), 288–308.

Strauss, M. A., Gelles, R. J., & Smith, C. (1990). *Physical violence in American families: Risk factors and adaptations to violence in 8,145 families*. New Brunswick, NJ: Transaction.

Tajfel, J. (1981). *Human groups and social categories*. London: Cambridge University Press.

Tannen, D. (1990). *You just don't understand: Women and men in conversation*. New York: Morrow.

Task Force of the National Advisory Council on Alcohol Abuse and Alcoholism. (2002, April). *A call to action: Changing the culture of drinking at U.S. colleges*. Bethesda, MD: National Institute on Alcohol Abuse and Alcoholism. Retrieved February 2007 from http://www.collegedrinkingprevention.gov/media/TaskForceReport.pdf.

Tavris, C., & Baumgartner, A. (1983, February). How would your life be different? *Redbook*, 92–95.

Taylor, S. E. (2002). *The tending instinct: Women, men, and the biology of relationships*. New York: Times Books.

Thelen, M. H., & Cormier, J. F. (1995). Desire to be thinner and weight control among children and their parents. *Behavior Therapy, 26*, 85–99.

Tjaden, P., & Thoennes, N. (2000, July). *Extent, nature, and consequences of intimate partner violence*. Washington, DC: National Institute of Justice and Centers for Disease Control and Prevention.

Trujillo, N. (1991). Hegemonic masculinity on the mound: Media representations of Nolan Ryan and American sports culture. *Critical Studies in Mass Communication, 8,* 290–308.

U.S. Census Bureau. (2004). Table MS-2: Estimated median age at marriage, by sex: 1890 to the present. Washington, DC. Available at http://www.census.gov/population/socdemo/hh-fam/tabMS-2.pdf.

U.S. Surgeon General. (2001). *Women and smoking: A report of the surgeon general.* Washington, DC: Office of the Surgeon General.

Wechsler, H., Lee, J. E., Kuo, M., Seibring, M., Nelson, T. F., & Lee, H. P. (2002). Trends in college binge drinking during a period of increased prevention efforts: Findings from four Harvard School of Public Health study surveys, 1993–2001. *Journal of American College Health, 50*(5): 203–217.

Weitzman, L. J. (1985). *The divorce revolution: The unexpected social and economic consequences for women and children in America.* New York: Free Press.

West, C. (1994). *Race matters.* New York: Vintage.

Whitehead, S. W., & Barrett, F. J. (Eds.). (2001). *The masculinities reader.* Cambridge: Polity.

Winston, R. B., Nettles, W. R., III, & Opper, J. H., Jr. (Eds.). (1987). *Fraternities and sororities on the contemporary college campus.* San Francisco: Jossey-Bass.

Wolfe, N. (1993). *Fire with fire: The new female power and how it will change the 21st century.* New York: Random House.

Wood, J. T. (1993). Engendered identities: Shaping voice and mind through gender. In D. Vocate (Ed.), *Intrapersonal communication: Different voices, different minds* (pp. 145–167). Hillsdale, NJ: Erlbaum.

Wood, J. T. (1999). *Gendered lives: Communication, gender, and culture* (3rd ed.). Belmont, CA: Wadsworth. (Original work published 1993)

Wood, J. T. (2005). *Gendered lives: Communication, gender, and culture* (6th ed.). Belmont, CA: Wadsworth. (Original work published 1993)

Wooley, S. C., & Wooley, O. W. (1984, February). Feeling fat in a thin society. *Glamour,* 198–252.

Workman, T. A. (2001). Finding the meanings of college drinking: An analysis of fraternity drinking stories. *Health Communication, 13*(4), 427–447.

World Health Organization (WHO). Department of Gender and Women's Health. (2003, November). *Gender, health, and tobacco.* Geneva. Available at http://www.who.int/gender/other_health/Gender_Tobacco_2.pdf.

Index

31–32; five gender themes and, 33–35; nurturing/caring aspects of, 34–35, 104–6; symmetrical pairing with masculinity, 36. *See also* hyperfemininity; women

fights: brotherhood and, 88–90; between fraternities, 77–78

focus group, 11, 14

food relationships: eating disorders and, 127–31; mother/daughter relationship and, 133–34; unhealthy, in sororities, 130–31; weight lifting and, 145–46; women and, 122–28

Forbes' 500 companies, Greek CEOs in, 7

Fortune 500 companies: Greek executives in, 7; desire to work for, 201

fraternal-centrism, 86–90

fraternities: aggression among, 80–86; alcohol consumption, excessive in, 242n4; anti-intellectual bias of, 204–6; black, 238n7; classroom performance, *191, 245n1, 245n2;* competition among, 80–86; discussion of sex among members, 43–44; as family, 161–63; GPA distribution in, *191;* intimate friendships in, 163–75; love, views of, 43–44, 154–55; marriage, views of, 210–14; meaningful communication in, 166; opposite-sex relationships in, 156–60; physical appearance and, 148–50; physical contact in, 244n3; professional, 3, 237n2; recognized, 237n5; relationships in, 43–44, 155; rituals of, 165–66, 217–18; same-sex relationships in, 160–63; self-disclosure in,

163–75; sex in, 43–44; structured activities of, 165–66; U.S. presidents and, *8;* violence among, 77–78; violence within, 90–92; weight lifting and, 139–44; on women/sex, 44–50, 74–75

frontiersmanship, as male attribute, 240n3

fund-raisers, as venue for exhibitionism, 69–70

future of Greek organizations: importance of stakeholders, 233–34. *See also* postcollege hopes; postcollege professions

Gadamer, Hans-Georg, 16

gender: cohesive fabric of, 37–38; as constant, 238n11; development, 38; differences, 178–79, 186–87; in elite Greek organizations, 219; as fluid variable, 25–26, 30; identity, 37–38; lessons, 28–29; lived, 219; pairings, symmetrical, 35–36; as performance, 26; popularity and, 38–39; scripts, rewriting of, 222–23; theorists, 72

gender constructs, 19; "bros before hos" mentality, 18, 153–55; "corporate dad," 18; "dyke," 175; female type of, 157–58; "gigolo," 175; male type of, 177–78; maternal qualities, 157–58; "old maid," 175; "playboy," 175; "player," 175; "soccer mom," 18, 191–92; "spinster," 175; "stud," 16–17, 43–44, 175; of unmarried women, 175; wife's role, 210–14; of working mother, 196–200; of working woman, 200–204

gender roles: blurring of, 36–37; challenging of, 2, 41–42; cultural,

of, 240n4; violence among, 78–
80; weight control and, 140–43;
on women/sex, 44–50, 74–75; on
women/weight, 134–37. *See also*
male aggression
Men's Health, 144
methodology, 9–16
"metrosexual" male type, 137–38
monogamy, 34; male view of, 50–54
mother/daughter relationship, food
relationships and, 133–34

nandrolone decanoate. *See* Deca
Durabolin
National Panhellenic Conference
(NPC), 62, 237n6, 240n1
National Panhellenic Council (NPHC),
238n7
New Guinea, 30
New York Times, 124
NIC. *See* North-American
Interfraternity Council
nonlifters, 143–44
nontraditional gender roles, 26–27
nonwhite students, pledges of, 22–24
North-American Interfraternity
Council (NIC), 171–73, 237n5
North American Plains Indians, 30
"not too emotional" male type, 177
NPC. *See* National Panhellenic
Conference
NPHC. *See* National Panhellenic
Council

obesity epidemic, 115
"old maid," as gender construct, 175
Omani Muslims, 30
opposite-sex relationships: in
fraternities, 156–60; in sororities,
175–83
oral sex, 46–47, 65–67, 241n2

organizations. *See* elite Greek
organizations; Greek-letter
organizations
Organon, 243n5
"Overcoming Obesity in America"
(*Time*), 115
overweight pledges, 120–21

parents: Greek system investigated by,
230–31; as stakeholders in Greek
system, 230; pressure from, to lose
weight, 132–34
performance: gender, 26;
performativity theory, 19, 25;
sexual, 69–73
personal intervention, controlling
sexual behavior by, 63–64
personal transformations, of Greek
graduates, 222–23
petite physical type, 35
Phi Beta Kappa, 3, 237n4
physical appearance: fraternities and,
148–50; men rate, 156; sororities
and, 177
physical contact, in fraternities, 244n3
physical type, imposing, 33
Pipher, Mary, 1
platonic relationships, 18, 51–52
"playboy," as gender construct, 175
"player," as gender construct, 175
pledges: activities for, 171–72;
criteria for, 118–21; early Greek
traditions, 5–6; homosexuality
and, 55; nonwhite, 22–24;
overweight, 120–21; sororities
and, 187–88; tough guy image
and, 92–94; women before
pledging, 115–17
point people, 11–12, 238n13
popularity, traditional gender
conceptions and, 38–39

postcollege hopes, 18, 208–10
postcollege professions, 201–2; gender
    roles and, 214–15; pressures
    about, 208–10; and stereotypes
    about women, 193–201
presidential cabinet members, Greek, 7
presidents of the United States, Greek,
    7, 8
professional fraternities, 3, 237n2
professional orientation, 33
professional sororities, 3, 237n2
promiscuity, 32–33, 43–44
public universities, 239n1

race: and Greek-letter organizations,
    4–5; nonwhite pledges, 22–24
*Raising Cain: Protecting the Emotional
    Life of Boys* (Kindlon), 1
ranking system, of Greek
    organizations, 38–39
rape: behavioral characteristics and,
    97–101; in Greek system, 97–104;
    statistics, 96–97. *See also* date
    rape
recruits, elite Greek organizations and,
    39–41
relational independence, 33, *36*
relational interdependence, 35, *36*, 37,
    188–89; masculine, 160–63
relational isolation, of men, 163–64
relationships: in fraternities, 43–44,
    155; monogamy and, male
    view of, 50–54; opposite-sex, in
    fraternities, 156–60; opposite-sex,
    in sororities, 175–83; platonic, 18,
    51–52; romantic, 18; same-sex, in
    fraternities, 160–63; same-sex, in
    sororities, 183–88; violence/abuse
    within, 96–97
*Reviving Ophelia: Saving the Selves of
    Adolescent Girls* (Pipher), 1

"Rise of the Metrosexual" (*The Age*),
    138, 150
rituals, Greek: candlelight ceremony,
    154–55; early, 5–6; of fraternities,
    165–66, 217–18; gossiping,
    43–44; treeing, 154–55
rush process: body image and, 118–21;
    competition in, 81–82; dry,
    241n2; early Greek traditions, 5–
    6; elite rushees, 40; homosexuality
    and, 55; identity during, 21–22;
    season of, 241n1; sex in, 61–62
rushed hard, defined, 149

same-sex relationships: in fraternities,
    160–63; in sororities, 183–88
Saudi Arabia, students from, 22
scapegoating, of elite sororities,
    131–32
self-definition, 20–21
self-disclosure, in fraternities, 163–75
senators, Greek, 7
Seventeen, 241n3
sex: in American advertising, 242n1;
    anal, 68; classification of, 64;
    Clinton scandal, 68; in fraternities,
    43–44; indiscriminate, 45–47;
    inequality in, 73–74; in media,
    242n1; men's view of, 44–50, 74–
    75; older views of, 64–65; oral,
    46–47, 65–67, 241n2; redefinition
    of, 64–69; in rush process, 61–62;
    women's view of, 58–64
sex drive, male, 44–50
sexual assaults, 96–104
sexual performances, 69–73
sexuality: appropriate, 59–61;
    appropriate, maintaining,
    61–64; controlling, by
    personal intervention, 63–64;
    hypersexuality, 44, 49–50; identity

university administrators, and Greek
system, 231–33
University of Alabama, 8
University of Chicago, 5
university professors, and Greek
system, 223–26
unmarried women, views of, 175
urban legends. *See* Greek lore

vaginal penetration, 65
verbal expression, male/female
differences in, 240n4
victimization, 150–51
violence: between fraternities, 77–78,
86–90; within fraternities, 90–92;
interrelationship, 96–97; among
men, 78–80
virgins, 16–17, 34, 43–44

Wall Street, 208. *See also* postcollege
professions
wardrobe, male, 147
Washington Post, 138
weight control, 121–28; of males, 140–
43; obsessive, 128–31; sororities
and, 124–31
weight lifting, 139–44; competitive
aspects, 142; food and, 145–46;
steroids and, 146–47; dietary
supplements and, 145, 243n5
weight loss: alcohol and, 127–28;
competitive aspects, 112–13;
men's view of, 134–37; obsessive,
115; parental pressure for, 132–
34; pressure for, 118–21; smoking
and, 127
Who's Who in America, 7
wife, role of, 210–14
Williams, Robin, 223
women: academic performance of,
191–93; attraction to male

aggression, 96–97; average
American body image of,
132–33; on "balanced life,"
199; competition among,
106–7; "cool/fun" type of,
158; cultural expectations of,
106, 117–18; define ideal man,
177–78; dieting of, 122–28,
130–31; food relationships and,
122–28; historical images of, 115;
ideal, defined by men, 156–58;
independence from, 156; male
hypersexuality and, 49–50; men's
view of, 44–50, 74–75; men's
view of weight of, 134–37; before
pledging, 115–17; postgraduate,
stereotypes of, 193–201;
professional, 201–2; sex, views
of, 58–64; unmarried, 175; verbal
expression of, 240n4; working,
200–201; working, men's response
to, 202–4. *See also* female
attributes, desirable; femininity
working mother, 196–200
working woman, 200–201; men's
response to, 202–4
world cultures, gender roles in, 30
World War II, 4–5
wrestling, 91

xanith, 30